# Learning SD-WAN with Cisco

## Transform Your Existing WAN Into a Cost-effective Network

Stuart Fordham

**Apress®**

*Learning SD-WAN with Cisco*

Stuart Fordham
Bedfordshire, UK

ISBN-13 (pbk): 978-1-4842-7346-3          ISBN-13 (electronic): 978-1-4842-7347-0
https://doi.org/10.1007/978-1-4842-7347-0

Managing Director, Apress Media LLC: Welmoed Spahr
Acquisitions Editor: Aditee Mirashi
Development Editor: Laura Berendson
Coordinating Editor: Aditee Mirashi

Cover designed by eStudioCalamar

Cover image designed by Freepik (www.freepik.com)

Distributed to the book trade worldwide by Springer Science+Business Media New York, 1 New York Plaza, Suite 4600, New York, NY 10004-1562, USA. Phone 1-800-SPRINGER, fax (201) 348-4505, e-mail orders-ny@springer-sbm.com, or visit www.springeronline.com. Apress Media, LLC is a California LLC and the sole member (owner) is Springer Science + Business Media Finance Inc (SSBM Finance Inc). SSBM Finance Inc is a **Delaware** corporation.

For information on translations, please e-mail booktranslations@springernature.com; for reprint, paperback, or audio rights, please e-mail bookpermissions@springernature.com.

Apress titles may be purchased in bulk for academic, corporate, or promotional use. eBook versions and licenses are also available for most titles. For more information, reference our Print and eBook Bulk Sales web page at http://www.apress.com/bulk-sales.

Any source code or other supplementary material referenced by the author in this book is available to readers on GitHub via the book's product page, located at www.apress.com/978-1-4842-7346-3. For more detailed information, please visit http://www.apress.com/source-code.

Printed on acid-free paper

*To my wife.*

# Table of Contents

# About the Author

 **Stuart Fordham, CCIE 49337** is the Network Manager and Infrastructure Team Leader for SmartCommunications SC Ltd, the only provider of a cloud-based, next-generation customer communications platform. Stuart has written a series of books on BGP, MPLS, VPNs, and NAT, as well as a CCNA study guide and the *Cisco ACI Cookbook*. He lives in the UK with his wife and twin sons.

# About the Technical Reviewer

 **David Samuel Peñaloza Seijas** works as a Principal Engineer at Verizon Enterprise Solutions in the Czech Republic, focusing on Cisco SD-WAN, ACI, OpenStack, and NFV. Previously, he worked as a Data Center Network Support Specialist in the IBM Client Innovation Center in the Czech Republic. As an expert networker, David has a wide diapason of interests, while his favorite topics include data centers, enterprise networks, and network design, including software-defined networking (SDN).

# Acknowledgments

I'd like to say thanks to the following:

My wife for her encouraging words: *"Well, if you played the guitar less, you'd have that book finished by now."* It's finished now. So back to playing the guitar!

My boys for being patient while "Daddy is working *again*." You guys are amazing.

David Peñaloza: The best technical editor a guy could ask for.

The team at Apress, for giving me another shot after I had finished freaking out about my workload.

My team at SmartCommunications. You guys are the best.

# Introduction

*Learning SD-WAN with Cisco* explores what SD-WAN is and how it will benefit modern networks and builds an example network.

This book covers the evolution of modern networks and how the software-defined wide area network (SD-WAN) has risen to the forefront. We will explore the components of SD-WAN for orchestration and management and look at the edge devices and then go on to build a network from the ground up, deploying cEdge and vEdge routers. We will apply policies and templates to manage the control and data planes as well as VPNs, Internet access, security, and quality of service.

We will also explore reporting and management, along with upgrading and troubleshooting.

This book is intended for those who would like to get an understanding of what SD-WAN is and how we deploy, configure, manage, and troubleshoot it.

# CHAPTER 1

# An Introduction to SD-WAN

In this chapter, we are going to look at what SD-WAN is and how it came about.

## The Traditional Network

The networks we rely on for both business and pleasure on a day-to-day basis are susceptible to many factors that can result in a slow and unreliable experience.

We can experience latency, which either refers to the time between a data packet being sent and received or the round-trip time, which is the time it takes for the packet to be sent and for it to get a reply, such as when we use ping.

We can also experience jitter, which is the variance in the time delay between data packets in the network, basically a "disruption" in the sending and receiving of packets.

We have fixed bandwidth networks that can experience congestion: with 5 people sharing the same Internet link, each could experience a stable and swift network, add another 20 or 30 people onto the same link and the experience will be markedly different.

© Stuart Fordham 2021
S. Fordham, *Learning SD-WAN with Cisco*, https://doi.org/10.1007/978-1-4842-7347-0_1

There are ways we can help manage the experience for all. We can implement quality of service (QoS), which we can use to prioritize traffic, such as voice and video, where fluctuations in the network due to these factors are noticeable. We can also use QoS to give each user their fair share of bandwidth and to ensure that the right amount of bandwidth is assured for our mission-critical applications.

QoS works well within the boundaries of the network but requires manual intervention. We need to know what our traffic is, where that traffic needs to go, and what our priority traffic is. We can help it get there faster and with a larger degree of assured delivery, but it still requires the network administrators to ensure that the paths the traffic is to take are present, working, and reliable. QoS, combined with policy-based routing (PBR), can also provide a way to route traffic out of different interfaces, making use of dedicated high-speed links for mission-critical traffic and other links for user traffic such as Internet browsing and media streaming. These do, again, require the network administrator to plan this traffic splitting out, and this method is not exactly "dynamic."

There are mechanisms to dynamically route traffic though, such as Multiprotocol Label Switching Traffic Engineering (MPLS-TE). Through the use of MPLS, a link-state protocol such as OSPF or IS-IS, RSVP (Resource Reservation Protocol), and CBR (Constraint-Based Routing), we can have a network that learns about changes in the network and reacts by performing path selection in the network.

MPLS-TE is very much in the realm of large enterprises and ISPs, though, and with it comes increased costs in both infrastructure and engineering.

Today, we are, however, deep into cloud adoption, where pretty much everything can now be offered "As a Service." Platform, infrastructure, and software are all deployable at a click of a button, and whole virtual data centers can be stood up in minutes. Names such as Microsoft Azure, Amazon Web Services (AWS), and Google Cloud are so embedded in 21st-century technology that it is fast approaching the time where we will soon not even begin to comprehend how we managed before "the cloud."

So how do we marry up the needs of today's cloud computing, the benefits of QoS, and MPLS-TE as well as the dynamism we need for modern networks, while, at the same time, increasing security, reducing costs, and having a technology that is easy to use? These seem like a lot of contradictory criteria to fulfil.

The answer is SD-WAN, or software-defined networking in a wide area network.

# SD-WAN

SD-WAN has taken the concept of software-defined networking (within a local area network) and cloud orchestration and applied it to the wide area network.

There are, according to Gartner,[1] four requirements for an SD-WAN:

- It must have the ability to support multiple connection types.

- It should be able to perform dynamic path selection.

- It should have the ability to support VPNs and third-party services (such as firewalls).

- It must have a simple interface.

It is not just Gartner that has put these requirements on paper. This is also the standard defined by MEF (which once stood for the Metro Ethernet Forum) in MEF 70. MEF is an international industry consortium that looks to promote the adoption of assured and orchestrated connectivity services across automated networks. Members of MEF include Cisco, Ericsson, Huawei, Juniper, Nokia Networks, VMWare, and more companies with "telecommunications" or "telecom" in their names than you can shake a stick at.

---

[1] www.networkworld.com/article/3031279/sd-wan-what-it-is-and-why-you-ll-use-it-one-day.html

MEF 70[2] is not the easiest document to understand. It uses many TLAs (three-letter acronyms) and contains nuggets like this:

*MEF Services, such as SD-WAN, are specified using Service Attributes. A Service Attribute captures specific information that is agreed on between the Service Provider and the Subscriber of a MEF Service, and it describes some aspect of the service behavior.*

Got that? Great, neither did I. However, if we take an SD-WAN deployment from a more practical angle and put it into some context, it does start to make sense. I will try to translate as we go through the various components.

We start with the SD-WAN edge device. These devices can either be physical ones or virtual appliances. The SD-WAN edge devices need to support multiple connection types, such as MPLS, Internet such as leased lines, and LTE. The edge device is *"situated between the SD-WAN UNI, on its Subscriber side, and UCS UNIs of one or more Underlay Connectivity Services on its network side,"* meaning that these devices live at the demarcation point between the business network (Customer Premises) and the ISP, the SD-WAN UNI (User Network Interface), and the Underlay Connectivity Service (UCS), or the Internet circuit.

Because we have an underlay service, it makes sense that we also have an overlay. The overlay is the network we are orchestrating, and we do this through the SD-WAN Controller and the SD-WAN Orchestrator; these devices control our policies concerning application flow and security. The overlay needs to be able to understand the network and feed information back to the edge devices so that they may choose the best paths across the network, as well as controlling our VPNs and other services.

So once we start looking at SD-WAN from a practical standpoint, MEF 70 actually starts to make sense.

---

[2]www.mef.net/resources/technical-specifications/download?id=122&fileid=file1

4

Cisco, along with Huawei, Nokia Networks, and Verizon, among others, participated in the development of MEF 70, but this was by no means Cisco's first step into the world of SD-WAN.

# Cisco and SD-WAN

Cisco had a product called iWAN (intelligent WAN), which provided traffic control and security and integrated into Cisco branch office routers. It offered QoS, WAN optimization, and VPN tunneling, without the cost of expensive MPLS VPNs.

iWAN made a lot of sense, as with the lowering cost of today's Internet links, along with the improvement in their SLAs, MPLS is becoming less attractive. iWAN could provide similar capabilities to MPLS VPN, such as WAN optimization, QoS, and VPN tunneling, all without affecting performance, security, or reliability.

The network overlay used by iWAN is DMVPN (Dynamic Multipoint VPN) and IPSec, which enables the use of any carrier service (MPLS, broadband, and 3G/4G/LTE).

Traffic is routed based on metrics such as SLA, endpoint type, and network conditions. This is achieved using PfRv3 (Performance Routing Version 3), which uses differentiated services code points (DSCP), and an application-based policy framework to optimize bandwidth and path control, protecting applications and increasing bandwidth utilization. PfRv3 looks at the application type, network performance in terms of jitter, packet loss, and delay and can make decisions to forward traffic over the best-performing path.

We can, with iWAN, make networks use MPLS networks for some traffic (e.g., business-critical and VoIP) and other traffic (less critical) use the public Internet, as shown in Figure 1-1.

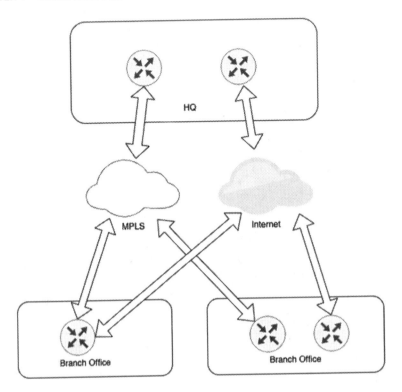

***Figure 1-1.***  *The iWAN network*

With PfR, border routers collect traffic and path information, sending it to a master controller (a dedicated router). The master controller is responsible for enforcing the service policies to match the requirements of the application.

Applications are optimized over the WAN using Cisco's Application Visibility and Control (AVC) and Wide Area Application Services (WAAS). AVC (which includes technologies such as Network-Based Application Recognition 2 [NBAR 2], NetFlow, and QoS) is essential here as many applications use the same ports (such as 443). Spotify, for example, uses a destination port of 4070 for its player, but will use port 443 or even 80 if the former port is unavailable, making the implementation of traffic control on Spotify impossible when based on the destination port. Because of this reuse of ports, we can no longer rely on static port classification, so AVC uses deep packet inspection to identify applications and to monitor their performance. iWAN also leverages Akamai for branch router caching.

iWAN is secured through IPSec encryption, zone-based firewalling, and ACLs (access control lists), protecting the WAN over the public Internet. It also uses Cisco's Cloud Web Security to provide a proxy to protect users over the Internet and is controlled using the APIC-EM (Application Policy Infrastructure Controller Enterprise Module).

All this sounds great. But why has Cisco rapidly moved to SD-WAN, instead of investing more in its existing product, iWAN?

The simple answer is that while all its benefits made it very attractive, in reality, iWAN was hard to deploy and manage. iWAN is not alone in technologies that have been sidelined, two more of which are PfR and NBAR, which, coincidentally, are two technologies used by iWAN.

The use of APIC-EM, for example, while great for managing iWAN, was only really useful in greenfield deployments. If you already had the building blocks of iWAN in place (DMVPN, QoS, PfR), then rolling out APIC-EM would pretty much require replacing all the existing configurations, which made switching to use the APIC-EM a tough and potentially expensive decision to make.

iWAN is not dead though, far from it. While new customers into the field will be steered toward SD-WAN, the ISR routers that are key to an iWAN deployment hold around 80% of the market share of branch office routers, and each year, Cisco sells around $1.6 billion of ISRs. There is too much invested by Cisco and its customers for iWAN to be ditched completely. However, the focus is now pointed directly at SD-WAN, which has some of the features that iWAN missed, such as an easy-to-use interface, which is, perhaps, why Cisco set its sights on Viptela.

# Viptela

Viptela was founded in 2012 by ex-Cisco directors Amir Khan and Khalid Raza. While it was in "stealth mode" and no one (in the general public) knew what it was doing, it received financial backing from Sequoia Capital. Considering the companies that Sequoia has backed in the past, such as Apple, Google, PayPal, YouTube, Instagram, and WhatsApp, Viptela was probably a surefire winner early on.

Over the next couple of years, Viptela emerged from stealth mode into the taking-the-network-world-by-storm mode. It garnered much praise and many customers. It was named several times in CRN's 10 Coolest Networking Startups, named a Gartner Cool Vendor and a Next Billion Dollar Startup by *Forbes*. Not a bad start (for a startup)!

Between 2012 and 2017, Viptela boasted customers such as Verizon, Singtel, and The Gap. Others were used in published case studies but preferred to remain unnamed, which is pretty common in the banking world.

The lure of Viptela is that it offers virtualization of the WAN and is carrier agnostic. Through the WAN overlay technology, communications are secured across whichever medium is used, even broadband and 4G/LTE. Similar to iWAN, in essence, but vastly different in deployment.

The report from clothing retailer The Gap makes for interesting reading and gives the reader a good idea about how and why Viptela was able to make such good ground within such a short amount of time.

The Gap started to roll out SD-WAN in 2015, to alleviate the reliance on the expensive MPLS lines and instead move to the cheaper public Internet. With SD-WAN, they could still do this, as well as keeping the traffic encrypted. Snehal Patel, Gap's network architect, said that they could connect up to 25 or more of their stores per night. Each upgraded store also had between ten and fifteen times the bandwidth it had previously. SD-WAN was also about 50% less expensive than their original method.

It is easy to see the benefits of Viptela's SD-WAN. You get the increased speed, at a lower cost, and rolling it out can be done at a very impressive pace.

You can read the original transcript from the *Wall Street Journal* here: `https://web.archive.org/web/20160726182850/http://blogs.wsj.com/cio/2015/11/05/gap-connects-stores-over-the-internet-with-software-defined-networking/`.

By 2017, Viptela had 16,000+ branch office deployments and proclaimed on its website the following benefits:

- 50% lower costs

- 10x more bandwidth

- 5x cloud performance

With such stores as The Gap putting their success story in the light, it's easy to see why Viptela did so well so quickly.

This brand-new network as a service offered seamless integration with Office 365, Azure, and AWS and used a simple interface (especially when compared to iWAN's APIC-EM). Policies can be used to send latency-sensitive traffic across dedicated MPLS lines and use the "regular" Internet for less critical applications, such as Office 365, and 4G/LTE for remote office where MPLS or broadband is not an option (Figure 1-2).

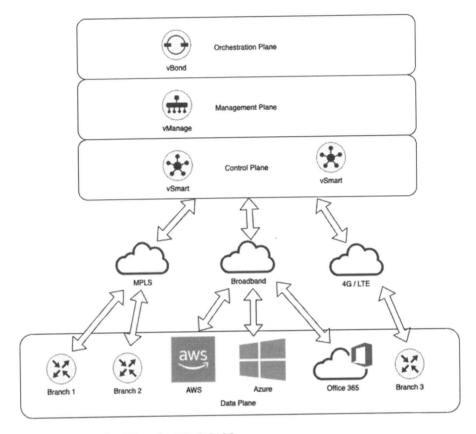

***Figure 1-2.***  *The Viptela SD-WAN*

The difference between Viptela's fabric and Cisco's iWAN is in the ease of connectivity into the likes of AWS, Azure, and Office 365, as well as the simplified management (again, compared to APIC-EM).

It is no wonder, therefore, that in 2017, Cisco bought Viptela for $610 million. Viptela aligned perfectly with Cisco's principles of security, virtualization, automation, and analytics, in their DNA (Digital Network Architecture).

Let's look at the different components that make up the (Cisco) SD-WAN (or SD-WAN Secure Extensible Network [SEN] as they also term it).

# Components of a Cisco SD-WAN

From Figure 1-2, you can see that there are four distinct areas to the SD-WAN. At the bottom, we have the connectivity aspect, the data plane. This can be offices or third-party services such as AWS and Office 365. For this connection, we need an "edge device."

## vEdge and cEdge

Because of the purchase by Cisco, the Cisco ISR, ASR, and CSR1000v routers are now part of the Viptela ecosystem (subject to running the correct software image); this is in addition to the products already made by Viptela, such as the low-cost vEdge 100b, which can be purchased for under $300.

The edge device takes care of the packet forwarding; they establish the secure virtual overlay network and come in many different flavors:

- vEdge 100b (Ethernet only)

- vEdge 100m (Ethernet and an integrated 2G/3G/4G modem)

- vEdge 100wm (as the 100m but with wireless LAN functionality)

- vEdge 1000 (8 fixed GE SFP ports)

- vEdge 2000 (2 pluggable interface modules)

- vEdge 5000 (4 Network Interface Modules)

- ISR 1100 4G (4 GE WAN ports)

- ISR 1100 6G (4 GE WAN ports and 2 SFP WAN ports)

- ISR 1000 series

- ISR 4000 series

11

- ASR 1000 series

- ENCS 5000

- vEdge Cloud

- CSR1000v

The vEdge Cloud device can run in VMWare ESXi (5.5. and 6.0), KVM, AWS, and Azure, and it is this image we will be using the most (along with the CSR1000v).

As well as looking after the routing (which can be either OSPF or BGP, or static), the vEdge devices also support AAA, bridging (802.1Q, VLANs, integrated routing-bridging), IPSec, DDOS prevention, NAT (network address translation) traversal, QoS, multicast and policies for routing, application awareness, control and data policies, ACL policies, VPN membership policies, and service advertisement and insertion policies. It also supports the standard set of functions that you would expect from any router, such as SNMP, NTP, DHCP (client, server, and relay), Syslog, SSH, NAT, and PAT.

The vEdge certainly feels like a very well-rounded and fully functioning replacement for most existing router deployments.

The next step-up in the overlay is the control plane, which uses vSmart devices.

## vSmart

The vSmart controller controls the data flowing through the network, it is the "routing brain," and once the vBond orchestrator has authenticated the vEdge devices, the vSmart controller manages the connectivity between vEdge devices.

The vSmart devices have a centralized policy engine that looks after the routing data, access control, segmentation, extranets, and service chaining.

There are six main functions provided by the vSmart controller:

- Control plane establishment and maintenance with each vEdge device.

  Each connection is a DTLS tunnel (Datagram Transport Layer Security) carrying the encrypted payload between the vSmart controller and the vEdge router. This information is what allows the vSmart controller to build up a picture of the network, the topology, and for the vSmart controller to perform route calculations to determine the best paths.

- Overlay Management Protocol (OMP). We will look in greater depth at OMP in Chapter 4, but essentially OMP facilitates the overlay network.

- Authentication. Using preinstalled credentials, the vSmart controller can communicate with each new vEdge device as they come online, ensuring that only authenticated devices can connect to the network.

- Key reflection and rekeying. vEdge routers send data-plane keys to the vSmart orchestrator which sends them to other vEdge routers.

- Policy engine. vSmart provides the inbound and outbound policies to look after routing and access control.

- Netconf and CLI. Netconf is used to provision vSmart controllers. Each vSmart controller provides local CLI access.

In Chapter 6, we will deploy a vSmart controller.

# vManage

vManage is a Network Management System (NMS) that is used to configure and manage the overlay network. We use this to configure and manage vEdge devices.

Like any good NMS, we can use vManage to create and store the configurations of our network devices. vManage will push down the certificate and configurations onto vEdge and cEdge devices as they come online (this is different in hardware devices, where the certificate is preinstalled on a SUDI or TPM chip during the manufacturing process). It can also generate bootstrap configurations and decommission vEdge devices if required.

We will deploy a vManage server (also referred to as a "controller" or "device" throughout this book) in Chapter 3.

# vBond

The vBond device performs functions such as the authentication and authorization of each element in the network, onboarding, and STUN. It is this piece of the topology that tells the rest of the network how they interconnect to the other components, essentially sitting between the vEdge and vSmart devices passing messages for them (initially at least, until the onboarding process has completed).

The functions performed by the vBond are

- Control plane connection. Each vBond orchestrator maintains a DTLS tunnel with each vSmart controller in the network. It also uses DTLS to communicate with the vEdge routers as they come online so that it can authenticate the router and aid the router to join the network.

- NAT traversal. vBond is also responsible for helping vEdge or vSmart devices that sit behind network address translation communicate with the rest of the network, orchestrating the NAT traversal (initially). For this to work, the vBond should live in a public address space.

- Load balancing. Where there are two or more vSmart controllers, the vBond performs load balancing of vEdge routers between the vSmart controllers.

We will deploy a vBond orchestrator in Chapter 5.

## Summary

In this, our first chapter, we looked at the driving forces behind the birth of SD-WAN, as well as the different parts that will make up our network. But first, we need to create that network, which we will do using EVE-NG (Emulated Virtual Environment Next Generation).

# CHAPTER 2

# Deployment Overview

In this chapter, we are going to set up EVE-NG, create our SmartNet account, and download the components we need to make our network. At the end of the chapter, we will look at VMWare and KVM as alternatives to EVE-NG.

## EVE-NG

EVE-NG (Emulated Virtual Environment Next Generation) is a virtual platform designed to run many different network devices, as well as Windows and Linux operating systems.

Many years ago there was a bit of software called Cisco IOU (IOS On Unix), and a very kind and clever guy called Andrea Dainese put a web front end on it and called it iou-web. It was very popular. Then he created UNetLab (Unified Networking Lab), which allowed the use of different vendor images.

UNetLab then forked into EVE-NG, which is where we are now.

There are two versions of EVE-NG: the community edition, which is free, and the professional edition. The professional edition, which costs 99EUR, can run up to 1024 nodes and has Docker support. The community version, which is free, can run up to 63 nodes and lacks Docker support, but this is fine for our purposes.

© Stuart Fordham 2021
S. Fordham, *Learning SD-WAN with Cisco*, https://doi.org/10.1007/978-1-4842-7347-0_2

The environment can run on vSphere, VMWare Workstation, or bare metal servers. If you have ever installed a Linux operating system, then it is all very straightforward, and there should be no surprises. For this chapter, I am assuming that you will be installing the server on a hypervisor.

Download the install ISO from `www.eve-ng.net/index.php/download/`. Again, the community version is more than suitable for our needs.

We need to properly size our server, so give it as much memory and CPU cores as you can. To get a rough idea of what we need, see Table 2-1.

***Table 2-1.*** *Hardware resource requirements*

|  | vCPU | Memory (GB) | Disk space (GB) |
|---|---|---|---|
| vBond | 2 | 4 | 10 |
| vManage | 16 | 32 | 30 + 100GB |
| vManage(2nd) | 16 | 32 | 30 + 100GB |
| vSmart | 2 | 4 | 16 |
| vEdge | 2 | 2 | 8 |
| **Total** | **38** | **74** | **294** |

We also need enough ram and CPU to run the actual operating system. While, thanks to hypervisor magic, we can over-provision memory and CPU, you still need something fairly capable.

The network we are going to run was created on a dual Xeon X5675 running at 3.06GHz with 48GB of memory. Running 15 QEMU nodes, CPU usage was around 28% and memory usage ran at around 79%. So there is some wiggle room in what can be run.

Once your VM has been created, boot it up using the ISO image downloaded from the link provided earlier. The first screen will be the Ubuntu installation window (Figure 2-1).

Select the option "*Install Eve VM*" (unless you are doing a bare metal, in which case choose the "*Install Eve Bare*" option).

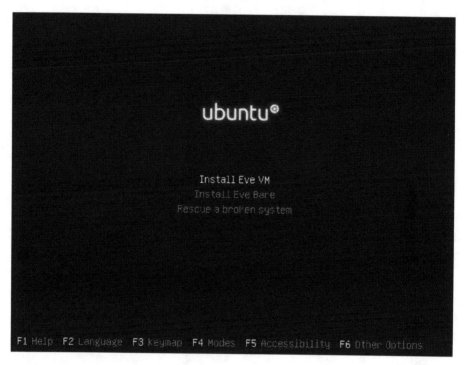

***Figure 2-1.*** *The initial install screen*

In the next window, choose your language (Figure 2-2).

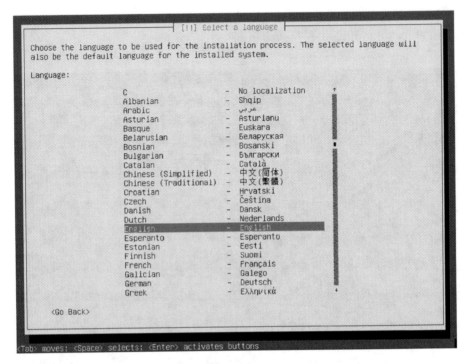

***Figure 2-2.*** *Choosing your language*

Then select your location (Figure 2-3).

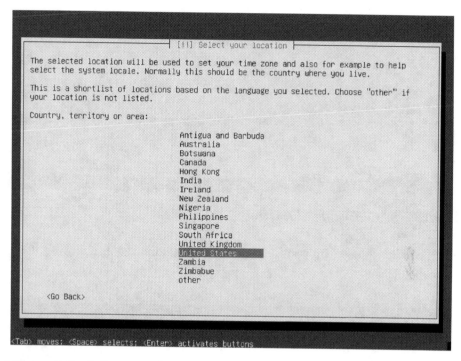

***Figure 2-3.***  *Select your location*

Set the hostname (Figure 2-4).

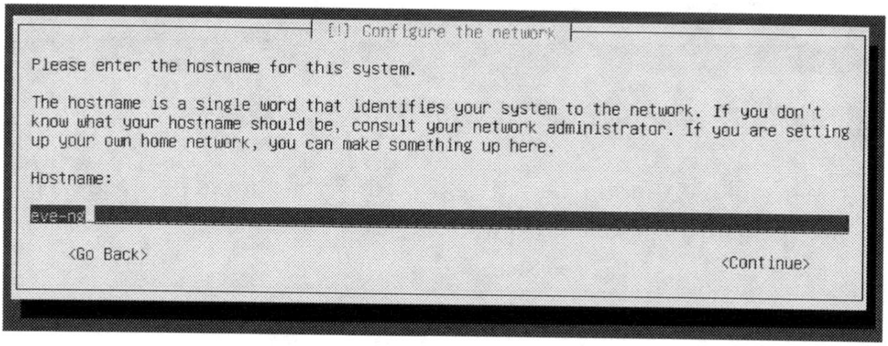

***Figure 2-4.***  *Setting the hostname*

Set the time zone (Figure 2-5).

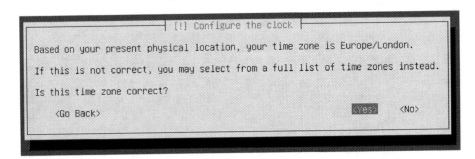

***Figure 2-5.*** *Setting the time zone*

If you use a proxy on your network, then set it in the following window (Figure 2-6).

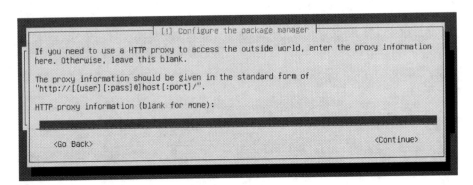

***Figure 2-6.*** *Setting the proxy information*

The installation should complete now, and you should be greeted with the login screen, as shown in Figure 2-7.

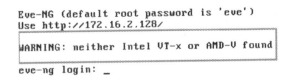

***Figure 2-7.*** *The EVE-NG logon screen*

If you see the same warning as the preceding, then you need to shut down your VM and edit your settings. Don't do this just yet though, as we need to complete the setup.

You will be prompted to enter the root password (Figure 2-8), so enter one of your choosing.

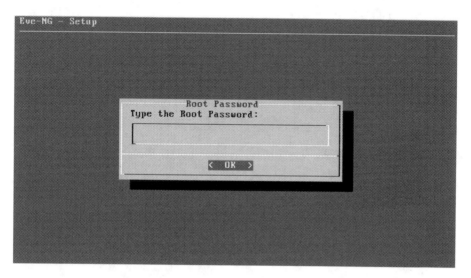

***Figure 2-8.*** *Setting the root password*

Type the password again, when prompted, and then set the hostname (again) (Figure 2-9).

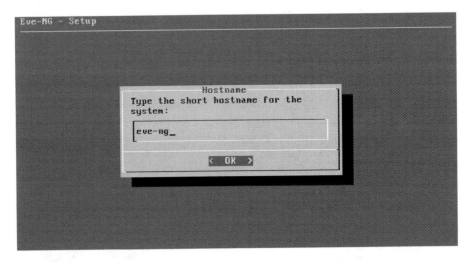

**Figure 2-9.**  *Setting the hostname*

Then set the DNS domain name, if you need to (Figure 2-10).

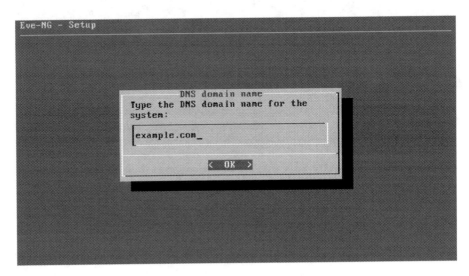

**Figure 2-10.**  *Setting the DNS domain name*

On the next page, we set our networking connectivity, either DHCP or static (Figure 2-11).

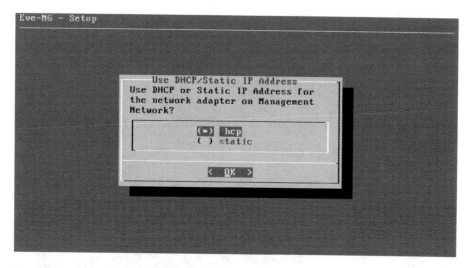

***Figure 2-11.*** *Setting the network adapter*

Set the NTP server, if you have one running in your network (Figure 2-12).

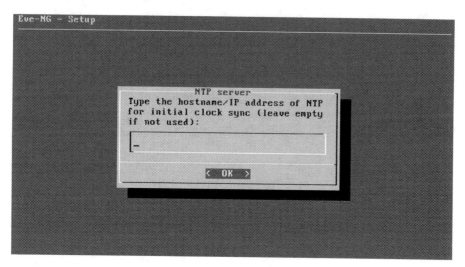

***Figure 2-12.*** *Setting the time servers*

Lastly, set the proxy details (or leave as the default if you do not have a proxy) as shown in Figure 2-13.

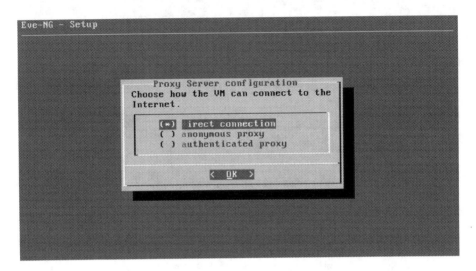

***Figure 2-13.*** *Proxy configuration*

If you did get the warning about "neither Intel VT-x or AMD-V found," then edit your VM settings to enable virtualization support.

In VMWare Fusion, it looks like this (Figure 2-14).

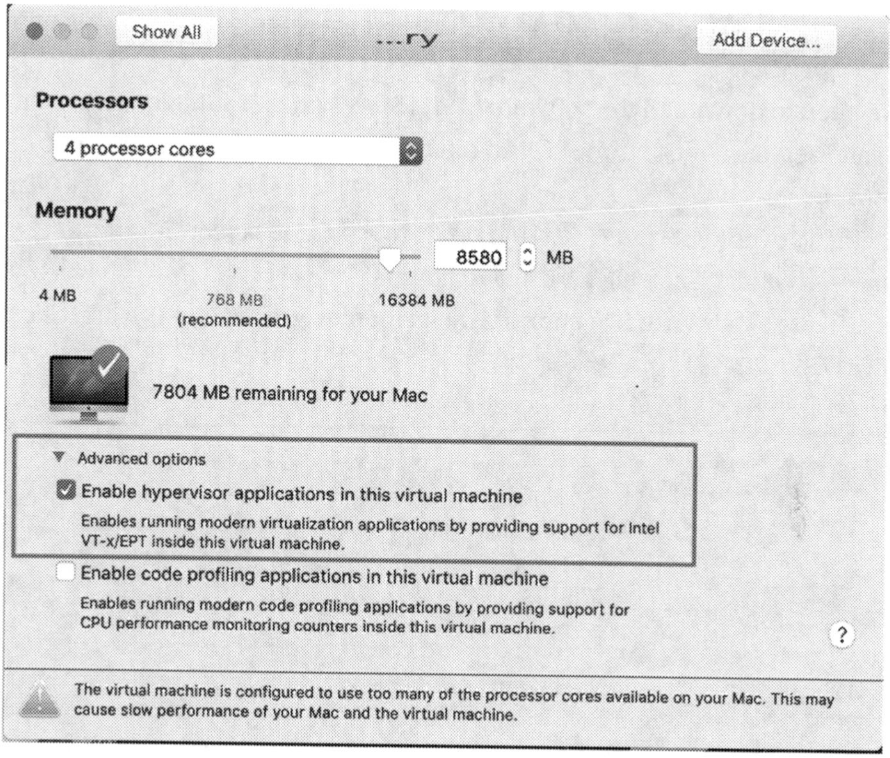

**Figure 2-14.** *Virtualization support*

Now your login page should look like this after a restart of the virtual machine (Figure 2-15).

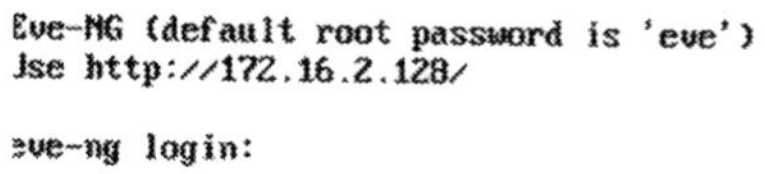

```
Eve-NG (default root password is 'eve')
Jse http://172.16.2.128/

eve-ng login:
```

**Figure 2-15.** *The EVE-NG login screen without warnings*

We are good to proceed.

# Getting the SD-WAN Software

We need to download the software from Cisco next. For this, you will need a valid service contract. Your Cisco rep may also be able to help you out here.

Head over to https://software.cisco.com, and select "*Manage Smart Account.*" Then click Virtual Accounts.

Create a new virtual account. Give it a name, and set it to Private. Click Save (Figure 2-16).

***Figure 2-16.*** *Creating the SmartNet virtual account*

Your virtual account should be visible (Figure 2-17).

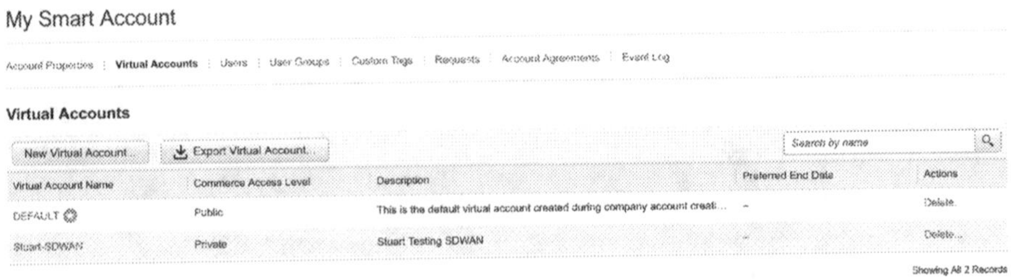

***Figure 2-17.*** *The virtual account has been created*

The next step is to create a vBond controller. Head back to the main software page where we started, and click the *"Plug and Play Connect"* link (Figure 2-18).

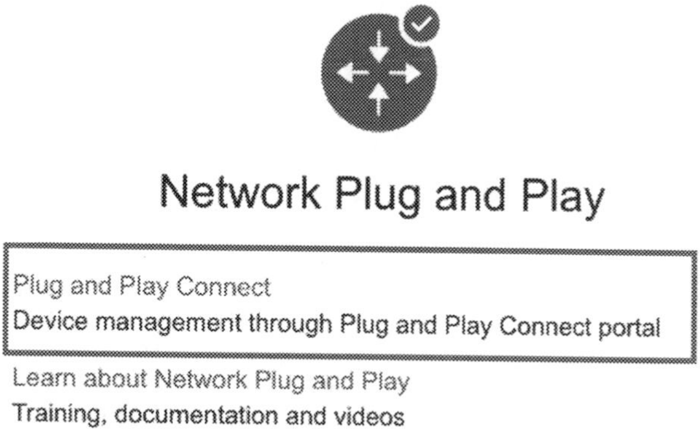

## Network Plug and Play

Plug and Play Connect
Device management through Plug and Play Connect portal

Learn about Network Plug and Play
Training, documentation and videos

***Figure 2-18.*** *The Plug and Play Connect portal*

Select the virtual account you created earlier (Figure 2-19).

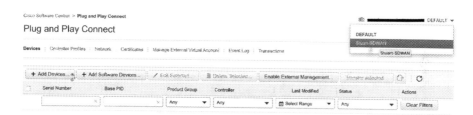

***Figure 2-19.*** *Selecting the virtual account*

Next, click "Controller Profiles" (Figure 2-20).

Cisco Software Central > **Plug and Play Connect**

## Plug and Play Connect

| **Devices** | Controller Profiles | Network | Certificates | Manage External Virtual Account | Event Log | Transactions |

***Figure 2-20.*** *Controller Profiles*

Click "Add Profile" (Figure 2-21).

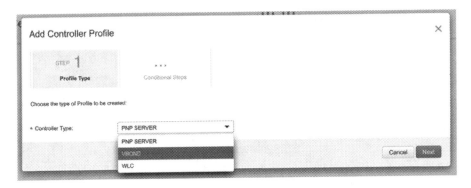

**Figure 2-21.** *Adding a profile*

Select VBOND from the drop-down menu (Figure 2-22).

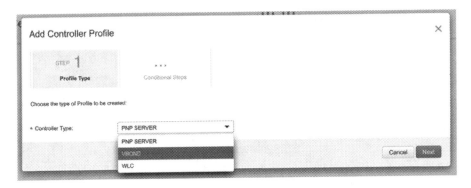

**Figure 2-22.** *Selecting vBond*

Give the profile a name, and set an organization name. Set the Primary controller to IPv4, and add an IP address. You can use any address you like here (Figure 2-23).

Click Next.

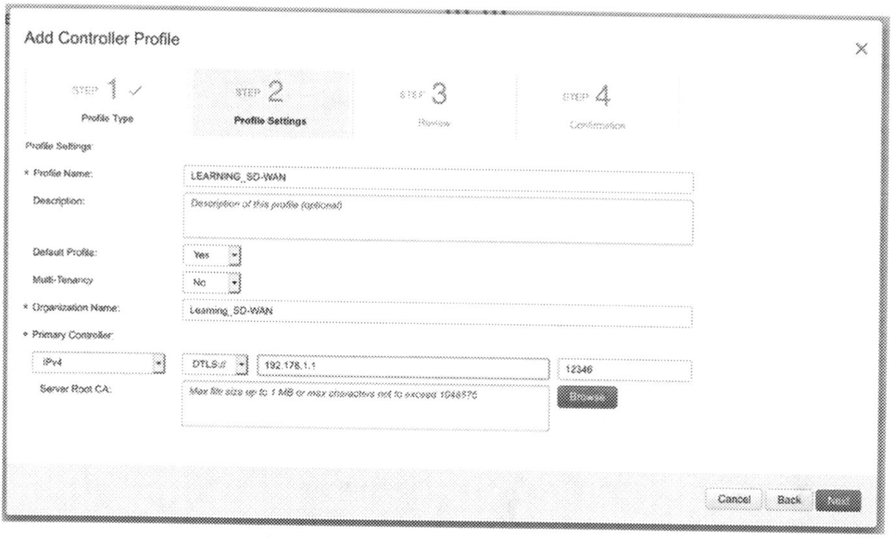

**Figure 2-23.** *Adding the controller profile*

Confirm your settings, and click Submit (Figure 2-24).

**Figure 2-24.** *Confirming the settings*

Click Done to confirm the profile (Figure 2-25).

*Figure 2-25.*  *Finishing the controller profile*

You should see the profile that has been created (Figure 2-26).

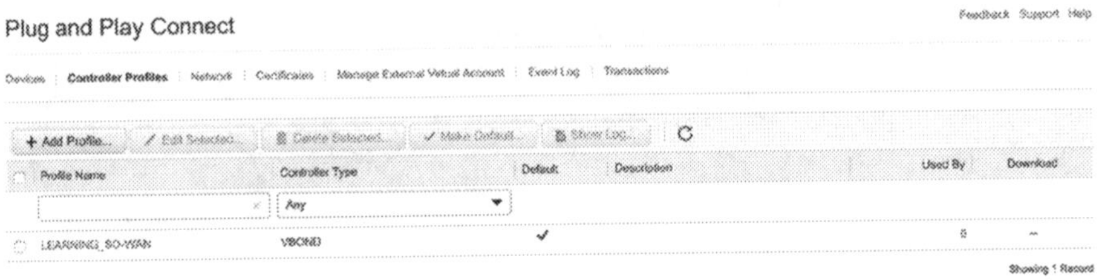

**Figure 2-26.**  *The new controller profile*

Go to Devices (Figure 2-27).

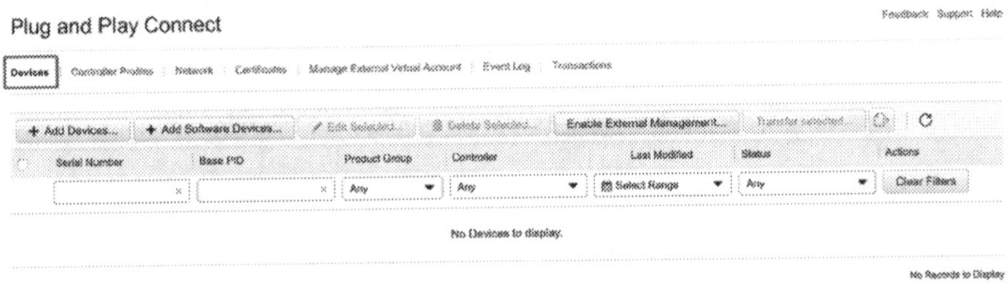

**Figure 2-27.**  *Devices*

Select "Add Software Devices" (Figure 2-28).

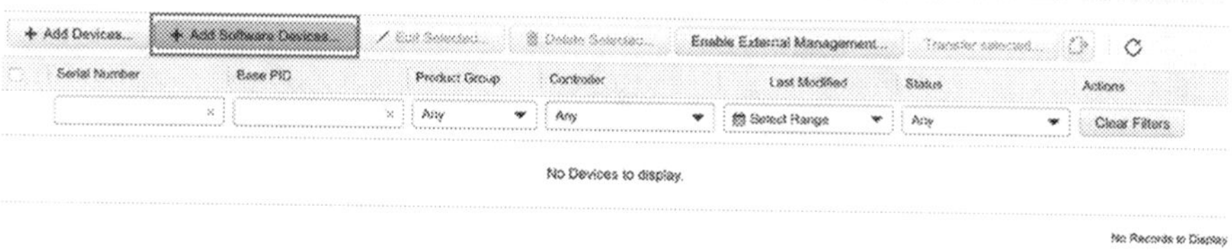

***Figure 2-28.*** *Add software devices*

Click "Add Software Device" (Figure 2-29).

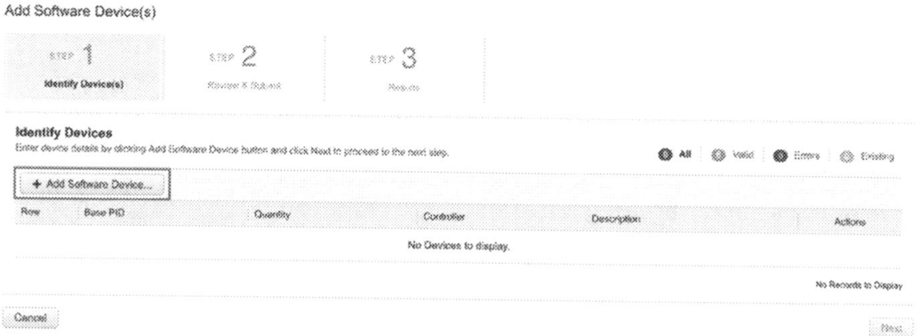

***Figure 2-29.*** *Identifying the devices*

In the Base PID box, start typing "VEDGE-CLOUD-DNA," and select it from the drop-down when it appears (Figure 2-30).

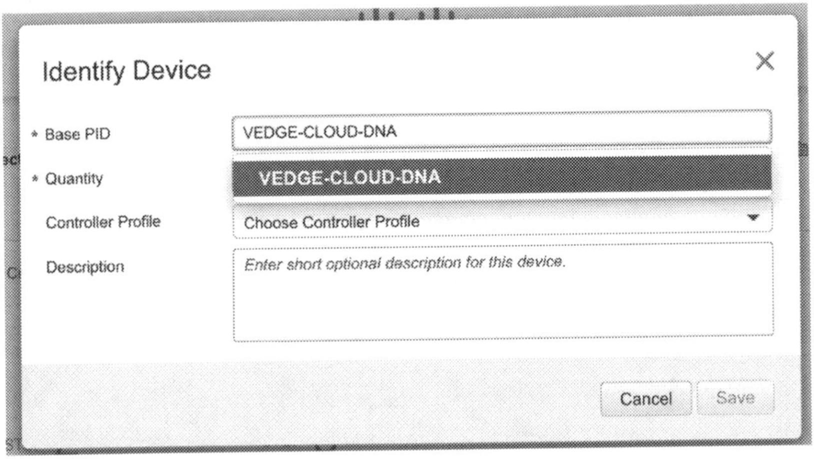

**Figure 2-30.** *Selecting vEdge*

Set the desired quantity (such as 5 which is a good number; there is a limit of 20 "free" nodes), and from the Controller Profile drop-down, select the profile name we created a moment ago (Figure 2-31).

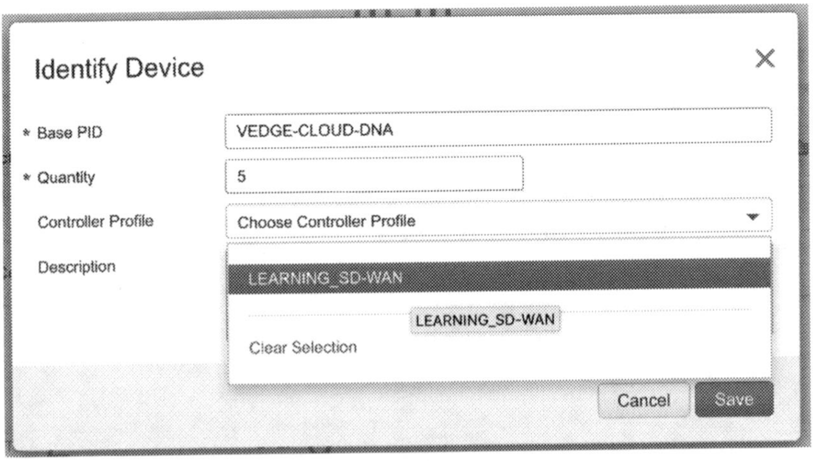

**Figure 2-31.** *Associating the device to the controller profile*

Click Save, and then click Next (Figure 2-32).

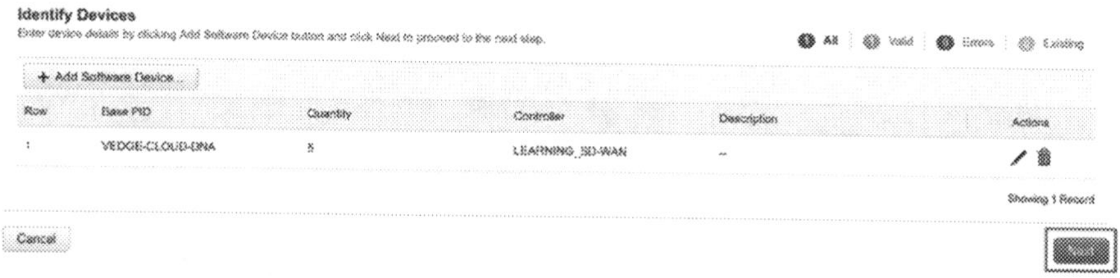

**Identify Devices**

Enter device details by clicking Add Software Device button and click Next to proceed to the next step.

● All   ◉ Valid   ● Errors   ◉ Existing

+ Add Software Device

| Row | Base PID | Quantity | Controller | Description | Actions |
|-----|----------|----------|------------|-------------|---------|
| 1 | VEDGE-CLOUD-DNA | 5 | LEARNING_SD-WAN | -- | ✏ 🗑 |

Showing 1 Record

Cancel                                                                 Next

*Figure 2-32. Setting the number of vEdge devices*

Click Submit (Figure 2-33).

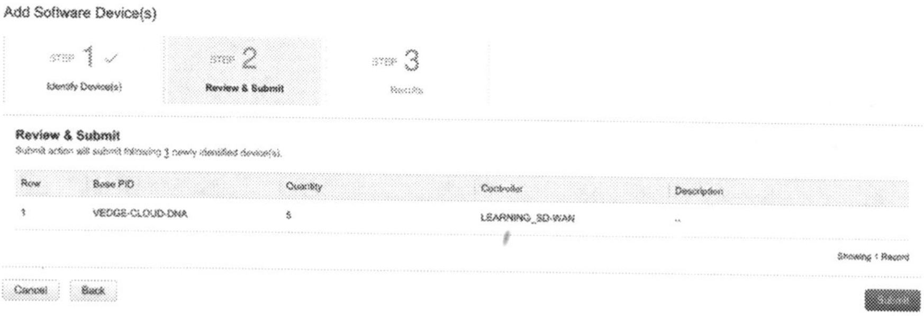

Add Software Device(s)

STEP 1 ✓   STEP 2   STEP 3
Identify Device(s)   Review & Submit   Results

**Review & Submit**

Submit action will submit following 3 newly identified device(s).

| Row | Base PID | Quantity | Controller | Description |
|-----|----------|----------|------------|-------------|
| 1 | VEDGE-CLOUD-DNA | 5 | LEARNING_SD-WAN | -- |

Showing 1 Record

Cancel   Back                                                         Submit

*Figure 2-33. Submitting the vEdge quantities*

Your request will be processed in the background, and you will receive an email once it has completed (I have obscured my work email address!) (Figure 2-34).

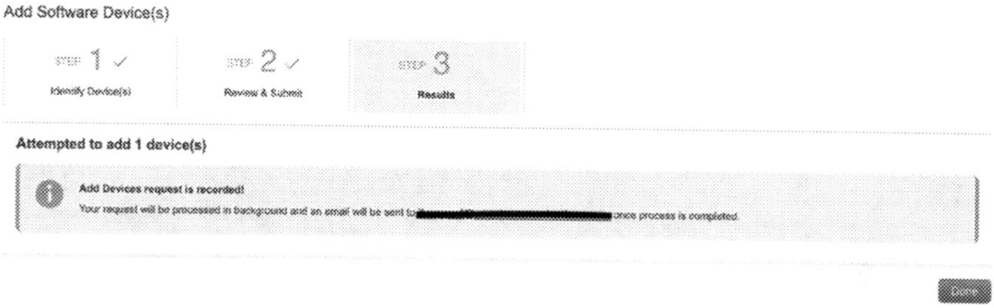

Add Software Device(s)

STEP 1 ✓   STEP 2 ✓   STEP 3
Identify Device(s)   Review & Submit   Results

**Attempted to add 1 device(s)**

ⓘ Add Devices request is recorded!
Your request will be processed in background and an email will be sent to ███████████ once process is completed.

Done

*Figure 2-34. Email confirmation*

Usually, this process is pretty quick, so give a few moments and refresh your page, and you should see your devices (Figure 2-35).

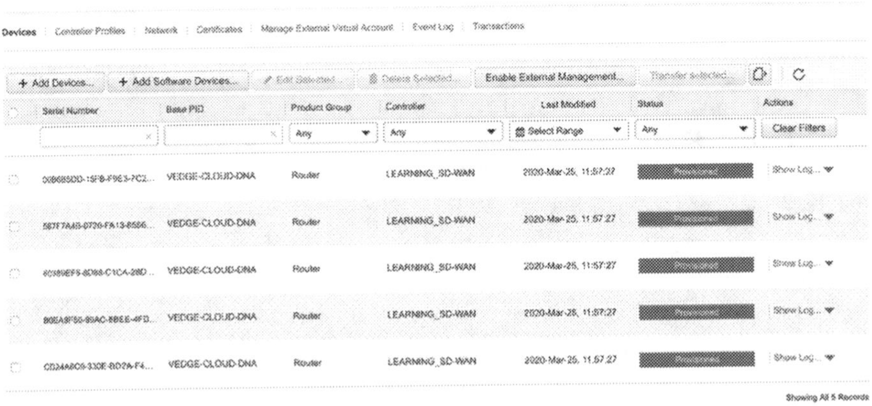

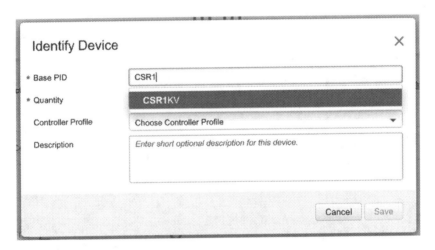

**Figure 2-35.** *Our device list*

Repeat the process, and add some CSR routers (Figure 2-36).

**Figure 2-36.** *Adding CSR devices*

Set the quantity and your profile (Figure 2-37).

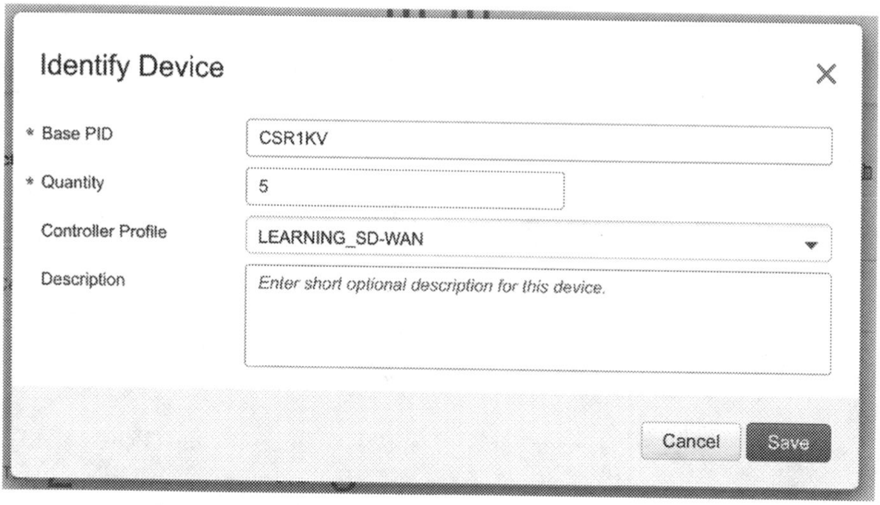

**Figure 2-37.** *5 CSR devices*

These should appear alongside the VEDGE devices (Figure 2-38).

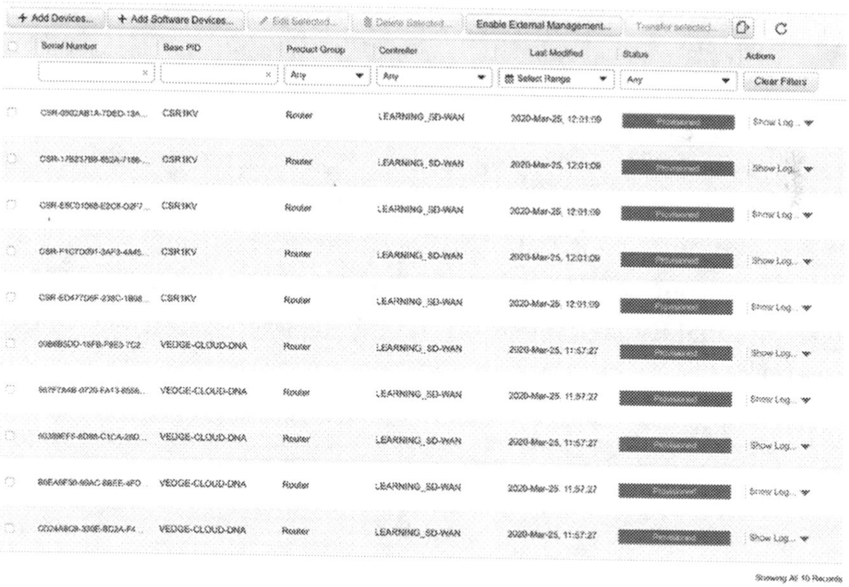

**Figure 2-38.** *Our device list in full*

Go back to Controller Profiles, and select the provisioning file (Figure 2-39).

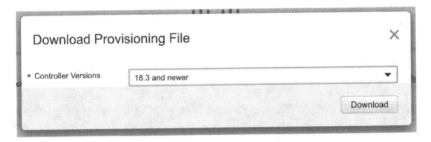

*Figure 2-39.* *Getting the provisioning file*

Select the "18.3 and newer" option, and download the file (Figure 2-40).

Download Provisioning File    ×

* Controller Versions    18.3 and newer ▼

Download

*Figure 2-40.* *Downloading the provisioning file*

The next step is to download the software. Because we are using EVE-NG, it is best to find the QCOW versions, so head back to the main Cisco website and search for "viptela qcow2" and download the vEdge, vSmart, vManage images. Also, download the SDWAN CSR1000v image (Figure 2-41).

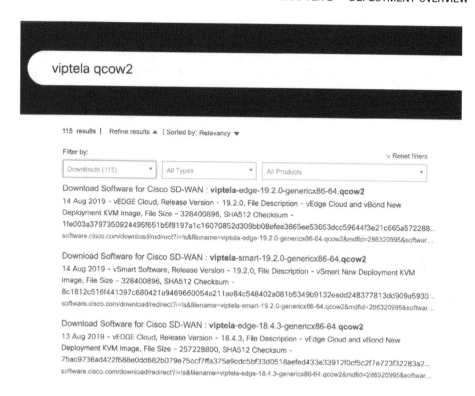

viptela qcow2

115 results | Refine results ▲ | Sorted by: Relevancy ▼

Filter by:                                                                                    × Reset filters

Downloads (115) ▼     All Types ▼     All Products ▼

Download Software for Cisco SD-WAN : **viptela-edge-19.2.0-genericx86-64.qcow2**
14 Aug 2019 ~ vEDGE Cloud, Release Version - 19.2.0, File Description - vEdge Cloud and vBond New
Deployment KVM Image, File Size ~ 328400896, SHA512 Checksum ~
1fe003a3797350924495f651b5f8197a1c16070852d309bb08efee3865ee53653dcc59644f3e21c665a572288...
software.cisco.com/download/redirect?i=!s&filename=viptela-edge-19.2.0-genericx86-64.qcow2&mdfid=286320995&softwar...

Download Software for Cisco SD-WAN : **viptela-smart-19.2.0-genericx86-64.qcow2**
14 Aug 2019 ~ vSmart Software, Release Version - 19.2.0, File Description - vSmart New Deployment KVM
image, File Size ~ 328400896, SHA512 Checksum ~
8c1812c516f441397c680421a9469660054a211ae84c548402a081b5349b9132eedd248377813dd909a5930...
software.cisco.com/download/redirect?i=!s&filename=viptela-smart-19.2.0-genericx86-64.qcow2&mdfid=286320995&softwar...

Download Software for Cisco SD-WAN : **viptela-edge-18.4.3-genericx86-64.qcow2**
13 Aug 2019 ~ vEDGE Cloud, Release Version - 18.4.3, File Description - vEdge Cloud and vBond New
Deployment KVM Image, File Size ~ 257228800, SHA512 Checksum ~
75ac9736ad422f688e0dd662b079e75ccf7ffa375a9cdc5bf33d051 8aefed433e33912f0cf5c2f7e723f32283a2...
software.cisco.com/download/redirect?i=!s&filename=viptela-edge-18.4.3-genericx86-64.qcow2&mdfid=286320995&softwar...

***Figure 2-41.***  *The downloads we need*

The versions used in the majority of the book are either 19.2.1 or 19.3.0 for the Viptela images and 16.12.2r for the CSR1000v.

---

**Note**    We do go through some upgrades later in the book, bumping all the "v" devices up to 20.1.1 and the CSR device up to 17.2.1r. The reasons for this is that firstly, upgrading is good practice, and secondly, the later versions include some features we need in the book, so the choice is yours as to whether to go straight for the later versions or follow along with the chapter on upgrades.

---

For the routers and switches, I am using vIOS 15.6 and vIOS-L2 15.2, respectively. Follow the steps on the EVE-NG website for how to generate these images from the VIRL originals: *www.eve-ng.net/index.php/ documentation/howtos/howto-add-cisco-vios-from-virl/*. You can use other router and switch images (such as Cumulus VX) should you so wish.

The Ubuntu image is the desktop version, 17.10.1. You need to have OpenSSL installed. You can either create your own or download a ready-built image from here: *www.eve-ng.net/index.php/ documentation/howtos/howto-create-own-linux-host-image/*.

If you are using different images, then please update the folder and file names accordingly.

Once you have downloaded the files, SSH onto your EVE-NG install and create the folders we will need:

```
cd /opt/unetlab/addons/qemu
```

```
mkdir vtbond-19.3.0
mkdir vtedge-19.3.0
mkdir vtsmart-19.3.0
mkdir vtmgmt19.3.0
mkdir csr1000vng-ucmk9.16.12.2r-sdwan
```

Then using FileZilla or WinSCP, copy the files as in Table 2-2.

***Table 2-2.***  *Appliance versions*

| Folder | Image |
| --- | --- |
| vtbond-19.3.0 | viptela-edge-19.3.0-genericx86-64.qcow2 |
| vtedge-19.3.0 | viptela-edge-19.3.0-genericx86-64.qcow2 |
| vtsmart-19.3.0 | viptela-smart-19.3.0-genericx86-64.qcow2 |
| vtmgmt-19.3.0 | viptela-vmanage-19.3.0-genericx86-64.qcow2 |
| csr1000vng-ucmk9.16.12.2r-sdwan | csr1000v-ucmk9.16.12.2r.qcow2 |

The next step is to rename the files and create a second disk for vManage:

```
cd csr1000vng-ucmk9.16.12.2r-sdwan
mv csr1000v-ucmk9.16.12.2r.qcow2 virtioa.qcow2
cd ..
cd vtbond-19.3.0/
mv viptela-edge-19.3.0-genericx86-64.qcow2 hda.qcow2
cd ..
cd vtedge-19.3.0/
mv viptela-edge-19.3.0-genericx86-64.qcow2 hda.qcow2
cd ..
cd vtsmart-19.3.0/
mv viptela-smart-19.3.0-genericx86-64.qcow2 hda.qcow2
cd ..
cd vtmgmt-19.3.0/
mv viptela-vmanage-19.3.0-genericx86-64.qcow2 hda.qcow2
/opt/qemu/bin/qemu-img create -f qcow2 hdb.qcow2 100G
cd ..
```

Lastly, update the wrappers using the command "unl_wrapper -a fixpermissions" (which corrects any permission issues after copying images around):

```
root@eve-ng:/opt/unetlab/addons/qemu# /opt/unetlab/wrappers/
unl_wrapper -a fixpermissions

root@eve-ng:/opt/unetlab/addons/qemu#
```

The resulting directory listing (with the router, switch, and Linux images) should look like this:

```
root@eve-ng:/opt/unetlab/addons/qemu# tree
.
├── csr1000vng-ucmk9.16.12.2r-sdwan
│   └── virtioa.qcow2
├── linux-ubuntu-desktop-17.10.1
│   └── virtioa.qcow2
├── vios-156
│   └── virtioa.qcow2
├── viosl2-152
│   └── virtioa.qcow2
├── vtbond-19.3.0
│   └── hda.qcow2
├── vtedge-19.3.0
│   └── hda.qcow2
├── vtmgmt-19.3.0
│   ├── hda.qcow2
│   └── hdb.qcow2
└── vtsmart-19.3.0
    └── hda.qcow2

8 directories, 9 files
root@eve-ng:/opt/unetlab/addons/qemu#
```

# Topology

Our initial topology looks like this (Figure 2-42).

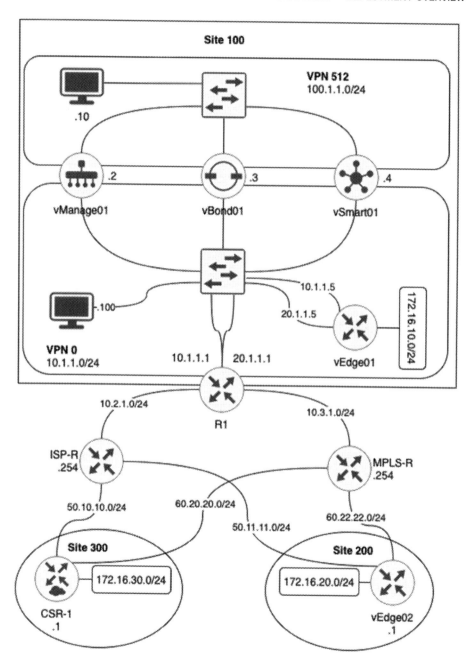

***Figure 2-42.***  *Our initial topology*

We have a central site, our headquarters, which is designated as "site 100." We also have two branch sites, site 200 and site 300. These are connected to our HQ using MPLS as well as standard Internet links.

We have three networks that we are going to use SD-WAN to provide connectivity for, and these are 172.16.10.0/24 in site 100, 172.16.20.0/24 in site 200, and 172.16.30.0/24 in site 300.

We have Linux machines connected to VPN 512 (for management) and also to VPN 0, which we will mainly be using as our certificate server; this is the one we will be using most. If resources are an issue, then you can just use the Linux server in VPN 0.

The topology will change as we move through this book.

You can download the lab file from www.apress.com.

# Importing the Lab File

To import the lab file, log into the EVE-NG GUI via your browser, and click the Import button. Browse to the zip file containing the lab and select it. Click the Upload button. You can then start the lab.

# Initial Configurations

The initial configurations for R1, ISP-R, and MPLS-R are as follows. They have been truncated to just show the important configurations.

# R1

```
R1#sh run
!
hostname R1
!
interface GigabitEthernet0/0
```

```
 description VPN0 Inside
 ip address 10.1.1.1 255.255.255.0
 no shut
!
interface GigabitEthernet0/1
 description VPN0 Outside
 ip address 10.2.1.1 255.255.255.0
 no shut
!
interface GigabitEthernet0/2
 description MPLS Outside
 ip address 10.3.1.1 255.255.255.0
 no shut
!
interface GigabitEthernet0/3
 description MPLS Inside
 ip address 20.1.1.1 255.255.255.0
 !
ip route 50.0.0.0 255.0.0.0 10.2.1.254
ip route 60.0.0.0 255.0.0.0 10.3.1.254
 !
end

R1#
```

# ISP-R

```
ISP-R#sh run
!
hostname ISP-R
!
interface GigabitEthernet0/0
```

```
 description VPNO
 ip address 10.2.1.254 255.255.255.0
 no shut
!
interface GigabitEthernet0/1
 Link to vEdge02
 ip address 50.11.11.254 255.255.255.0
 no shut
!
interface GigabitEthernet0/2
 no ip address
!
interface GigabitEthernet0/3
 Link to CSR-1
 ip address 50.10.10.254 255.255.255.0
 no shut
!
ip route 10.1.1.0 255.255.255.0 10.2.1.1
!
end

ISP-R#
```

# MPLS-R

```
MPLS-R#sh run
!
hostname MPLS-R
!
interface GigabitEthernet0/0
 description MPLS
 ip address 10.3.1.254 255.255.255.0
```

```
 no shut
!
interface GigabitEthernet0/1
 Link to vEdge02
 ip address 60.22.22.254 255.255.255.0
 no shut
!
interface GigabitEthernet0/2
 Link to CSR-1
 ip address 60.20.20.254 255.255.255.0
 no shut
!
ip route 10.1.1.0 255.255.255.0 10.3.1.1
!
end

MPLS-R#
```

# ESXi and KVM Configuration

This network can also be set up on VMWare and KVM. While the steps for creating each of the SD-WAN VMs will be given for both platforms at the end of each respective chapter, explaining the full set up of ESXi, vCenter, and KVM is beyond the scope of this book.

# Summary

We have set up our EVE-NG server, created our smart account, generated our serial file list so that we can run some edge devices, and downloaded our device images. We should also have the routers configured, ready to start sending traffic around our network. With that in mind, let's get started with our vManage server.

# CHAPTER 3

# Deploying vManage

In this chapter, we will set up our vManage servers. vManage is the NMS (Network Management System) which controls our SD-WAN, so it makes sense that we start here. We will set up our organization, the certificates we need to add and authenticate our devices, and look at how to control our users, implementing clustering for high availability and resilience. We will also look at single- and multi-tenancy options, installation of vManage on ESXi and KVM, and how to install the serial file we generated from the Smart account.

## Installing vManage

Because we are using a ready-made appliance, all the heavy lifting has been done for us, so just right-click vManage01 in EVE-NG and select "Start," and then left-click it to start the telnet console session.

After a while, you will be prompted to log in; use the default username and password of "admin", setting a new password when prompted. The next step is to format the storage disk, so select the 100G disk created earlier, and press "y" to format it. Once this is done, the system will reboot.

```
vmanage login: admin
Password:
Welcome to Viptela CLI
admin connected from 127.0.0.1 using console on vmanage
```

© Stuart Fordham 2021
S. Fordham, *Learning SD-WAN with Cisco*, https://doi.org/10.1007/978-1-4842-7347-0_3

```
Available storage devices:
hdb        100GB
hdc        3GB
1) hdb
2) hdc
Select storage device to use: 1
Would you like to format hdb? (y/n): y
mke2fs 1.43.8 (1-Jan-2018)
Creating filesystem with 26214400 4k blocks and 6553600 inodes
Filesystem UUID: bc995938-6aeb-49c9-aeba-48d70b18235b
Superblock backups stored on blocks:
        32768, 98304, 163840, 229376, 294912, 819200, 884736,
        1605632, 2654208,
        4096000, 7962624, 11239424, 20480000, 23887872

Allocating group tables: done
Writing inode tables: done
Creating journal (131072 blocks): done
Writing superblocks and filesystem accounting information: done

vmanage# wall: cannot get tty name: Success

Broadcast message from root@vmanage (somewhere) (Mon Mar 30
09:35:19 2020):

Mon Mar 30 09:35:19 UTC 2020: The system is going down for
reboot NOW!

Stopping services...
acpid: exiting
```

When the system has come back up again, log in and set the system IP address (100.100.1.2), the site-id (100), the organization name (Learning_ SD-WAN), and the hostname (vManage01) (as shown in Figure 2-42 in the previous chapter).

```
Mon Mar 30 09:36:19 UTC 2020: System Ready

viptela 19.3.0

vmanage login: admin
Password:
Welcome to Viptela CLI
admin connected from 127.0.0.1 using console on vmanage
vmanage#
vmanage#
vmanage# config
Entering configuration mode terminal
vmanage(config)# system
vmanage(config-system)# system-ip 100.100.1.2
vmanage(config-system)# site-id 100
vmanage(config-system)# organization-name Learning_SD-WAN
vmanage(config-system)#
vmanage(config-system)# host-name vManage01
vmanage(config-system)#
```

The next step is to create the management VPN (VPN 512).

```
vmanage(config-system)# vpn 512
vmanage(config-vpn-512)# interface eth0
vmanage(config-interface-eth0)# ip address 100.1.1.2/24
vmanage(config-interface-eth0)# no shutdown
vmanage(config-interface-eth0)#
vmanage(config-interface-eth0)# exit
vmanage(config-vpn-512)#
```

The management VPN carries the out-of-band network management traffic for the SD-WAN devices.

Now we can create our WAN overlay VPN (VPN 0):

```
vmanage(config-vpn-512)# vpn 0
vmanage(config-vpn-0)# no interface eth0
vmanage(config-vpn-0)# interface eth1
vmanage(config-interface-eth1)# ip address 10.1.1.2/24
vmanage(config-interface-eth1)# tunnel-interface
vmanage(config-tunnel-interface)# exit
vmanage(config-interface-eth1)# no shutdown
vmanage(config-interface-eth1)#
vmanage(config-interface-eth1)# exit
vmanage(config-vpn-0)#ip route 0.0.0.0/0 10.1.1.1
vmanage(config-vpn-0)# exit
vmanage(config)#
```

VPN 0 carries our control traffic. By default, all of our interfaces will be added to VPN 0, and the interfaces are disabled. We, therefore, have to remove eth0 from VPN 0 (because we need eth0 to be in VPN 512) and enable eth1, configuring the IP address and setting it as a tunnel interface. We also add a default route. You will notice that no default route was added to our VPN 512 configuration, but this is due to the size of our topology; in a real-world set up, this may be required.

The last step of our configuration is to save our settings. Before we try and commit our changes, we should confirm that the settings are valid, which we can do by using the "validate" command or "commit check".

```
vmanage(config)# validate
Validation complete
vmanage(config)# commit check
Validation complete
vmanage(config)# commit and-quit
Commit complete.
vManage01#
```

If all is working, we should have connectivity to the R1 router:

```
vManage01# ping 10.1.1.1
Ping in VPN 0
PING 10.1.1.1 (10.1.1.1) 56(84) bytes of data.
64 bytes from 10.1.1.1: icmp_seq=1 ttl=64 time=1.61 ms
64 bytes from 10.1.1.1: icmp_seq=2 ttl=64 time=0.825 ms
64 bytes from 10.1.1.1: icmp_seq=3 ttl=64 time=0.787 ms
64 bytes from 10.1.1.1: icmp_seq=4 ttl=64 time=0.680 ms
64 bytes from 10.1.1.1: icmp_seq=5 ttl=64 time=0.743 ms
^C
--- 10.1.1.1 ping statistics ---
6 packets transmitted, 6 received, 0% packet loss, time 5001ms
rtt min/avg/max/mdev = 0.680/0.897/1.611/0.322 ms
vManage01#
```

From the Linux machine in VPN 0, launch the browser and connect to the management interface on https://10.1.1.2 (Figure 3-1).

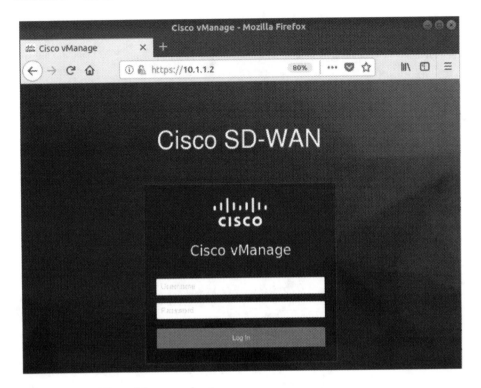

*Figure 3-1.  The vManage login page*

You can also use the Linux machine in VPN 512 and connect using the URL https://100.1.1.2. Log in using the username admin and the password you set during setup.

---

**TIP**   There is a lot of information on the dashboard, so if you find your screen resolution is too small, as it can be with QEMU devices, then you can change it if you set your QEMU VM properties to use "-vga virtio" instead of "-vga std", as shown in Figure 3-2. You will need to stop and then start the Linux VM for the change to take effect.

---

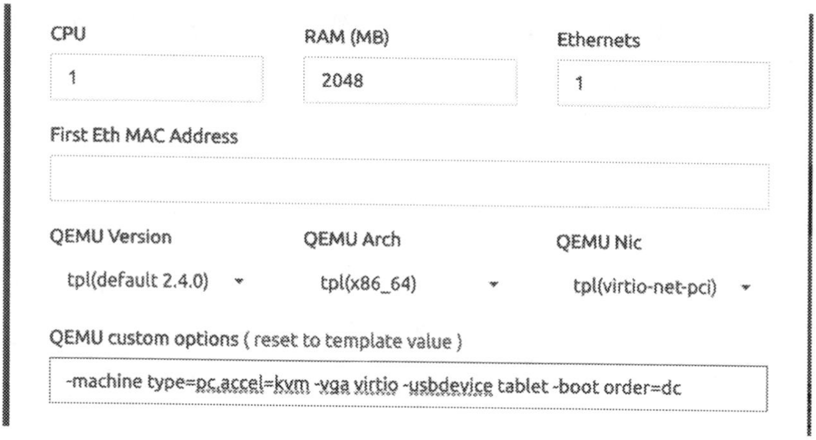

| CPU | RAM (MB) | Ethernets |
|---|---|---|
| 1 | 2048 | 1 |

First Eth MAC Address

| QEMU Version | QEMU Arch | QEMU Nic |
|---|---|---|
| tpl(default 2.4.0)  ▾ | tpl(x86_64)  ▾ | tpl(virtio-net-pci)  ▾ |

QEMU custom options ( reset to template value )

-machine type=pc,accel=kvm -vga virtio -usbdevice tablet -boot order=dc

***Figure 3-2.*** *Use -vga virtio for a bigger window size*

The vManage interface (Figure 3-3) shows us our connected devices at the top, listing the vSmart, WAN Edge, vBond devices, and vManage servers.

The middle sections show us our WAN status and site health, and at the bottom, we have our applications and application-aware routing.

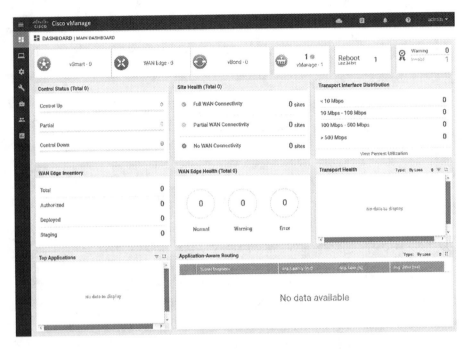

**Figure 3-3.** *The main vManage dashboard*

There is an issue at the moment, though. We can tell this as there is a (invalid) warning at the top right-hand corner (Figure 3-4).

**Figure 3-4.** *Certificate invalid message*

Clicking the number takes us into the error detail, where we can see that we have a problem with our certificate (Figure 3-5).

***Figure 3-5.*** *Certificate issue detail*

# Certificates

Certificates in the SD-WAN network are hugely important; they form a very large role in the authentication of devices.

We need to generate the CA certificates and upload them to the vManage server. The easiest way to do this is to enable SSH on the vManage server so that we can use SCP (Secure Copy Protocol) to upload the files we need. We enable this under the VPN 0 tunnel interface.

```
vManage01(config)# vpn 0
vManage01(config-vpn-0)# interface eth1
vManage01(config-interface-eth1)# tunnel-interface
vManage01(config-tunnel-interface)# allow-service sshd
vManage01(config-tunnel-interface)#
vManage01(config-tunnel-interface)# end
Uncommitted changes found, commit them? [yes/no/CANCEL] yes
Commit complete.
vManage01#
```

We will be using the Linux host to be our certificate authority (CA) so that it can sign our certificates.

The first step is to set it up as our CA. Open the console window on the Linux host, and enter the following:

```
openssl genrsa -out CA.key 2048
openssl req -new -x509 -days 1000 -key CA.key -out CA.crt
```

As mentioned in the previous chapter, your Linux VM will need to have the OpenSSL packages installed for this to work. This will generate our CA certificate. Next, copy it across to the vManage server using SCP ("scp CA.crt admin@10.1.1.2:"), typing in the vManage admin password when prompted.

Switching back to the vManage server, install the CA certificate, using the command "request root-cert-chain install":

```
vManage01# request root-cert-chain install /home/admin/CA.crt
Uploading root-ca-cert-chain via VPN 0
Copying ... /home/admin/CA.crt via VPN 0
Updating the root certificate chain..
Successfully installed the root certificate chain
vManage01#
```

Now that the vManage server knows that we have a CA, we can use it to sign our CSRs.

We must have our organization name set at this stage. If it is not set, then go to *Administration* ➤ *Settings* and set it.

As we are running this in a virtual lab, we need to switch how our certificates are provisioned to us. Go to *Administration* ➤ *Settings*, and click "edit" next to "Controller Certificate Authority."

By default, it is set to "Cisco" as shown in Figure 3-6.

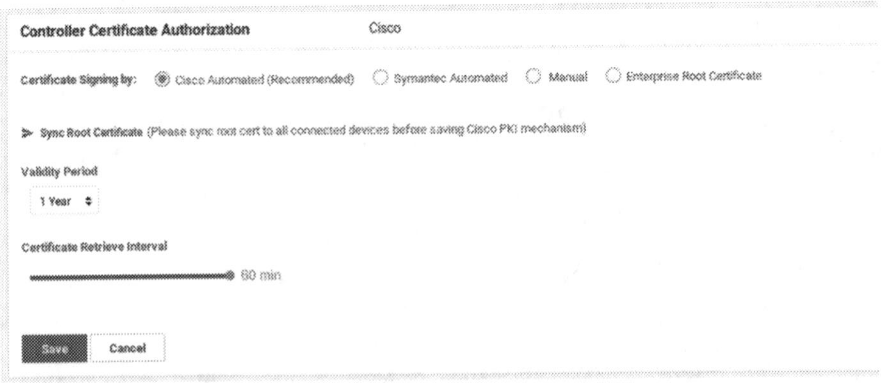

*Figure 3-6. Default certificate authority*

Click the "Enterprise Root Certificate" option (Figure 3-7), and confirm the change by clicking "Proceed."

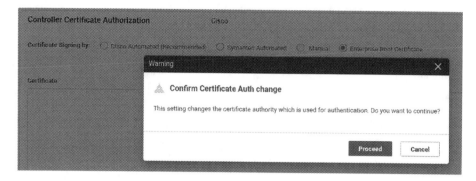

***Figure 3-7.***  *Confirm the change*

Upload the CA.crt file next (Figure 3-8).

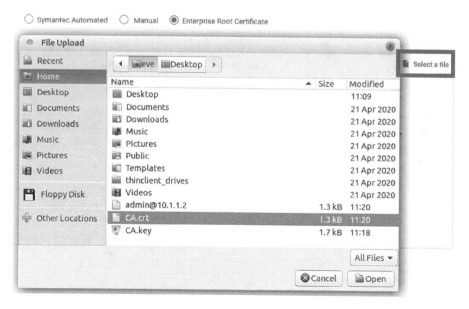

***Figure 3-8.***  *Upload the CA certificate*

Click "Import & Save" (Figure 3-9).

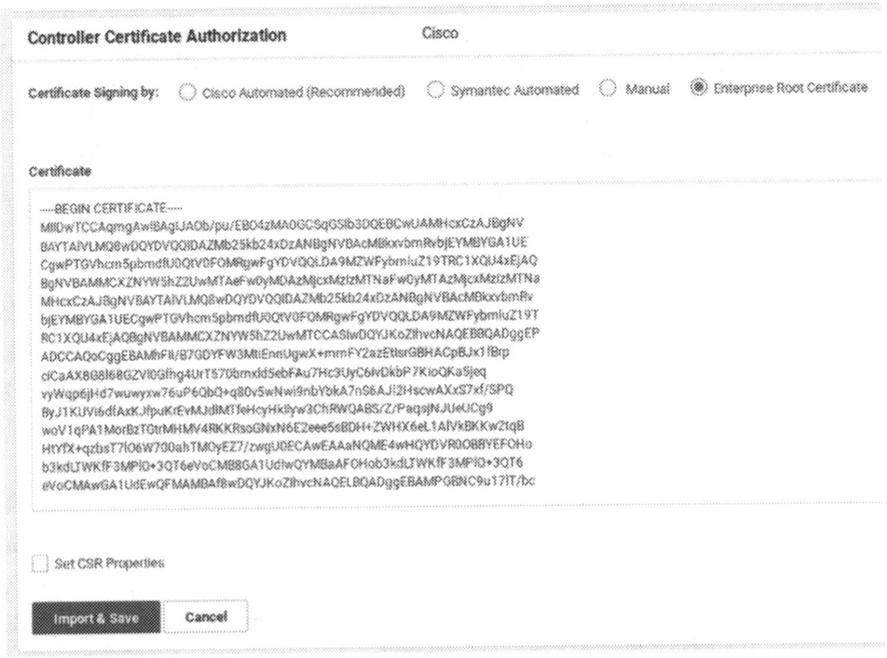

*Figure 3-9.* *Import and save the CA certificate*

Generate a certificate request by going to *Configuration* ➤ *Certificates* (Figure 3-10).

***Figure 3-10.*** *The certificates menu*

There won't be any certificates for the WAN Edge yet (Figure 3-11), so click "Controllers."

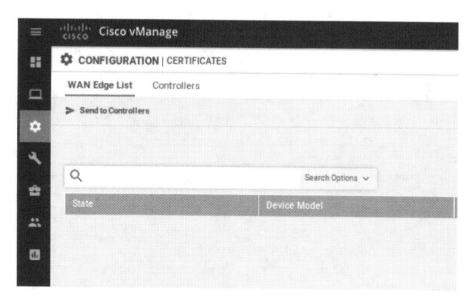

***Figure 3-11.*** *Certificates (or lack of)*

The Controllers page will show "No certificate installed." Click the three buttons on the right-hand side, and select "Generate CSR"; vManage will generate a certificate (Figure 3-12).

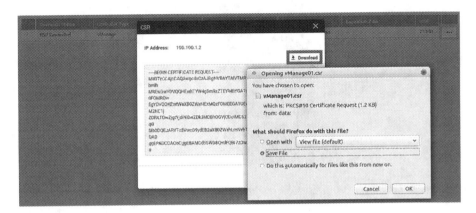

***Figure 3-12.***  *vManage CSR*

Download the CSR and save it. Back on the Linux machine, sign the CSR, making sure that the CSR is in the right directory (Figure 3-13):

```
openssl x509 –req –in vManage01.csr –CA CA.crt –CAkey CA.key –
CAcreateserial –out vManage01.crt –days 1000 –sha256
```

```
user@user-virtual-machine:~/Downloads$ openssl x509 -req -in vManage01.csr -CA
CA.crt -CAkey CA.key \
> -CAcreateserial -out vManage01.crt -days 1000 -sha256
Signature ok
subject=/C=US/ST=California/L=San Jose/OU=Learning_SD-WAN/O=Viptela LLC/CN=vman
age-b63aa480-37f6-4589-ba5e-961c9115c8fe-1.viptela.com/emailAddress=support@vip
tela.com
Getting CA Private Key
user@user-virtual-machine:~/Downloads$
```

***Figure 3-13.***  *Signing the vManage CSR*

Once the certificate has been generated, go back to the vManage GUI, and select the "Install Certificate" option. Click "Select a file," and select the vManage01.crt file we just created (Figure 3-14).

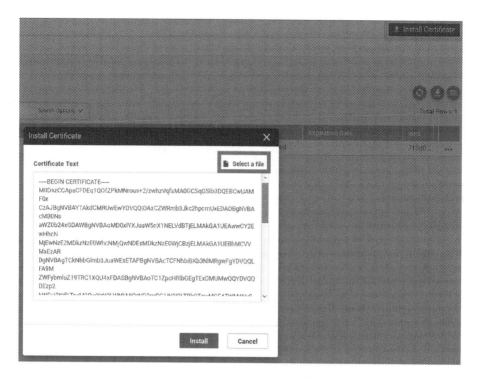

***Figure 3-14.*** *Installing the signed vManage certificate*

Click Install. The certificate will then synchronize (Figure 3-15).

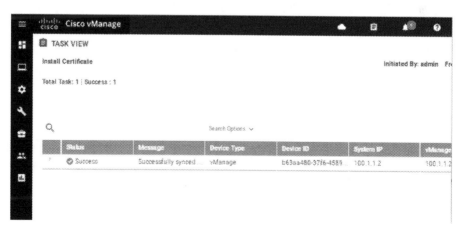

***Figure 3-15.*** *Certificate synchronization*

If the certificate takes a while to synchronize, you can speed it up using the API, by going to `https://10.1.1.2/dataservice/system/device/sync/rootcertchain` (Figure 3-16).

***Figure 3-16.*** *Certificate synchronization through the API*

While our certificate synchronizes, let's take a moment to look at users and clustering.

# Users

We only have one user at the moment, the admin user. We can create more, if we want to, by going to *Administration ➤ Manage Users.*

There are three groups (by default) that we add users into, and these are basic, netadmin, and operator. The NetAdmin role has full rights over every aspect of the SD-WAN software. The operator has read-only rights, and the basic role can only look at the interface and the system. The full list of privileges is listed in Table 3-1.

***Table 3-1.*** *User privileges*

| | Basic | NetAdmin | Operator |
|---|---|---|---|
| Alarms | – | Full | Read |
| Audit Log | – | Full | Read |
| Certificates | – | Full | Read |
| Cloud OnRamp | – | Full | Read |
| Cluster | – | Full | Read |
| Colocation | – | Full | Read |
| Device inventory | – | Full | Read |
| Device monitoring | – | Full | Read |
| Device reboot | – | Full | Read |
| Events | – | Full | Read |
| Interface | Read | Full | Read |
| Manage users | – | Full | Read |
| Policy | – | Full | Read |
| Policy configuration | – | Full | Read |
| Policy deploy | – | Full | Read |
| Routing | – | Full | Read |
| Security | – | Full | Read |
| Security policy configuration | – | Full | Read |
| Settings | – | Full | Read |
| Software upgrade | – | Full | Read |

(*continued*)

**Table 3-1.** (*continued*)

|  | Basic | NetAdmin | Operator |
|---|---|---|---|
| System | Read | Full | Read |
| Template configuration | – | Full | Read |
| Template deploy | – | Full | Read |
| Tools | – | Full | Read |
| vAnalytics | – | Full | Read |

We can create custom groups by clicking the "Add User Group" button, and we can also create new users, by clicking the "Add User" button. Here, we can create an account for "monitoring," which is a member of the "basic" user group (Figure 3-17).

*Figure 3-17.* *A basic user*

Our new user is visible along with the default admin account (Figure 3-18).

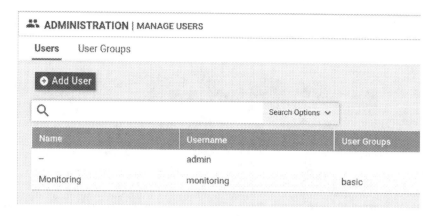

*Figure 3-18.* A new user

# vManage Clustering

As vManage is the linchpin of the SD-WAN, it needs to be resilient. We can have multiple vManage servers and cluster them to ensure the configuration among them is consistent.

Navigate to *Administration* ➤ *Cluster Management* (Figure 3-19).

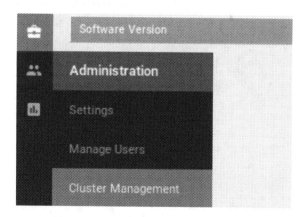

*Figure 3-19.* Cluster Management

By default, the local vManage server will show an IP address of "localhost" as shown in Figure 3-20.

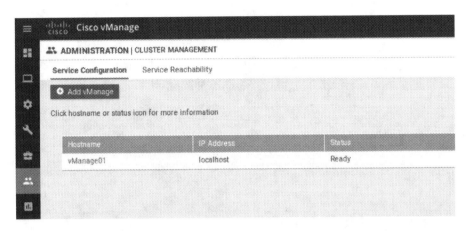

***Figure 3-20.*** *vManage as localhost*

We need to be able to distinguish between our vManage servers, so we have to change the IP address first, before we can add any new servers to our cluster.

Click the triple dots at the right-hand side of the server, and select "Edit" (Figure 3-21).

***Figure 3-21.*** *Editing the vManage server*

Select the IP address (10.1.1.2) from the drop-down, and enter the
username and password (Figure 3-22).

***Figure 3-22.*** *Setting the vManage IP address*

Click "Update." In the next window, you will be prompted to reboot the
vManage server (Figure 3-23).

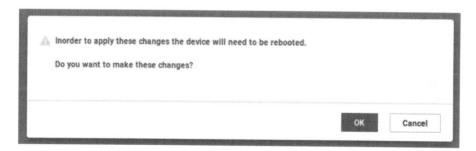

***Figure 3-23.*** *Rebooting the vManage*

Click OK. You will see now that the IP address has changed (Figure 3-24).

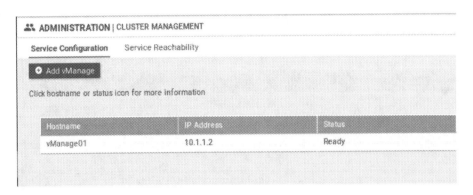

*Figure 3-24.* *New vManage IP address*

We can now add a new vManage node, and we can do this by copying the existing one on the EVE-NG server:

```
root@eve-ng:~# cd /opt/
root@eve-ng:/opt# cd unetlab/addons/qemu/
root@eve-ng:/opt/unetlab/addons/qemu# cp -R vtmgmt-19.3.0
vtmgmt-19.3.0-2
root@eve-ng:/opt/unetlab/addons/qemu# /opt/unetlab/wrappers/
unl_wrapper -a fixpermissions

root@eve-ng:/opt/unetlab/addons/qemu#
```

Add a new vManage server to our topology by right-clicking on a blank area of the topology in EVE-NG and selecting "Node" (Figure 3-25).

***Figure 3-25.*** *Adding a new node to EVE-NG*

Scroll down until you see "Viptela vManage," and click it (Figure 3-26).

***Figure 3-26.*** *Adding the second vManage server*

Select the second instance we just created (Figure 3-27).

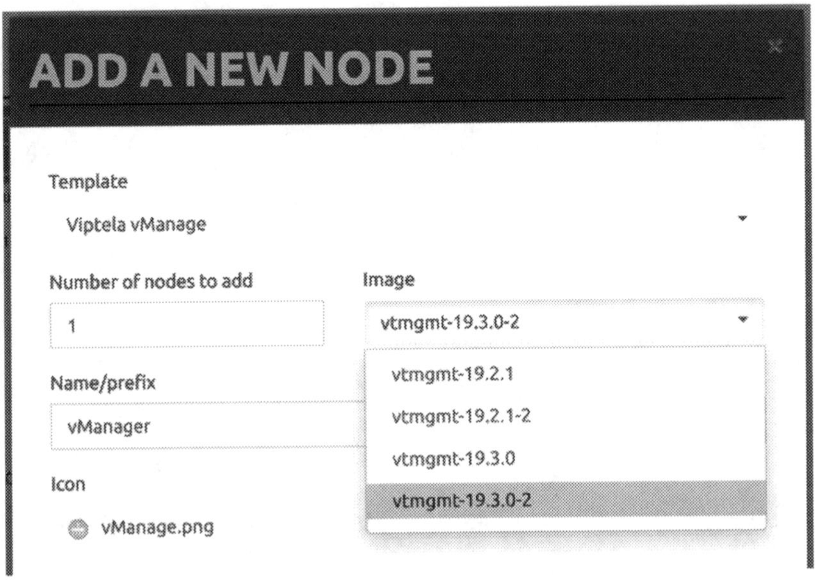

## ADD A NEW NODE

Template

Viptela vManage

Number of nodes to add

1

Image

vtmgmt-19.3.0-2

vtmgmt-19.2.1

vtmgmt-19.2.1-2

Name/prefix

vManager

vtmgmt-19.3.0

vtmgmt-19.3.0-2

Icon

vManage.png

*Figure 3-27.* *Select the second vManage node*

Name it "vManage02" and click Save.

Hover over the new instance with your mouse and then drag the orange network cable icon over to Net100, making sure that eth0 is connected to Net100. You will need to right-click on the VPN0 switch and stop it, then connect the eth1 interface from vManage02 to Gi1/0 on the switch. Start the switch again.

Right-click the topology, and add a text object of ".22". The new topology should look like Figure 3-28.

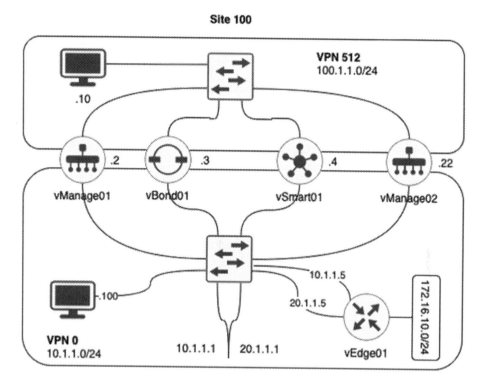

**Figure 3-28.** *The new topology*

Right-click vManage02 and select start (Figure 3-29).

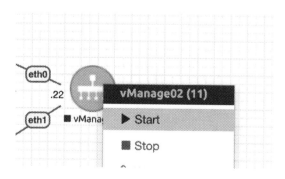

**Figure 3-29.** *Starting vManage02*

Left-click it to launch a telnet connection.

Once the console has loaded, you will be prompted to change the password and format the disk, as we did at the start of the chapter. Once the VM has rebooted, configure it as follows:

```
vmanage# config
Entering configuration mode terminal
vmanage(config)# system
vmanage(config-system)# system-ip 100.100.1.22
vmanage(config-system)# site-id 100
vmanage(config-system)# organization-name Learning_SD-WAN
vmanage(config-system)# host-name vManage02
vmanage(config-system)#
vmanage(config-system)# vpn 512
vmanage(config-vpn-512)# interface eth0
vmanage(config-interface-eth0)# ip address 100.1.1.22/24
vmanage(config-interface-eth0)# no shutdown
vmanage(config-interface-eth0)# exit
vmanage(config-vpn-512)#
vmanage(config-vpn-512)# vpn 0
vmanage(config-vpn-0)# no interface eth0
vmanage(config-vpn-0)# interface eth1
vmanage(config-interface-eth1)# ip address 10.1.1.22/24
vmanage(config-interface-eth1)# no shut
vmanage(config-interface-eth1)# tunnel-interface
vmanage(config-tunnel-interface)# allow-service all
vmanage(config-tunnel-interface)# exit
vmanage(config-interface-eth1)# ip route 0.0.0.0/0 10.1.1.1
vmanage(config-vpn-0)# end
Uncommitted changes found, commit them? [yes/no/CANCEL] yes
Commit complete.
vManage02# ping 10.1.1.2
```

```
Ping in VPN 0
PING 10.1.1.2 (10.1.1.2) 56(84) bytes of data.
64 bytes from 10.1.1.2: icmp_seq=1 ttl=64 time=0.623 ms
64 bytes from 10.1.1.2: icmp_seq=2 ttl=64 time=0.647 ms
^C
--- 10.1.1.2 ping statistics ---
2 packets transmitted, 2 received, 0% packet loss, time 1000ms
rtt min/avg/max/mdev = 0.623/0.635/0.647/0.012 ms
vManage02#
```

I have been a bit lazy with the preceding settings and allowed all services, but this does make life a lot easier when setting up a cluster. In production, I would say that as a minimum, SSHD and NetConf should be allowed, but each deployment will have its separate requirements.

Before we can add this new vManage server to the cluster, we need to complete the setup, which means we need to follow the same steps as we did with vManage01 and add the enterprise root certificates and create a certificate for vManage02.

Once this is complete, we should not have any warnings on the main dashboard on vManage02.

Repeat the process of setting the IP address under *Administration* ➤ *Cluster Management* as we did for vManage01, and wait for vManage02 to come back up again.

Returning to vManage01, we can now add vManage02 to the cluster, click the "Add vManage" button, and enter the IP address of vManage02 and the username and password (Figure 3-30).

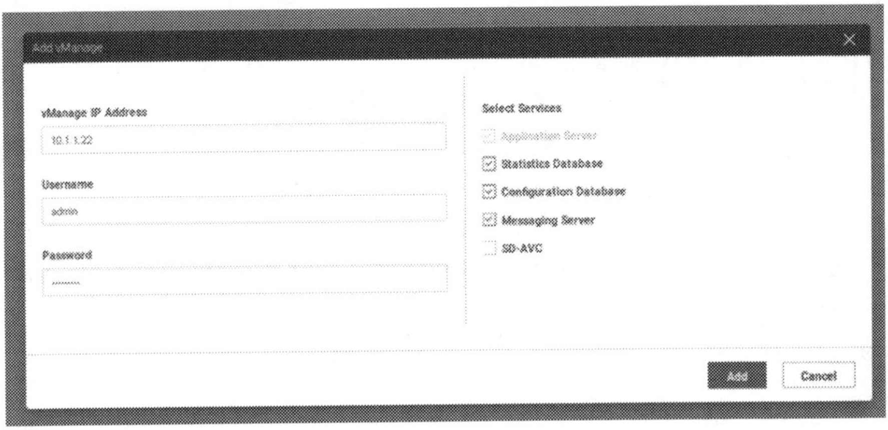

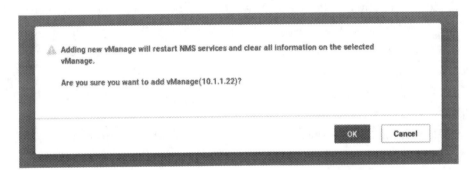

***Figure 3-30.*** *Adding vManage02 to the cluster*

Click "Add" and accept the prompt to reboot vManage02 (Figure 3-31).

***Figure 3-31.*** *Rebooting vManage02*

The new server will have a state of pending until it has rebooted (Figure 3-32).

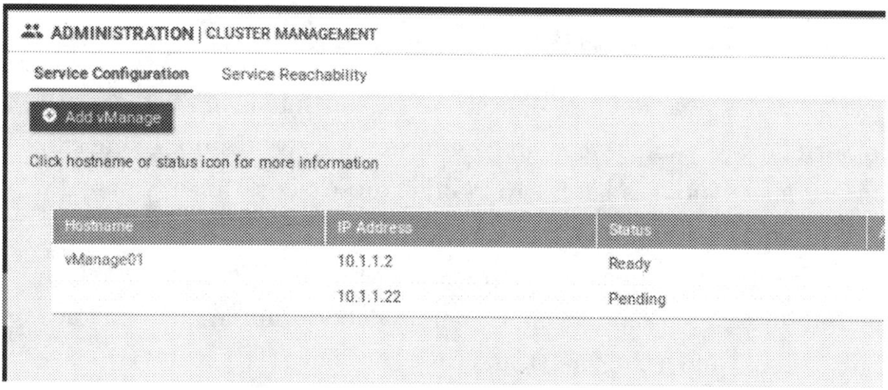

**ADMINISTRATION | CLUSTER MANAGEMENT**

Service Configuration    Service Reachability

⊕ Add vManage

Click hostname or status icon for more information

| Hostname | IP Address | Status |
|----------|-----------|--------|
| vManage01 | 10.1.1.2 | Ready |
| | 10.1.1.22 | Pending |

***Figure 3-32.*** *vManage02 is pending*

Once the server has rebooted, it should be part of the cluster. This will be reflected in the dashboard, as the number of vManage systems should now be 2. We can also see this in the cluster details, as the hostname has changed and the status is now "Ready" (Figure 3-33).

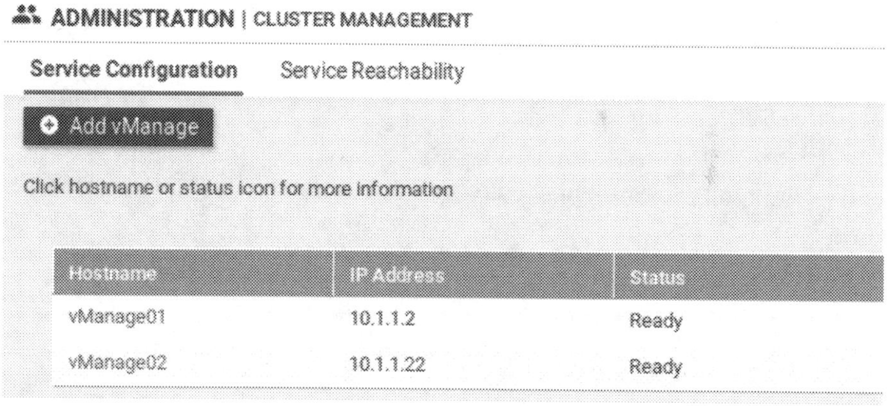

**ADMINISTRATION | CLUSTER MANAGEMENT**

Service Configuration    Service Reachability

⊕ Add vManage

Click hostname or status icon for more information

| Hostname | IP Address | Status |
|----------|-----------|--------|
| vManage01 | 10.1.1.2 | Ready |
| vManage02 | 10.1.1.22 | Ready |

***Figure 3-33.*** *Both vManage servers are ready*

# Single- and Multi-tenancy Options

Cisco's SD-WAN has tenancy options, so we can enable multi-tenancy support; however, once we enable multi-tenancy, we cannot go back to single-tenancy mode, so don't go through these steps (unless you really fancy rebuilding your vManage servers)!

To enable multi-tenancy, go to *Administration* ➤ *Settings*. Select the Edit button next to "Tenancy Mode," and select "Multitenant," enter a domain name and a cluster-ID, and then click Save (Figure 3-34).

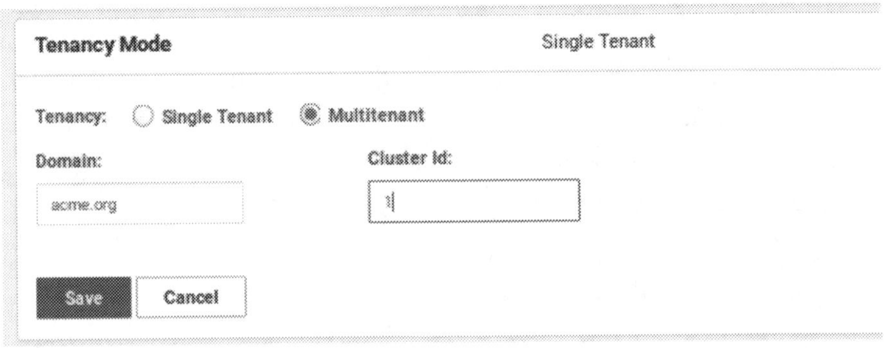

**Figure 3-34.**  *Setting up tenancies*

The vManage server will then reboot and come up in multi-tenancy mode.

To create tenants, go to the new vManage URL, which, in this example, would be https://1.acme.org. From the main screen, go to *Administration* ➤ *Tenant Management* and click "Add Tenant." Enter the details for the new tenant, such as the tenant name, description, the organization name, and the domain name for the tenant, and then click save.

# Alternative vManage Deployments

## VMWare

Installing vManage on VMWare is very straightforward. In vCenter, click *File ➤ Deploy OVF Template...* (Figure 3-35).

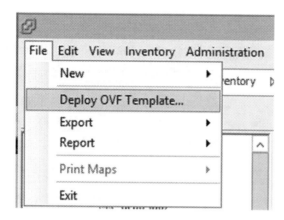

***Figure 3-35.*** *Deploying OVF templates*

Select the viptela-vmanage-19.3.0-genericx86_64.ova file (Figure 3-36).

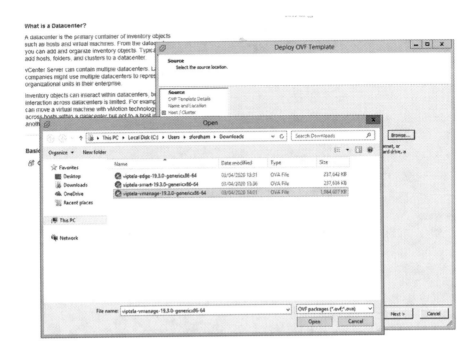

***Figure 3-36.*** *Selecting the OVF*

Click Next to see the OVF details (Figure 3-37).

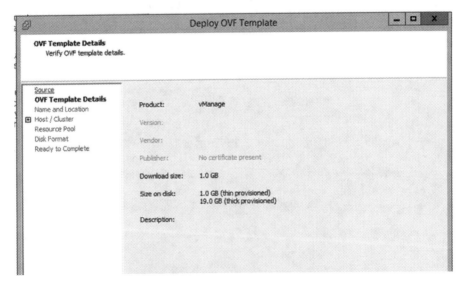

***Figure 3-37.*** *The OVF details*

Name the VM and select a location (Figure 3-38).

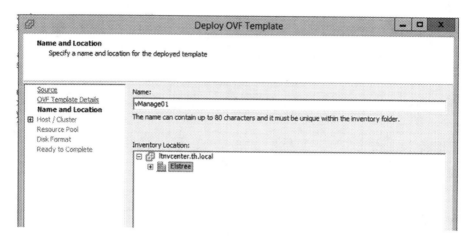

***Figure 3-38.*** *Setting the virtual machine name*

Select an ESXi host (if you have more than one) (Figure 3-39).

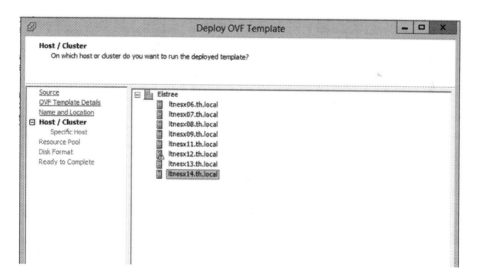

***Figure 3-39.*** *Selecting an ESXi host*

Select a datastore (Figure 3-40).

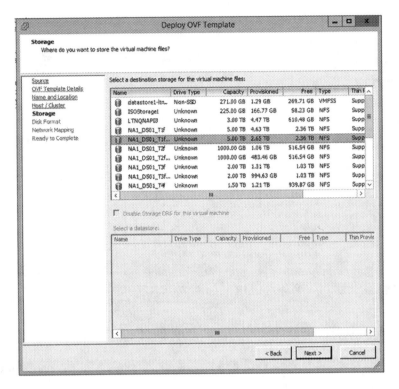

**Figure 3-40.** *Selecting the datastore*

Click Next through the disk format (Figure 3-41).

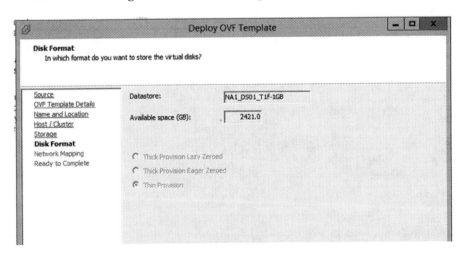

**Figure 3-41.** *VM disk format*

Select the networks to use (Figure 3-42).

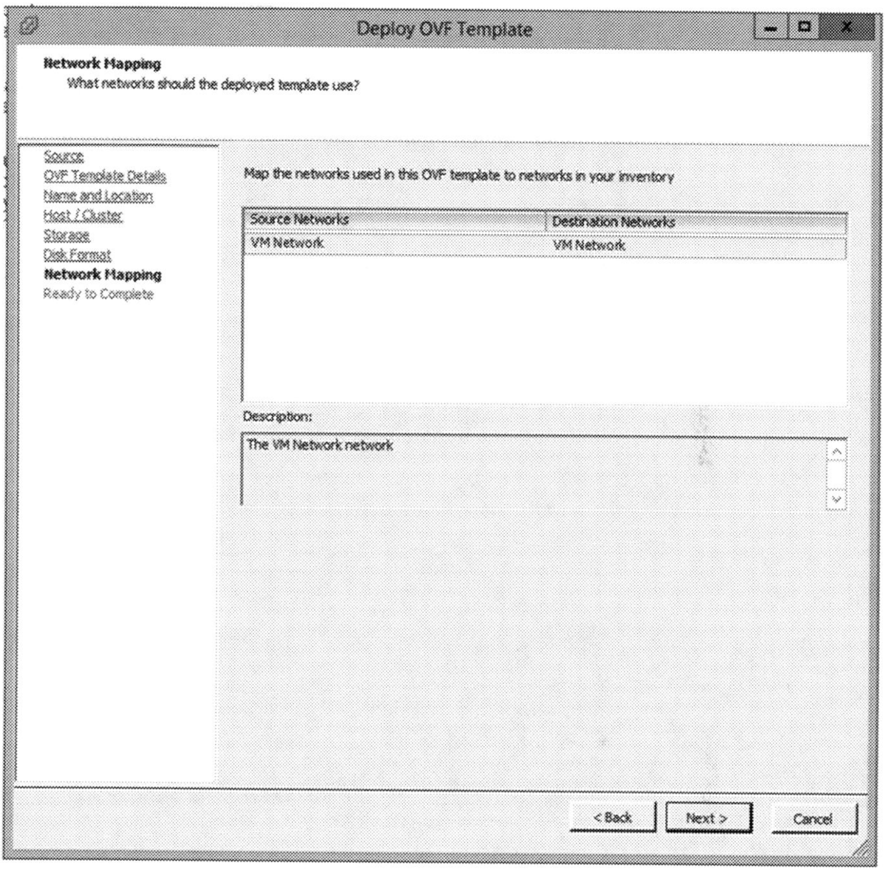

*Figure 3-42.* *VMWare networks*

Click Finish (Figure 3-43).

***Figure 3-43.*** *Finishing the setup*

The VM will be deployed (Figure 3-44).

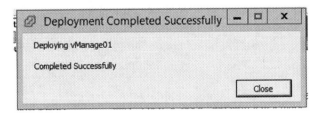

***Figure 3-44.*** *Deploying the vManage server in VMWare*

The next step is to add the second hard disk for storage.

Select the vManage01 VM, and click "Edit virtual machine settings" (Figure 3-45).

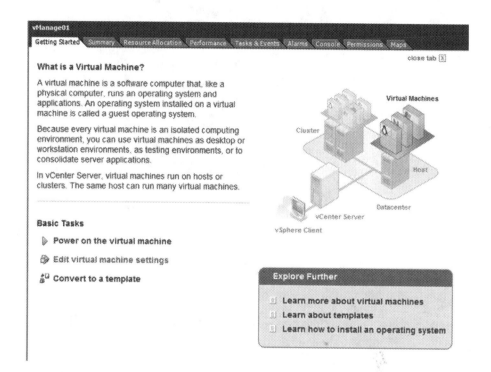

***Figure 3-45.*** *Editing the virtual machine settings*

Click "Add..." (Figure 3-46).

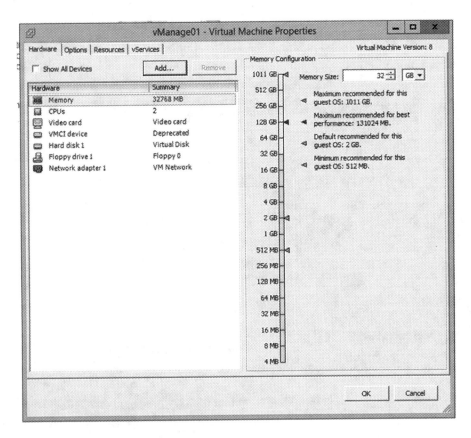

*Figure 3-46.*  *Adding new hardware*

In the Add Hardware dialog box, click Hard Disk (Figure 3-47).

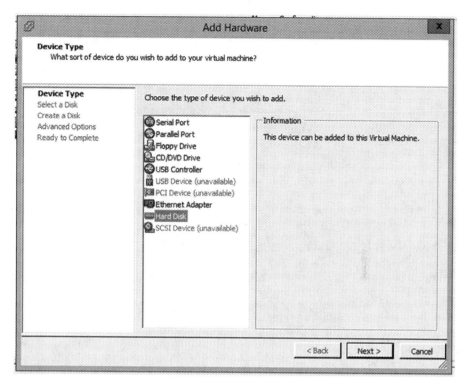

***Figure 3-47.*** *Adding a hard disk*

Click Next to select the option to create a new virtual disk (Figure 3-48).

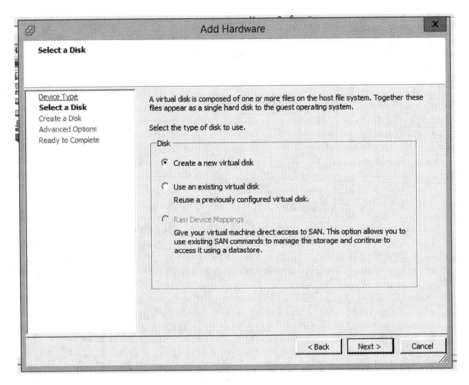

***Figure 3-48.*** *Create a virtual disk*

Set the size to be 100GB, and click Next (Figure 3-49).

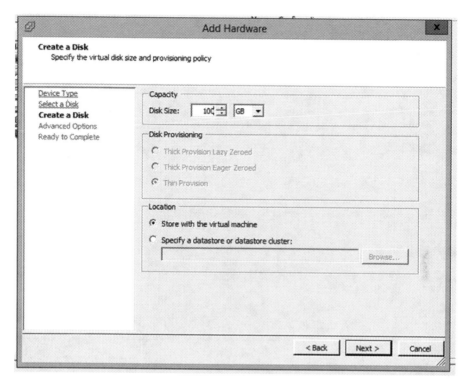

***Figure 3-49.*** *Set the disk size*

Set the Virtual Device Node to be "IDE"; SCSI is not supported (Figure 3-50).

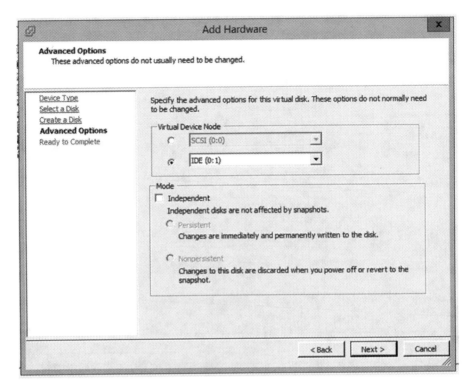

***Figure 3-50.***  *Make sure you select IDE!*

Click Next and then click Finish (Figure 3-51).

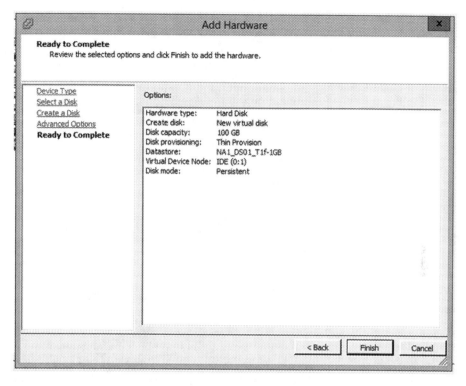

***Figure 3-51.*** *Finishing the additional hard disk*

The next and final stage is to add a second NIC, for the out-of-band management (VPN 512).

Click "Edit virtual machine settings," and then click Add and select "Ethernet Adapter" (Figure 3-52).

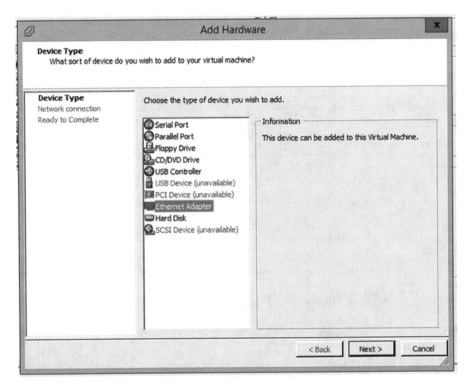

***Figure 3-52.***  *Adding a new Ethernet adapter*

The type should be "VMXNET 3" (Figure 3-53).

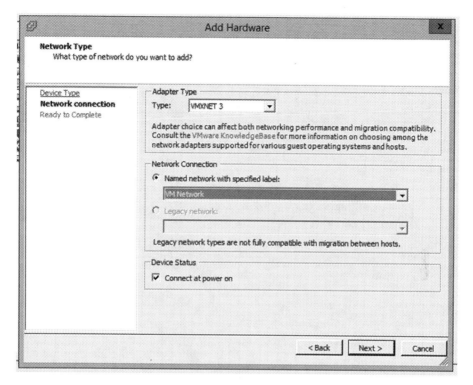

***Figure 3-53.*** *Selecting the network*

Click "Next" and then "Finish" (Figure 3-54).

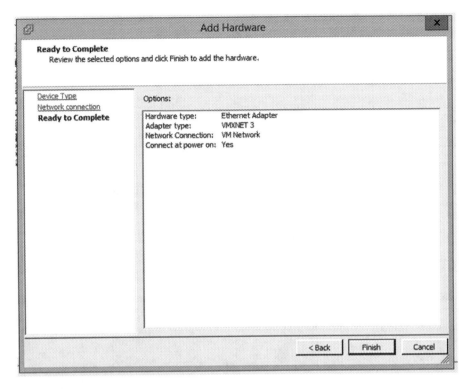

*Figure 3-54.* *Finishing the vManage hardware changes*

vManage is ready to run on ESXi now.

# KVM

Using the qemu-img command, create a second disk:

```
qemu-img create -f qcow2 vmanage-disk2.qcow2 100G
```

Setup vManage as follows:

```
virt-install \
    --name vManage01 \
    --os-type linux \
    --os-variant ubuntu14.04 \
```

```
--cpu host \
--vcpus=2 \
--hvm \
--arch=x86_64 \
--ram 16384 \
--disk path=viptela-vmanage-19.3.0-genericx86-64.qcow2,size=
   16,device=disk,bus=ide,format=qcow2 \
--disk path=vmanage-disk2.qcow2,size=16,device=disk,bus=ide,
   format=qcow2 \
--network=network:default,model=virtio \
--network=network:default,model=virtio \
--graphics none \
--import
```

# The Viptela Serial File

In the previous chapter, we downloaded a serial file from the Smart account portal. We now need to get this file into vManage.

The first step is to copy the file over to the VM directory, using something like FileZilla. Once it is there, we should be able to see it along with the virtioa.qcow2 file (I have edited the folder name to make it easier to read the output in the following):

```
root@eve-ng:~# cd /opt/unetlab/addons/qemu/linux-ubun-
dsktp-17.10.1/
root@eve-ng:/opt/unetlab/addons/qemu/linux-ubun-dsktp-17.10.1# ls
serialFile.viptela  virtioa.qcow2
root@eve-ng:/opt/unetlab/addons/qemu/linux-ubun-dsktp-17.10.1#
```

You need to install the MKISOFS utility, which you can do by following the guide on this page: www.802101.com/how-to-get-files-into-qemu-vm/

The next stage is to create a CD ROM for our Linux machine:

```
root@eve-ng:/opt/unetlab/addons/qemu/linux-ubun-dsktp-17.10.1#
mkisofs -o cdrom.iso serialFile.viptela
I: -input-charset not specified, using utf-8 (detected
in locale settings)
Total translation table size: 0
Total rockridge attributes bytes: 0
Total directory bytes: 0
Path table size(bytes): 10
Max brk space used 0
176 extents written (0 MB)
root@eve-ng:/opt/unetlab/addons/qemu/linux-ubun-dsktp-17.10.1# ls
cdrom.iso  serialFile.viptela  virtioa.qcow2
root@eve-ng:/opt/unetlab/addons/qemu/linux-ubun-dsktp-17.10.1#
```

Reboot the Linux VM and the CD Rom should be visible (Figure 3-55).

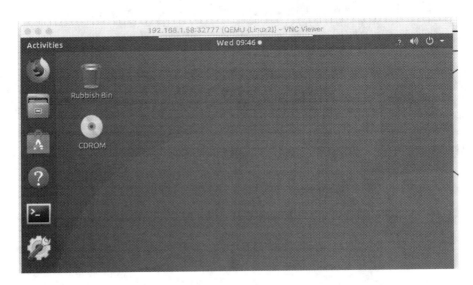

***Figure 3-55.***  *We have a CDROM!*

The serialFile.viptela will have had the name truncated as we used the standard format (ISO 9660) when creating our ISO file, so file names have a maximum of eight characters with a three-character extension. Later on, we'll use Joliet extensions so that this does not happen again. Copy the serialfi.vip file to /tmp, and rename it back to serialFile.viptela (Figure 3-56).

```
user@user-virtual-machine:~$ cp /media/user/CDROM/serialfi.vip /tmp/serialFile.
viptela
user@user-virtual-machine:~$ ▮
```

***Figure 3-56.*** *Renaming our serial file*

On vManage01, navigate to *Configuration ➤ Devices,* and click "Upload WAN Edge List" (Figure 3-57).

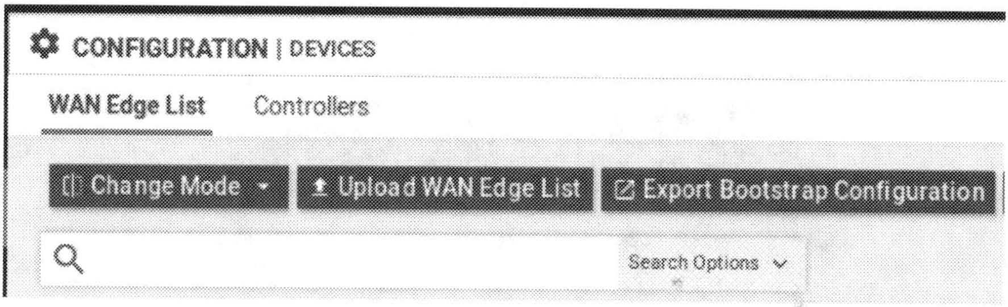

***Figure 3-57.*** *Uploading the WAN edge list*

Select the serialFile.viptela file that is in the /tmp directory (Figure 3-58).

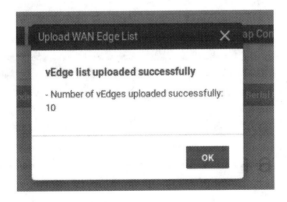

*Figure 3-58.* *Yes, we are sure*

The file will upload (Figure 3-59).

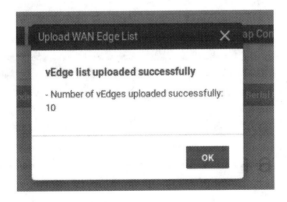

*Figure 3-59.* *The successful upload*

We can check this in the *Configuration* ➤ *Devices* page (Figure 3-60).

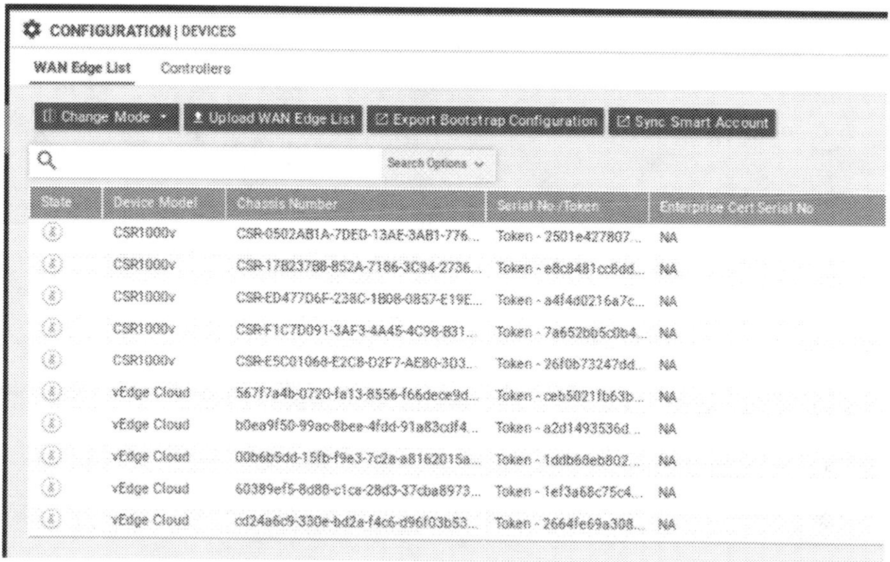

*Figure 3-60.* *Our edge device list!*

Now that we have our vManage server up and running and loaded with our serial file, we can start to build out the rest of the network.

# Summary

In this chapter, we set up our vManage NMS cluster and set the certificate authority using our Linux server in VPN 0. We set up some extra users and looked at tenancy options. We then uploaded the Viptela serial which will enable us to add our edge devices. Next up, we should look at how the SD-WAN network will operate.

# CHAPTER 4

# Understanding the Overlay

During our setup of the vManage server(s), we created two VPN connections, VPN 0 and VPN 512. These have different purposes; we use VPN 512 for out-of-band management, whereas VPN 0 is our transport VPN, but can also be used for management purposes.

In this chapter, we are going to look at these two VPNs in greater detail and the OMP routing protocol, which forms the overlay network used by the SD-WAN, as well as BFD and NETCONF (Network Configuration Protocol).

## VPN 512

This management VPN is enabled by default on all Viptela devices, but will be unconfigured, such as here on the vSmart controller:

```
vSmart01# sh run vpn 512
vpn 512
!
vSmart01#
```

Typically, on vEdge devices, the Gigabit Ethernet interface will be used; on other devices, such as vBond, the Ethernet interface will be used.

© Stuart Fordham 2021
S. Fordham, *Learning SD-WAN with Cisco*, https://doi.org/10.1007/978-1-4842-7347-0_4

The IP address configuration can be configured for static or DHCP IP addressing:

```
vBond01# sh run vpn 512
vpn 512
 interface eth0
  ip address 100.1.1.3/24
  ipv6 dhcp-client
  no shutdown
 !
!
vBond01#
```

Apart from a little bit of routing, there is little we can do with VPN 512, so let's look at VPN 0 instead.

# VPN 0

VPN 0 is where all the magic happens; this is the WAN transport VPN. All the control plane traffic is carried by this VPN through the overlay network, within OMP sessions.

---

**Note**    If a device is to be part of the overlay network, then at least one interface must be connected to VPN 0.

---

We start by defining the interface to be used for VPN 0 and then set the IP address; this address can be IPv4 or IPv6 (or both if you are so inclined):

```
vBond01# sh run vpn 0
vpn 0
 interface ge0/0
  ip address 10.1.1.3/24
  ipv6 dhcp-client
```

Next, we define our tunnel interface. On the vBond and vEdge devices, we need to set an encapsulation method, which can be IPSec or GRE (this is for the TLOC, or Transport Location). We do not need to specify the encapsulation on all devices. It is mandatory on the vBond device, but not required (or even available as a command) on the vSmart or vManage devices.

```
tunnel-interface
 encapsulation ipsec
```

Within the tunnel interface, we specify the allowed services. Routing-wise we can enable BGP and OSPF. To overcome issues with NAT, we can enable the STUN (Session Traversal Utilities for NAT) protocol. For management, we can enable SSH (sshd), NTP, NETCONF, ICMP, HTTP, DNS, and DHCP.

We can enable all of the services (using the command "allow-service all"), but even so, will still see those commands that have not been explicitly permitted or denied showing in the configuration as having their default values. Hopefully, this will be changed in future versions:

```
allow-service all
no allow-service bgp
allow-service dhcp
allow-service dns
allow-service icmp
no allow-service sshd
no allow-service netconf
no allow-service ntp
no allow-service ospf
no allow-service stun
allow-service https
!
```

Access such as SSH will be available over VPN 512 by default; however, we can also enable this over VPN 0. NETCONF should be enabled on edge devices as this is how vManage provisions virtual devices, as well as the edge devices using NETCONF to send notifications back to vManage.

The VPN 0 interface will, by default, be placed in a shutdown state. We need to enable it.

```
no shutdown
!
```

Lastly, we (may) need to provide routing information, which is done under the interface, where we set the IP address:

```
ip route 0.0.0.0/0 10.1.1.1
!
vBond01#
```

The options available under the tunnel interface differ depending on the platform. There are, however, some constants, such as the allowed services, the Hello interval, and Hello tolerance, which set the time (in seconds) that we send hello packets and the control tolerance of these packets.

The Hello interval is the time between Hello packets. These packets are used to check that tunnels between devices are still active and act to keep the tunnel alive. These are sent every one second, by default. If no Hello packet is received, then we use the Hello tolerance to keep the tunnel up that little bit longer. The Hello tolerance is set to 11 seconds (again by default), so if no Hello packet is received within 12 seconds (the original Hello interval plus the tolerance), the tunnel is taken down.

If the interval and tolerance have different values at each end of the DTLS tunnel, then the *lower* hello interval and *higher* tolerance interval will be used between controller devices (vManage, vBond, and vSmart). If one side of the tunnel is an edge router, then the tunnel will use the values configured on the router. This is to minimize the amount of traffic sent over the tunnel.

# DTLS

The Viptela/Cisco SD-WAN uses DTLS or TLS tunnels between devices
(Figure 4-1). DTLS (Datagram Transport Layer Security) is based on
TLS and was designed to do what SSL could not, namely, create a secure
protocol under UDP. The vBond will *only* use DTLS, though.

***Figure 4-1.*** *A DTLS tunnel*

TCP has measures built into it to make it reliable. It will request
missing packets, and it will reorder packets received so they are in the
correct order. These are all excellent ways of giving us a network we can
use. However, once we start putting TCP within TCP (like in tunnels), then
these reliability measures can be detrimental. This is referred to as "*TCP
meltdown.*"

With TCP meltdown, when the underlying protocol has an issue, it tries
to recover (by requesting a missing packet, for example); this can cause the
preceding layer to also compensate, which can, in turn, cause delays on
the network.

To avoid this, UDP is used instead. While UDP is connectionless and
lacks recovery mechanisms, issues with loss of datagrams and out-of-order
packets have to be offloaded to the application (SD-WAN), instead of having
TCP do this for us. But at least we avoid TCP meltdown.

Within the tunnel are the OMP messages (Figure 4-2).

# OMP

OMP is the Overlay Management Protocol. This is the control plane of the
SD-WAN and runs between the vEdges and the vSmart controllers.

***Figure 4-2.*** *DTLS tunnel carrying OMP messages*

OMP performs the following functions:

- Network overlay orchestration, such as site connectivity

- Distribution of routing information and location
  mappings (the TLOCs)

- Data-plane security parameter distribution

- Control and distribution of routing policy

OMP is enabled by default, as we can see on the vSmart controller:

```
vSmart01# show omp summary
oper-state          UP
admin-state         UP
personality         vsmart
omp-uptime          4:19:03:49
routes-received     0
routes-installed    0
routes-sent         0
tlocs-received      0
tlocs-installed     0
```

```
tlocs-sent                 0
services-received          0
services-installed         0
services-sent              0
mcast-routes-received      0
mcast-routes-installed     0
mcast-routes-sent          0
hello-sent                 0
hello-received             0
handshake-sent             0
handshake-received         0
alert-sent                 0
alert-received             0
inform-sent                0
inform-received            0
update-sent                0
update-received            0
policy-sent                0
policy-received            0
total-packets-sent         0
total-packets-received     0
vsmart-peers               0
vedge-peers                0
vSmart01#
```

OMP advertises the following:

- OMP routes/vRoutes

- Service routes

- TLOCs

To understand these three different types of routes a little easier, we can break our network into two halves: the service side and the transport side.

## OMP Routes/vRoutes

OMP routes are also known as vRoutes; these will be the service prefixes mentioned earlier. These routes are advertised to the vSmart controller as they are collected from the edge devices. Any connected, static, OSPF inter-area or intra-area routes will be automatically injected into OMP. BGP and OSPF external routes will need to be manually redistributed within OMP.

Looking at our topology, in Figure 4-3, the lines in black would be our OMP routes.

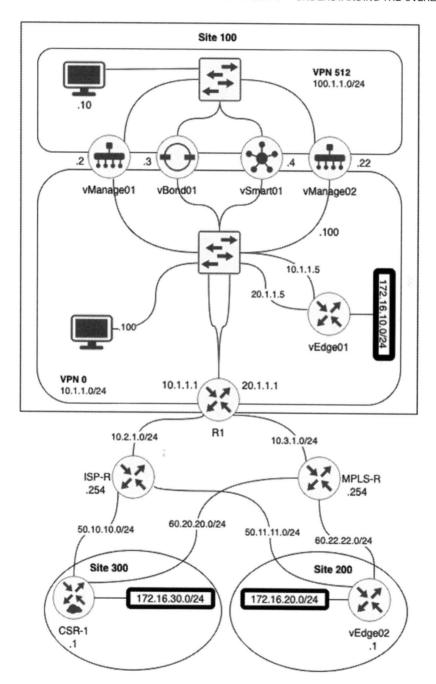

*Figure 4-3.* *Our OMP routes*

## Service Routes

Service routes are identifiers that link an OMP route to a service on a vEdge router or within the site that the vEdge router is in. These services could be a firewall, IPS/IDS, or a load balancer, for example. These routes specify the location of the service. We do not have any of these in our topology, but if we did (such as a firewall inside site 100), the service routes would look like in Figure 4-4.

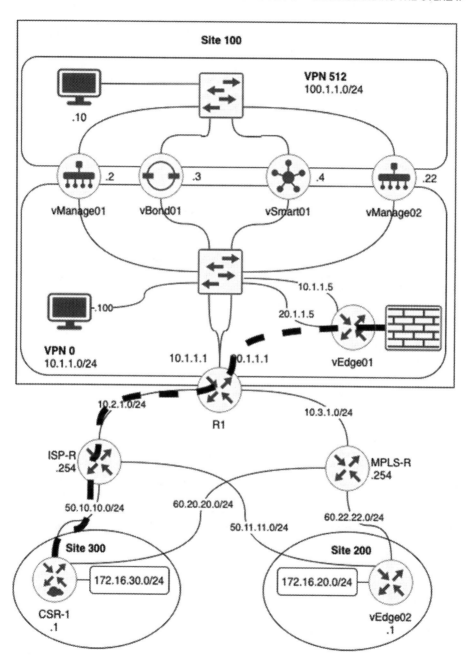

***Figure 4-4.*** *Service routes*

Service routes use the Subsequent Address Family Identifier (SAFI), which include the following attributes:

- VPN ID

- Service ID

- FW

- IDS

- IDP

- Generic net-svc

- Label

- Originator ID

- TLOC

- Path ID

# TLOC

TLOC stands for Transport Location, and it is a way of separating the route from the endpoint on which it sits; routes are based on location, not on specific router interfaces. TLOCs are our next hops and WAN attachment points, they are the only part of the OMP that is visible to the physical network, and these TLOCs must be reachable by the routing domain.

Figure 4-5 shows these TLOCs.

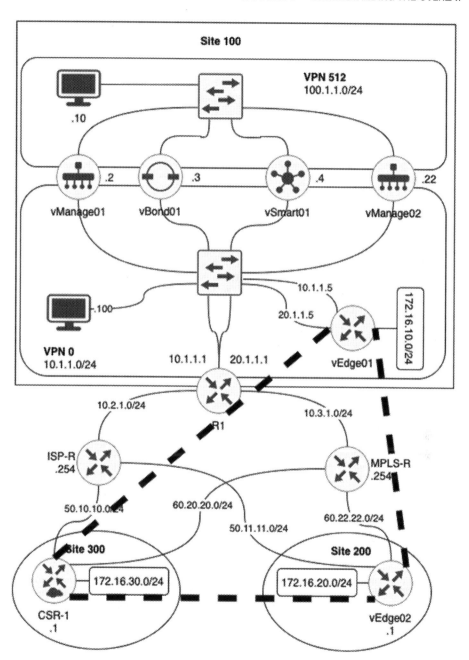

***Figure 4-5.***  *TLOCs*

A TLOC has three components:

- System IP. We have seen these already when we set up our vManage NMS. This "IP" does not have to be routable or reachable; it is for identification only, similar to a BGP router ID. It is not an IP in the proper sense, it is purely a dotted decimal set of numbers. We set this in the system properties.

- Color. The color is used to distinguish between different transports.

- Encapsulation type, which will either be GRE or IPSec.

The TLOC will advertise the following:

- TLOC private address

- TLOC public address

- Carrier

- Color

- Encapsulation type

- Preference

- Site ID

- Tag

- Weight

The carrier attribute is an identifier, and there are eight options to choose from (carrier1 through to carrier8). The carrier attribute is used, when we are using NAT and private colors, to control whether we use the private or public IP address for session establishment. If the carrier setting is the same, then the private IP address is used. If the carrier setting is different, then then public IP address is used:

```
vBond01(config-tunnel-interface)# carrier ?
Description: Set carrier for TLOC
Possible completions:
  <default carrier1 carrier2 carrier3 carrier4 carrier5
carrier6 carrier7 carrier8>[default]
vBond01(config-tunnel-interface)#
```

The color identifies the link type from a predefined list:

```
vBond01(config-tunnel-interface)# color ?
Description: Set color for TLOC
Possible completions:
  <3g  biz-internet  blue  bronze  custom1  custom2  custom3
  default  gold  green  lte  metro-ethernet  mpls public-
  internet  red  silver private1 private2 private3 private4
  private5 private6>[default]
vBond01(config-tunnel-interface)# color
```

Color does more than link identification; it defines the VPN tunnel establishment logic, as we will see later. Color is an important area to understand, so we will go into this in greater detail in Chapter 9 when we can see it in action.

Preference is used to differentiate OMP routes advertised by two different TLOCs; the TLOC with the highest preference will be advertised out. If an OMP route is reachable through two (or more TLOCs), then we can use the weight attribute to control our outbound traffic.

**Note**   By default, traffic will be balanced equally across multiple TLOCs, and each of these will have a value of 1. If this value is increased (to a maximum of 255), then more traffic will be sent to this TLOC. We can use this to perform unequal cost multi-pathing, for example, to send more flows across higher-bandwidth lines, by configuring one TLOC with a weight of 100 and the other with a weight of 10, to get a 10:1 traffic ratio.

The tag is used for TLOC filtering; this is an optional, transitive path attribute.

We will look closer at TLOCs in Chapter 7 when we set up our edge routers.

# BFD

BFD, or Bidirectional Forwarding Detection, is used to quickly detect path failures. BFD is used by several technologies such as OSPF and BGP as well as SD-WAN.

BFD sessions are created automatically when edge routers come up and they run inside IPSec connections:

```
vEdge01# show bfd summary
sessions-total          1
sessions-up             1
sessions-max            2
sessions-flap           2
poll-interval           600000
vEdge01# show bfd tloc-summary-list
```

```
IF            SESSIONS  SESSIONS  SESSIONS
NAME   ENCAP  TOTAL     UP        FLAP
-----------------------------------------------
ge0/0  ipsec  1         1         2

vEdge01#
```

We can use the "show bfd history" and "show bfd sessions" commands to look at the BFD details. The history command (Figure 4-6) shows us the state changes and when they occurred.

```
vEdge01# show bfd history
                                      DST PUBLIC  DST PUBLIC                      RX     TX
SYSTEM IP     SITE ID  COLOR   STATE  IP          PORT    ENCAP  TIME             PKTS   PKTS  DEL

60.100.100.1  200      red     down   50.11.11.1  12426   ipsec  2020-04-09T13:44:15+0000  4       5      0
60.100.100.1  200      red     up     50.11.11.1  12426   ipsec  2020-04-09T13:44:16+0000  1014693  1014717  0
60.100.100.1  200      red     down   50.11.11.1  12426   ipsec  2020-04-15T10:36:32+0000  1014698  1014765  0
60.100.100.1  200      red     up     50.11.11.1  12426   ipsec  2020-04-15T10:37:16+0000  1014698  1014765  0
60.100.100.1  200      red     down   50.11.11.1  12426   ipsec  2020-04-15T10:37:16+0000  0       0      0
60.100.100.1  200      red     down   50.11.11.1  12426   ipsec  2020-04-15T10:37:16+0000  0       0      0
60.100.100.1  200      red     down   50.11.11.1  12346   ipsec  2020-04-15T10:37:19+0000  10      10     0
60.100.100.1  200      red     up     50.11.11.1  12346   ipsec  2020-04-15T10:37:20+0000  0       0      0

vEdge01#
```

***Figure 4-6.*** *BFD history*

The sessions command (Figure 4-7) shows us our current sessions.

```
vEdge01# show bfd sessions
                         SOURCE TLOC  REMOTE TLOC              DST PUBLIC          DST PUBLIC       DETECT   TX
SYSTEM IP     SITE ID  STATE  COLOR  COLOR  SOURCE IP         IP                  PORT  ENCAP  MULTIPLIER  INTERVAL(msec)  UPTIME      TRANSITIONS
60.100.100.1  200      up    blue   red    10.1.3.5          50.11.11.1          12346  ipsec  7           5000            2:01:35:50  0

vEdge01#
```

***Figure 4-7.*** *BFD sessions*

BFD is used to confirm that remote TLOCs are active. We have one BFD session per TLOC *per destination TLOC,* and if the BFD session fails, then the vSmart controller will remove all the routes which point to that particular TLOC as a next hop.

# NETCONF

NETCONF (Network Configuration Protocol) is the last topic for this chapter. NETCONF is a *"simple mechanism through which a network device can be managed"* (RFC 4741[1]). It allows us to pull configuration data out and push configuration data in and uses XML to encode a remote procedure call (RPC).

The RFC for NETCONF (RFC 4741) was published in 2006 by Rob Enns, then of Juniper Networks. We then have another couple of useful RFCs, such as RFC 4742[2] for using NETCONF over SSH and RFC 5539[3] for NETCONF over TLS.

NETCONF can be seen as four different layers:

- Content (configuration data and notification data)

- Operations (retrieve and edit the configuration data)

- Messages (for encoding RPCs and notifications)

- Secure transport (secure and reliable transport of messages between a client and a server)

The basic NETCONF operations are shown in Table 4-1.

---

[1] https://tools.ietf.org/html/rfc4741
[2] https://tools.ietf.org/html/rfc4742
[3] https://tools.ietf.org/html/rfc5539

*Table 4-1.* *NETCONF commands*

| Operation | Purpose |
|---|---|
| <get> | Retrieve the running configuration and device state information |
| <get-config> | Retrieve all or part of a specific configuration datastore |
| <edit-config> | Edit the configuration through creating, deleting, merging, or replacing |
| <copy-config> | Copy the configuration datastore to another configuration datastore |
| <delete-config> | Delete a configuration datastore |
| <lock> | Lock the configuration datastore of a device |
| <unlock> | Unlock a locked configuration datastore |
| <close-session> | Close a NETCONF session (gracefully) |
| <kill-session> | Close a NETCONF session (ungracefully) |

When we send configurations to our edge devices, these configurations are sent as NETCONF messages, within IPSec tunnels. NETCONF is also used to send the signed certificate to the vEdge devices during the onboarding process and then to push localized policies from vManage to the vEdge devices.

# Summary

We have looked at the overlay network, including VPN 512 and 0, and covered the DTLS tunnels and the OMP messages carried within them. We then looked at BFD and NETCONF. In the next chapter, we will set up our vBond controller.

# CHAPTER 5

# Deploying vBond

In this chapter, we are going to set up the vBond server. The basic setup is very similar to the vManage, as all the devices share the same basic configuration.

As with all the devices, you will be prompted to change the password for the admin account when you first log in.

Because vBond and vEdge share the same software image, the device will default to the hostname of "vedge" when it starts up for the first time.

## Basic vBond Configuration

Start by entering the hostname, system IP, site ID, and organization name:

```
vedge# config
Entering configuration mode terminal
vedge(config)# system
vedge(config-system)# host-name vBond01
vedge(config-system)# system-ip 100.100.1.3
vedge(config-system)# site-id 100
vedge(config-system)# organization-name "Learning_SD-WAN"
vedge(config-system)#
```

Next, set the vBond IP address. This must match the IP address we set on our VPN 0 interface. We also specify that we are the "local" vBond controller. Commit your configuration.

© Stuart Fordham 2021
S. Fordham, *Learning SD-WAN with Cisco*, https://doi.org/10.1007/978-1-4842-7347-0_5

```
vedge(config-system)#
vedge(config-system)# vbond 10.1.1.3 local
vedge(config-system)# commit
```

---

**Note**   You may see some documentation also using the option of
"vbond-only" as well as "local." You can still use this option,
and it will work in the configuration, but it was deprecated in Viptela
version 16.2.

---

In a real-life deployment, the vBond IP address should be a publicly
reachable IP address. Next, we move on to our network configuration.

## vBond Network Configuration

Type the following:

```
vBond01(config-system)# vpn 0
vBond01(config-vpn-0)# ip route 0.0.0.0/0 10.1.1.1
vBond01(config-vpn-0)# interface ge0/0
vBond01(config-interface-ge0/0)# ip address 10.1.1.3/24
vBond01(config-interface-ge0/0)# no tunnel-interface
vBond01(config-interface-ge0/0)# commit and-quit Commit complete.
vBond01#
```

We need to remove the tunnel interface from VPN 0; otherwise, we will
not be able to add vBond to vManage, and we will just get a Java exception
error.

We should also set up our management connectivity:

```
vBond01# conf t
Entering configuration mode terminal
vBond01(config)# vpn 512
```

```
vBond01(config-vpn-512)# interface eth0
vBond01(config-interface-eth0)# ip address 100.1.1.3/24
vBond01(config-interface-eth0)# no shutdown
vBond01(config-interface-eth0)# exit
vBond01(config-vpn-512)# commit and-quit
Commit complete.
vBond01#
```

We should now be able to copy over our CA certificate, so, from the Linux server's command prompt, CD into the Downloads directory and type, filling in the authentication details when prompted:

```
scp CA.crt admin@10.1.1.3:
```

Switch back to the vBond01 VM and install the certificate:

```
vBond01# request root-cert-chain install /home/admin/CA.crt
Uploading root-ca-cert-chain via VPN 0
Copying ... /home/admin/CA.crt via VPN 0
Updating the root certificate chain..
Successfully installed the root certificate chain
vBond01#
```

We should now be able to add the vBond device to vManage.

## Adding vBond to vManage

Firstly, make sure that vManage has been set up with a vBond device.

Go to *Administration* ➤ *Settings*, and edit the vBond configuration, adding the IP address of our vBond controller. This must be the VPN 0 address we configured earlier (Figure 5-1).

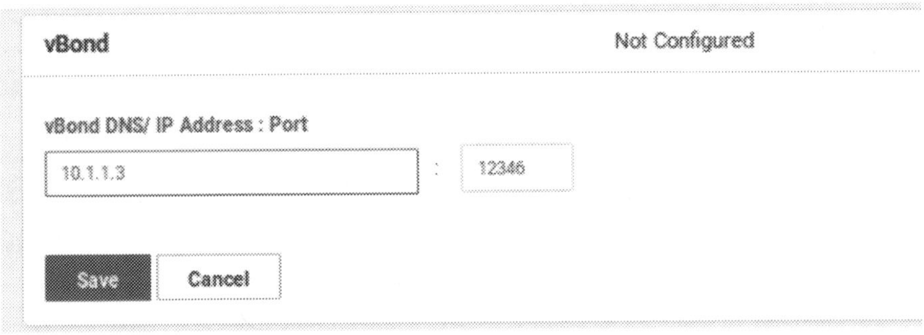

**vBond**                                              Not Configured

**vBond DNS/ IP Address : Port**

| 10.1.1.3 | : | 12346 |

Save      Cancel

***Figure 5-1.*** *Adding the IP address of the vBond controller to vManage*

Click Save.

Next, navigate to *Configuration* ➤ *Devices* (Figure 5-2).

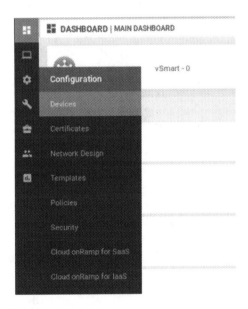

***Figure 5-2.*** *The Devices menu*

Click "*Controllers*" (Figure 5-3).

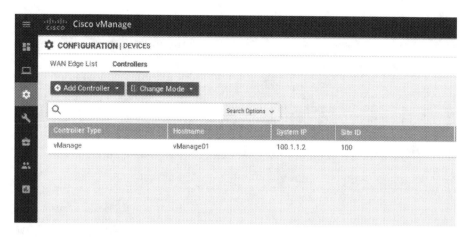

***Figure 5-3.*** *Controllers*

Click "*Add Controller,*" and select the vBond option (Figure 5-4).

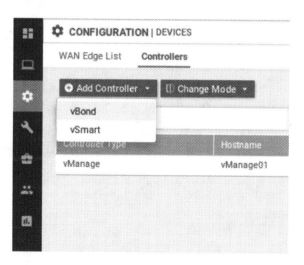

***Figure 5-4.*** *Adding a new controller*

Enter the IP address and username and password of the vBond device, and click "*Add*" (Figure 5-5).

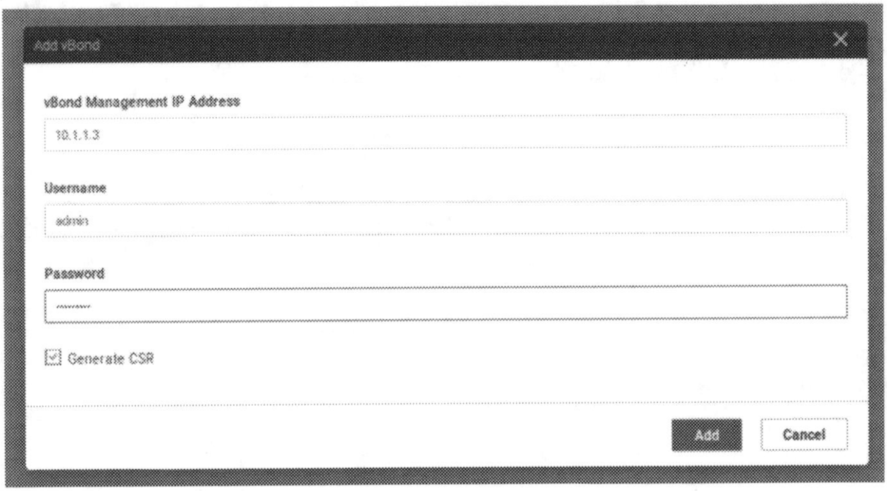

**Figure 5-5.** *The name is Bond. vBond*

We should see the vBond controller added to our list now as seen in Figure 5-6.

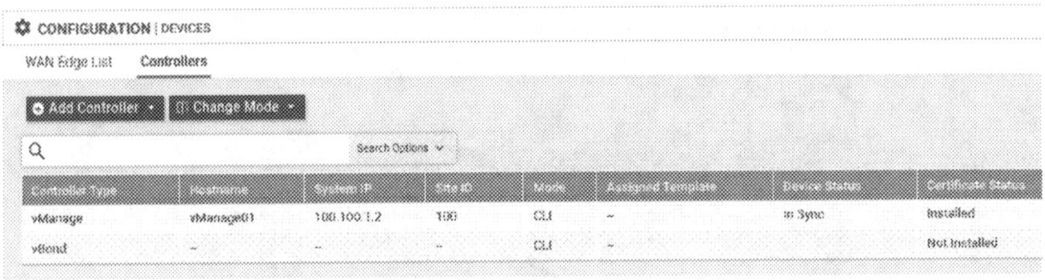

**Figure 5-6.** *Our controller list*

We still have some work to do, as the vBond server details are missing, and we do not have a certificate installed.

Navigate to *Configuration* ➤ *Certificates* ➤ *Controllers*. The vBond controller will have an operation status of "CSR generated," so click the triple dots and select "View CSR." Download it to the Linux server (Figure 5-7).

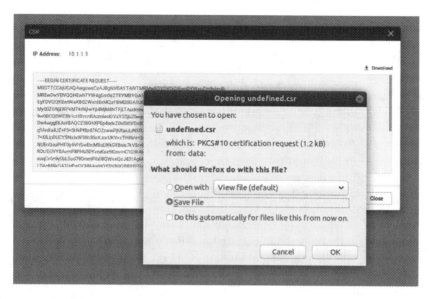

***Figure 5-7.*** *The vBond CSR*

Sign the certificate using the Linux server:

```
openssl x509 -req -in undefined.csr -CA CA.crt -CAkey CA.key
-CAcreateserial -out vBond01.pem -days 1000 -sha256
```

Back on vManage, navigate to *Configuration* ➤ *Certificates* ➤
*Controllers.* Click "Install Certificate." Select the vBond01.pem certificate
and install it.

The task view will first show that the install is scheduled (Figure 5-8).

***Figure 5-8.*** *vBond certificate install scheduled*

Then, it will show that it was (hopefully) successful (Figure 5-9).

*Figure 5-9.*  *vBond certificate install success*

Head back to *Configuration ➤ Devices ➤ Controllers*; we will see that
the Certificate Status now shows as "Installed," and we should be fully
populated with the hostname and system IP (Figure 5-10).

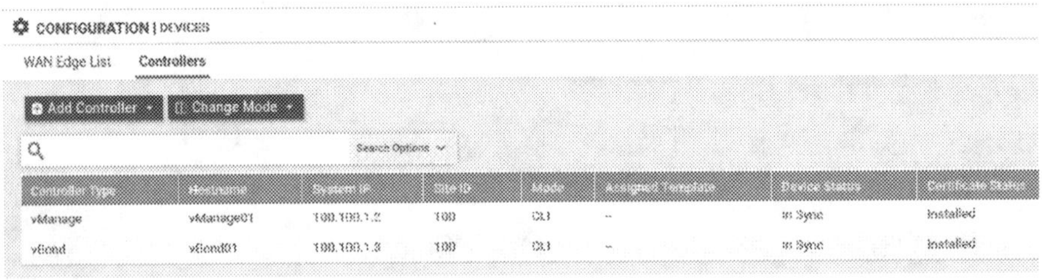

*Figure 5-10.*  *All the vBond details!*

If you don't get the same result, then head over to the troubleshooting
chapter (Chapter 14).

Assuming all is well, we should see that our dashboard has updated to
reflect the new vBond orchestrator (Figure 5-11).

*Figure 5-11.*  *We have a vBond*

Our Network page (Monitor ➤ Network) will also show the new
controller (Figure 5-12).

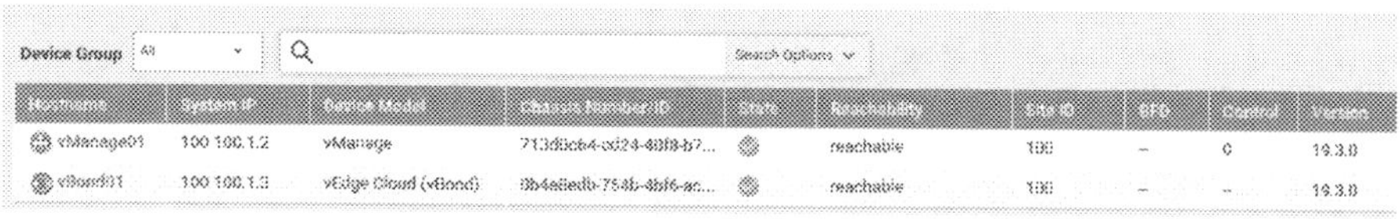

**Figure 5-12.**  *The Network monitoring page*

We can use the console to check our orchestrator properties ("show orchestrator local-properties"), which is great for troubleshooting certificate issues, as well as misconfiguration such as organization names that do not match.

```
vBond01#  show orchestrator local-properties
personality               vbond
sp-organization-name      Learning_SD-WAN
organization-name         Learning_SD-WAN
system-ip                 100.100.1.3
certificate-status        Installed
root-ca-chain-status      Installed

certificate-validity      Valid
certificate-not-valid-before Apr 01 08:23:30 2020 GMT
certificate-not-valid-after  Dec 27 08:23:30 2022 GMT
chassis-num/unique-id     87563514-cc06-47a9-85ea-
                          03d4cf2e0a24
serial-num                C024D682372213FA
number-active-wan-interfaces 1
protocol                  dtls

INSTANCE INDEX  PORT  VSMARTS  VMANAGES  STATE
-----------------------------------------------
0        0      12346 0        4         up

vBond01#
```

We can also check out the connections we have using the command "show orchestrator connections". The output for this is quite long, as shown in Figure 5-13!

```
vBond01# show orchestrator connections

                                                                PEER              PEER
            PEER      PEER      PEER      SITE    DOMAIN  PEER    PRIVATE PEER      PUBLIC                            ORGANIZATION
INSTANCE TYPE PROTOCOL SYSTEM IP  ID      ID      PRIVATE IP PORT   PUBLIC IP  PORT   REMOTE COLOR   STATE           NAME            UPTIME
0           vmanage   dtls    100.100.1.2  100     0      10.3.3.2  12346  10.3.3.2   12346  default        up      Learning_SD-WAN  0:03:55:19
0           vmanage   dtls    100.100.1.2  100     0      10.3.3.2  12346  10.3.3.2   12346  default        up      Learning_SD-WAN  0:03:55:19
0           vmanage   dtls    100.100.1.2  100     0      10.3.3.2  12346  10.3.3.2   12346  default        up      Learning_SD-WAN  0:01:55:19
0           vmanage   dtls    100.100.1.2  100     0      10.1.1.2  12646  10.1.1.2   12646  default        up      Learning_SD-WAN  0:01:55:19

vBond01#
```

**Figure 5-13.**  *The output from "show orchestrator connections"*

By now, the serial number list we downloaded from SmartNet and uploaded to vManage should have downloaded to vBond (this output has been truncated to avoid sharing serial numbers):

vBond01# show orchestrator valid-vedges serial-number

| CHASSIS NUMBER | SERIAL NUMBER |
| --- | --- |
| 00B6B5DD-15FB-123FFFF | 1ddb68eb80270123FFFF |
| 567F7A4B-0720-123FFFF | ceb5021fb63bd123FFFF |
| 60389EF5-8D88-123FFFF | 1ef3a68c75c43123FFFF |
| B0EA9F50-99AC-123FFFF | a2d1493536d8f123FFFF |
| CD24A6C9-330E-123FFFF | 2664fe69a308c123FFFF |
| CSR-0502AB1A-123FFFF | 2501e42780753123FFFF |
| CSR-17B237B8-123FFFF | e8c8481cc8dda123FFFF |
| CSR-E5C01068-123FFFF | 26f0b73247dd4123FFFF |
| CSR-ED477D6F-123FFFF | a4f4d0216a7cb123FFFF |
| CSR-F1C7D091-123FFFF | 7a652bb5c0b47123FFFF |

vBond01#

The final stage of setting up the vBond controller is to enable the tunnel interface under VPN 0. We need this for the vSmart and edge devices to be able to connect to vBond.

```
vBond01# config
Entering configuration mode terminal
vBond01(config)# vpn 0
vBond01(config-vpn-0)# interface ge0/0
vBond01(config-interface-ge0/0)# tunnel-interface
vBond01(config-tunnel-interface)# allow-service all
vBond01(config-tunnel-interface)# encapsulation ipsec
vBond01(config-tunnel-interface)# commit and-quit
Commit complete.
vBond01#
```

# Alternative vBond Deployments

We can also set up the vBond appliance on VMWare and KVM.

## VMWare

Within vSphere, click *File* ➤ *Deploy OVF Template...*, then select viptela-edge-19.3.0-genericx86-64.ova, and click Next (Figure 5-14).

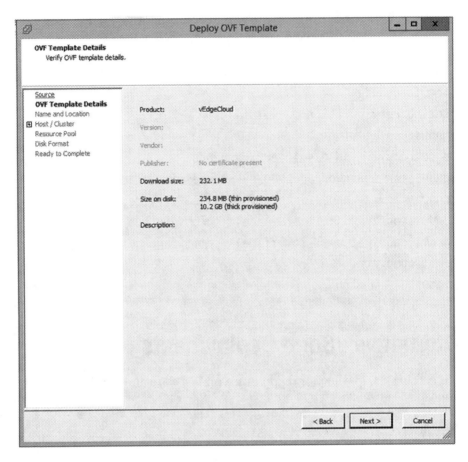

***Figure 5-14.***  *vBond install on ESXi*

Click Next.

Name the new VM, and select a location (Figure 5-15).

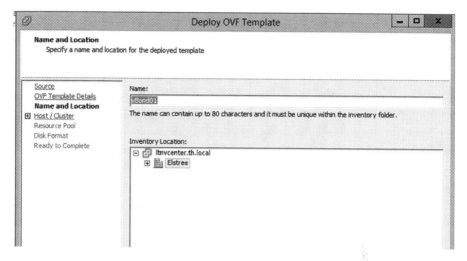

***Figure 5-15.*** *Naming the vBond controller on ESXi*

Select a host and click Next.

Select a datastore.

Click next on Disk Format.

Select the networks you will be using; each should be mapped to different networks (ideally) (Figure 5-16).

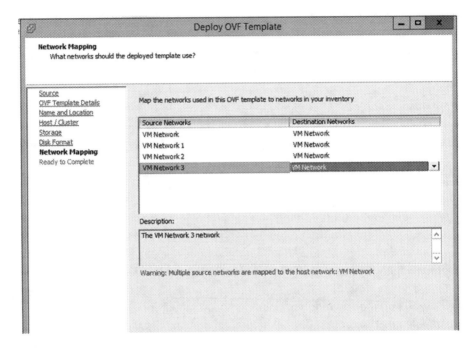

***Figure 5-16.*** *vBond networks*

Click Next to complete the deployment settings, and finally, click Finish (Figure 5-17).

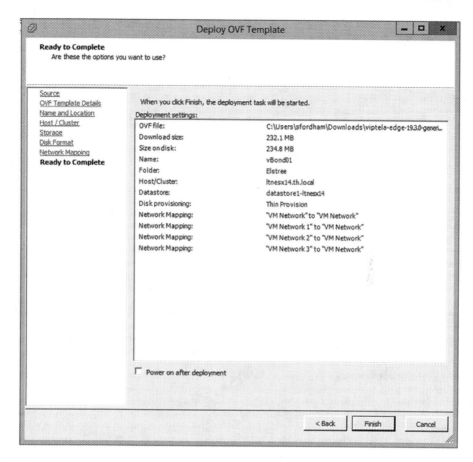

***Figure 5-17.*** *vBond configuration*

The deployment will complete (Figure 5-18).

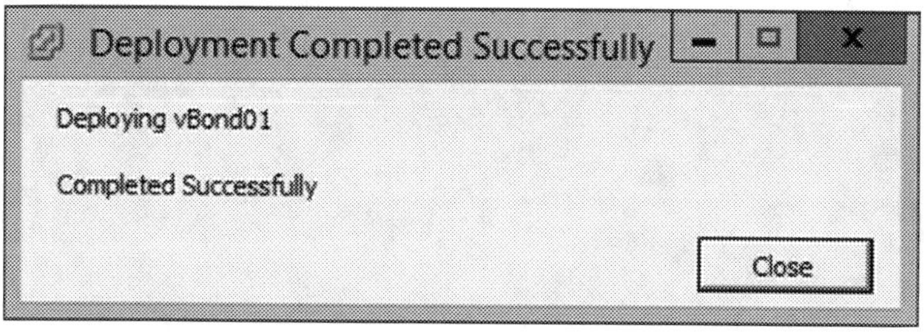

***Figure 5-18.*** *vBond successful deployment*

## KVM

If you want to install vBond on KVM, use the following:

```
virt-install \
    --name vbond01 \
    --os-type linux \
    --os-variant ubuntu14.04 \
    --cpu host \
    --vcpus=2 \
    --hvm \
    --arch=x86_64 \
    --ram 2048 \
    --disk path=viptela-bond-19.3.0-genericx86-64.qcow2,
      size=16,device=disk,bus=ide,format=qcow2 \
    --network=network:default,model=virtio \
    --network=network:default,model=virtio \
    --graphics none \
    --import
```

## Summary

In this chapter, we have set up our vBond controller. The next step in building our topology is to set up vSmart.

# CHAPTER 6

# Deploying vSmart

The vSmart controller sits between the vEdge devices and the vBond orchestrator; it helps with the authentication of edge devices to the vBond and manages the connectivity between the edge devices.

## vSmart Basic Config

The vSmart configuration follows the same steps as the vBond from the previous chapter:

```
vsmart# config
Entering configuration mode terminal
vsmart(config)# system
vsmart(config-system)# host-name vSmart01
vsmart(config-system)# organization-name Learning_SD-WAN
vsmart(config-system)# site-id 100
vsmart(config-system)# system-ip 100.100.1.4
vsmart(config-system)#
vsmart(config-system)# vbond 10.1.1.3
vsmart(config-system)#
```

© Stuart Fordham 2021
S. Fordham, *Learning SD-WAN with Cisco*, https://doi.org/10.1007/978-1-4842-7347-0_6

For the VPN 0 configuration, we need to enable the NETCONF service in the tunnel interface:

```
vsmart(config-system)# vpn 0
vsmart(config-vpn-0)#
vsmart(config-vpn-0)# no interface eth0
vsmart(config-vpn-0)# interface eth1
vsmart(config-interface-eth1)# ip address 10.1.1.4/24
vsmart(config-interface-eth1)# no shut
vsmart(config-interface-eth1)# ip route 0.0.0.0/0 10.1.1.1
vsmart(config-interface-eth1)# tunnel-interface
vsmart(config-tunnel-interface)# allow-service netconf
vsmart(config-tunnel-interface)# commit and-quit
Commit complete.
vSmart01#
```

Whereas the vBond IP address should be a public IP (in a real-life deployment), the IP address we assign to the eth1 interface does not have to, but will be determined by your deployment needs. We can now test connectivity.

```
vSmart01# ping 10.1.1.2
Ping in VPN 0
PING 10.1.1.2 (10.1.1.2) 56(84) bytes of data.
64 bytes from 10.1.1.2: icmp_seq=1 ttl=64 time=3.41 ms
64 bytes from 10.1.1.2: icmp_seq=2 ttl=64 time=1.48 ms
^C
--- 10.1.1.2 ping statistics ---
2 packets transmitted, 2 received, 0% packet loss, time 1000ms
rtt min/avg/max/mdev = 1.484/2.450/3.416/0.966 ms
vSmart01#
```

Let's set up our management connectivity:

```
vSmart01# config
vSmart01(config)# vpn 512
vSmart01(config-vpn-512)# interface eth0
vSmart01(config-interface-eth0)# ip address 100.1.1.4/24
vSmart01(config-interface-eth0)# no shutdown
vSmart01(config-interface-eth0)# exit
vSmart01(config-vpn-512)# commit and-quit
Commit complete.
vSmart01#
```

# vSmart Certificates

This is the same process as the other devices. We start by copying the CA certificate from the Linux server to the vSmart controller.

```
scp CA.crt admin@10.1.1.4:
```

Then we install the certificate:

```
vSmart01# request root-cert-chain install /home/admin/CA.crt
Uploading root-ca-cert-chain via VPN 0
Copying ... /home/admin/CA.crt via VPN 0
Updating the root certificate chain..
Successfully installed the root certificate chain
vSmart01#
```

The next step is to add vSmart to vManage. Navigate to *Configuration* ➤ *Devices Controllers*, click "*Add Device*," and select vSmart. Add the IP address, username, and password, and set the protocol, which can be left as the default of "DTLS" (Figure 6-1).

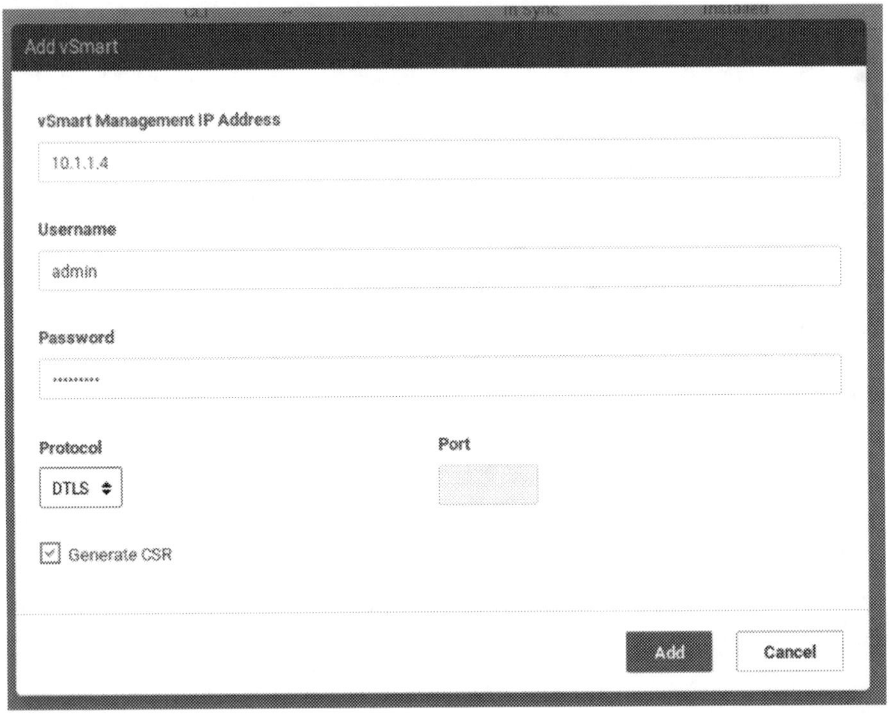

***Figure 6-1.*** *Adding a vSmart controller*

View and save the CSR (Figure 6-2).

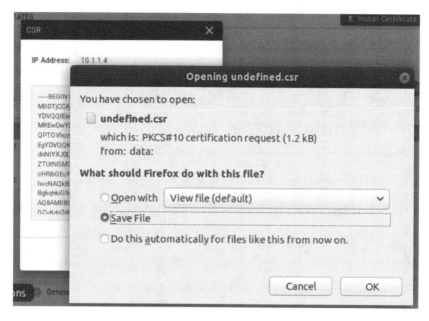

***Figure 6-2.***   *The vSmart CSR*

Because we will already have a file called "undefined.csr", we should rename this new file when we generate the certificate (Figure 6-3).

```
user@user-virtual-machine:~/Downloads$ mv undefined\(1\).csr vSmart.csr
user@user-virtual-machine:~/Downloads$ openssl x509 -req -in vSmart.csr -CA CA.
crt -CAkey CA.key -CAcreateserial -out vSmart01.pem -days 1000 -sha256
Signature ok
subject=/C=US/ST=California/L=San Jose/OU=Learning_SD-WAN/O=Viptela LLC/CN=vsma
rt-611a5b84-b2e5-4c7f-951b-a91c93520063-0.viptela.com/emailAddress=support@vipt
ela.com
Getting CA Private Key
user@user-virtual-machine:~/Downloads$ █
```

***Figure 6-3.***   *Generating the vSmart certificate*

Upload the certificate back into vManage, by going to *Configuration* ➤ *Certificates* ➤ *Controllers,* clicking "*Upload certificate,*" and selecting the vSmart01.pem certificate we just created.

The vSmart should then be fully populated with the hostname and system IP (Figure 6-4).

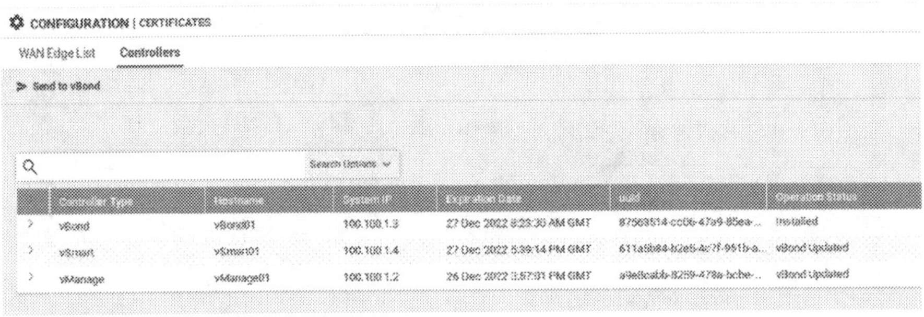

**Figure 6-4.** *vSmart showing in the NMS*

Similarly, the Devices page should show also be updated (Figure 6-5).

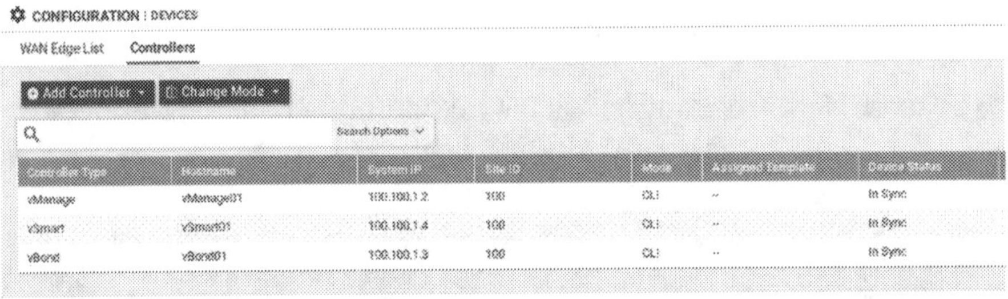

**Figure 6-5.** *vSmart in Devices*

If you are missing the hostname and system IP, then head over to the troubleshooting chapter.

Our dashboard should now show that we have one vSmart (Figure 6-6).

**Figure 6-6.** *vSmart in the dashboard*

This should be reflected in the Network page (Figure 6-7).

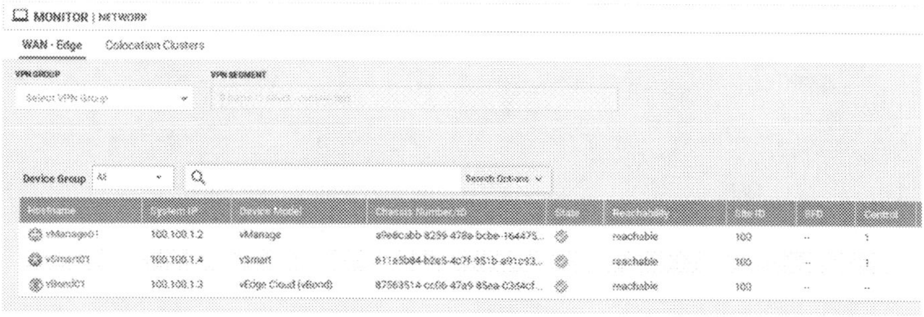

***Figure 6-7.*** *The Network page*

We can also use the CLI to gauge the health of our vSmart controller, by checking the connections to our vBond device, using the command "show transport connection":

```
vSmart01# show transport connection
```

```
TRACK
TYPE     SOURCE  DESTINATION  HOST  INDEX  TIME            STATE
-----------------------------------------------------------------
system   -       10.1.1.3           0      Wed Apr 1 20    up
vSmart01#
```

As well as looking at this (truncated) output from "show control local-properties":

```
vSmart01# show control local-properties
personality                 vsmart
sp-organization-name        Learning_SD-WAN
organization-name           Learning_SD-WAN
root-ca-chain-status        Installed
```

```
certificate-status                    Installed
certificate-validity                  Valid
certificate-not-valid-before          Apr 01 17:39:14 2020 GMT
certificate-not-valid-after           Dec 27 17:39:14 2022 GMT

dns-name                              10.1.1.3
site-id                               100
domain-id                             1
protocol                              dtls
tls-port                              23456
system-ip                             100.100.1.4
chassis-num/unique-id                 611a5b84-b2e5-4c7f-951b-
a91c93520063
serial-num                            CO24D682372213FB
token                                 -NA-
retry-interval                        0:00:00:17
no-activity-exp-interval              0:00:00:20
dns-cache-ttl                         0:00:02:00
port-hopped                           FALSE
time-since-last-port-hop              0:00:00:00
cdb-locked                            false
number-vbond-peers                    1

INDEX    IP                                        PORT
-----------------------------------------------------------
0        10.1.1.3                                  12346

number-active-wan-interfaces    2
```

vSmart01#

The output has been truncated due to the connection details at the end, which have been removed to preserve print formatting. From here, we can check our certificate validity.

We can also check our control connections using the command "show control connections" (Figure 6-8).

```
vSmart01# show control connections
                                                      PEER                      PEER
        PEER    PEER PEER        SITE   DOMAIN PEER   PRIV  PEER                 PUB
INDEX   TYPE    PROT SYSTEM IP   ID     ID     PRIVATE IP   PORT  PUBLIC IP       PORT  REMOTE COLOR   STATE UPTIME
0       vbond   dtls 0.0.0.0     0      0      10.1.1.3      12346 10.1.1.3       12346 default        up    0:15:12:44
0       vmanage dtls 100.100.1.2 100    0      10.1.1.2      12346 10.1.1.2       12346 default        up    0:15:12:40
1       vbond   dtls 0.0.0.0     0      0      10.1.1.3      12346 10.1.1.3       12346 default        up    0:15:12:44
vSmart01#
```

***Figure 6-8.*** *Show control connections*

We have full connections to the vBond and vManage over DTLS.

# vSmart Authentication and Validation

Behind the scenes, the vSmart controller and the vBond start a mutual process of validation and authentication between each other. We start this process when we add the IP address (or DNS name) of the vBond device during the initial configuration of the vSmart device:

```
vsmart(config-system)# vbond 10.1.1.3
```

The second part of this initial validation and authentication is performed when we add vSmart to vManage and issue the certificates. vManage then initiates an update of vBond (Figure 6-9).

| | Controller Type | Hostname | System IP | Expiration Date | uuid | Operation Status |
|---|---|---|---|---|---|---|
| > | vBond | vBond01 | 100.100.1.3 | 27 Dec 2022 8:23.30 AM GMT | 87568514-cc96-47a9-85ea-... | Installed |
| ∨ | vSmart | vSmart01 | 100.100.1.4 | 27 Dec 2022 8:39.14 PM GMT | 611a5b84-b2e5-4e7f-98 1b-a... | vBond Updated |
| | -vBond Updated | | | | | |
| > | vManage | vManage01 | 100.100.1.2 | 26 Dec 2022 3:57:01 PM GMT | a9e8cabb-8259-478a-bcbe-... | vBond Updated |

***Figure 6-9.*** *vManage updating vBond with the details of vSmart*

vManage has now sent the serial number of vSmart to vBond, priming it for vSmart to start talking to it over a DTLS tunnel, which is encrypted using RSA private- and public-key pairs.

With the tunnel in place, vBond sends the root CA to vSmart, along with the vEdge serial number file. vSmart checks the organization name in the certificate against its own configured organization name. If the organization name is the same, then vSmart will check the certificate against the CA root chain (which explains why we have uploaded the CA.crt file every time we have started a new device up). If the certificate signature is correct, the DTLS tunnel stays up and the authentication of the vBond orchestrator to vSmart has completed.

Naturally, vBond must perform similar checks. So vSmart also sends the root CA certificate to vBond, and vBond checks the serial number, organization name, and certificate signature as well. If these checks pass, then authentication of vSmart to vBond has completed.

The temporary DTLS tunnel that was created for this initial authentication now transitions to a permanent tunnel.

If the vBond orchestrator has not started when the vSmart controller is in the position to start the authentication sequence, then the vSmart will periodically attempt to start the sequence, until it is eventually successful.

If we have more than one vSmart controller, then the process is much the same. Each vSmart controller learns of the other vSmart controller(s) from vBond. Once each vSmart controller receives the serial number file from the vBond orchestrator, it initiates a DTLS connection to the other vSmart controller. The first vSmart will send its trusted root CA-signed certificate to the other vSmart controller. The second vSmart controller checks the serial number of the first vSmart controller against the serial number file it has received from vBond and checks the organization name in the certificate and the signature of the certificate. This process is also performed by the other vSmart controller so that there is a two-way trust between the controllers. Again, if each step is completed successfully, the temporary DTLS tunnel is replaced with a permanent one. vBond will then balance the control connections between the vEdge devices and the vSmart controllers automatically.

If any of the steps fail, and the same is true for the authentication sequence between vSmart and vBond devices, then the temporary DTLS tunnel will be torn down and the authentication attempt stops.

# Alternative vSmart Deployments

Like the other appliances, we can run the vSmart on VMWare or KVM.

## VMWare

As the steps for installing the vSmart are no different than those of vManage or vBond, there is no benefit in showing you all the steps.

## KVM

From the Linux command prompt type, the following:

```
virt-install \
    --name vSmart01 \
    --os-type linux \
    --os-variant ubuntu14.04 \
    --cpu host \
    --vcpus=2 \
    --hvm \
    --arch=x86_64 \
    --ram=2048 \
    --disk path=viptela-smart-19.3.0-genericx86_64.qcow2,
      size=16,device=disk,bus=ide,format=qcow2 \
```

```
--network=network:default,model=virtio \
--network=network:default,model=virtio \
--graphics none \
--import
```

## Summary

We have now set up our vSmart controller which acts as the gateway between the vBond and vManage devices and the vEdge devices. We will look at the role of the vSmart controller further, when we start to provision policies in Chapter 10, but for now, we are at a position where we can start adding our vEdge devices.

# CHAPTER 7

# Edge Devices

In this chapter, we will set up two vEdge devices and one cEdge device. vEdge means that it is a Viptela device, and cEdge means that it is a Cisco device (a CSR1000v in this instance). Although they are technically now the same company, vEdge and cEdge are still used to distinguish between the two different router types and the OS that they run.

We begin with the vEdge router, in our HQ, in the same way as the other devices we have previously configured, by changing the password:

```
vedge login: admin
Password:
Welcome to Viptela CLI
admin connected from 127.0.0.1 using console on vedge
You must set an initial admin password.
Password:
Re-enter password:
vedge#
```

The basic set up is the same as the other devices we have configured:

```
vedge# config
Entering configuration mode terminal
vedge(config)# system
vedge(config-system)# host-name vEdge01
vedge(config-system)# site-id 100
vedge(config-system)# system-ip 100.100.1.5
vedge(config-system)# vbond 10.1.1.3
```

© Stuart Fordham 2021
S. Fordham, *Learning SD-WAN with Cisco*, https://doi.org/10.1007/978-1-4842-7347-0_7

```
vedge(config-system)# organization-name Learning_SD-WAN
vedge(config-system)#
vedge(config-system)# commit and-quit
Commit complete.
vEdge01#
```

We can then move on to VPN 0:

```
vEdge01(config)# vpn 0
vEdge01(config-vpn-0)# ip route 0.0.0.0/0 10.1.1.1
vEdge01(config-vpn-0)# interface ge0/0
vEdge01(config-interface-ge0/0)# ip address 10.1.1.5/24
vEdge01(config-interface-ge0/0)# no shut
vEdge01(config-interface-ge0/0)#
vEdge01(config-interface-ge0/0)# tunnel-interface
vEdge01(config-tunnel-interface)# encapsulation ipsec
vEdge01(config-tunnel-interface)# color blue
vEdge01(config-tunnel-interface)#
vEdge01(config-tunnel-interface)# validate
Validation complete
vEdge01(config-tunnel-interface)# commit and-quit
Commit complete.
vEdge01#
```

Once the changes have been committed, confirm that you can reach the vBond and vSmart devices:

```
vEdge01# ping 10.1.1.3
Ping in VPN 0
PING 10.1.1.3 (10.1.1.3) 56(84) bytes of data.
64 bytes from 10.1.1.3: icmp_seq=1 ttl=64 time=26.2 ms
64 bytes from 10.1.1.3: icmp_seq=2 ttl=64 time=28.8 ms
^C
```

```
--- 10.1.1.3 ping statistics ---
2 packets transmitted, 2 received, 0% packet loss, time 1000ms
rtt min/avg/max/mdev = 26.239/27.525/28.811/1.286 ms
vEdge01#
vEdge01# ping 10.1.1.4
Ping in VPN 0
PING 10.1.1.4 (10.1.1.4) 56(84) bytes of data.
64 bytes from 10.1.1.4: icmp_seq=1 ttl=64 time=1.36 ms
64 bytes from 10.1.1.4: icmp_seq=2 ttl=64 time=1.31 ms
^C
--- 10.1.1.4 ping statistics ---
2 packets transmitted, 2 received, 0% packet loss, time 1001ms
rtt min/avg/max/mdev = 1.316/1.340/1.365/0.044 ms
vEdge01#
```

Next, on the vManage server, navigate to *Configuration* ➤ *Devices* ➤ *WAN Edge List*. Select the first vEdge Cloud device (not the CSR1000v), and click the three dots on the right-hand side, and select "Generate Bootstrap Configuration" from the drop-down list (Figure 7-1).

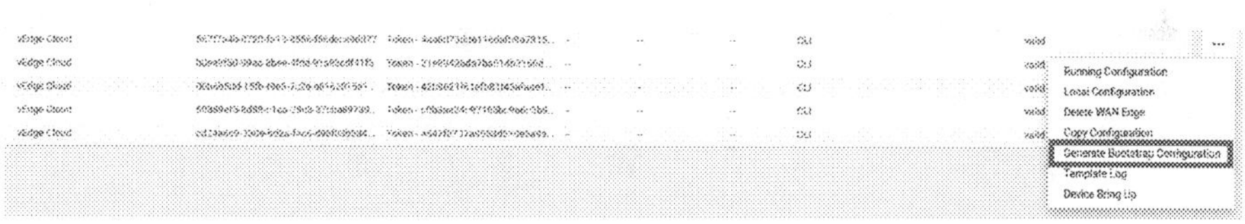

*Figure 7-1.* *Generating the vEdge bootstrap configuration*

We need the configuration to be in "Cloud-Init" format. Click OK (Figure 7-2).

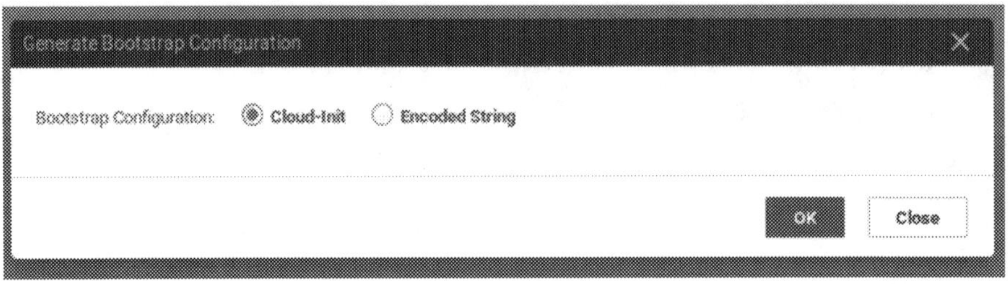

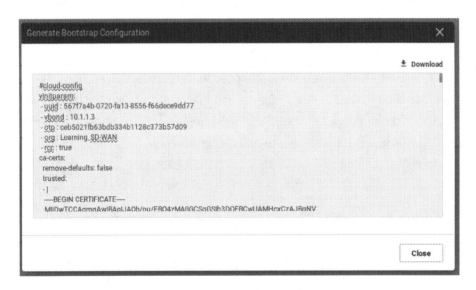

***Figure 7-2.*** *Select Cloud-Init*

The file contains a few lines of text as well as the certificates we need for the communication to occur between the edge device and the control devices (Figure 7-3).

***Figure 7-3.*** *The vEdge bootstrap configuration*

Save the file locally, and open it up in a text editor, so that we can copy the parts we need, which are the UUID and the OTP (one-time password). The UUID is our chassis number, and the OTP is the one-time token code. The OTP is referred to as a "token" in the CLI and as an "OTP" in the vManage GUI, so these terms may be used interchangeably.

Back on the vEdge router, request activation using the "request vedge-cloud activate chassis-number <UUID> token <OTP>" command using the UUID and the OTP from the file we just downloaded:

```
vEdge01# request vedge-cloud activate chassis-number 577f7a4b-
0720-fa13-8556-f66dece9dd77 token ceb5021fb63bdb334b1128c373b5
7d09
```

As we are using an OTP, the command can only be run once. If the activation fails, then the device must be decommissioned from vManage, so that the serial is released for reuse and a new OTP must be generated. The UUID will remain the same though.

For the certificate chain to be valid, we need to upload the CA certificate from the Linux server. Start by enabling SSH on the vEdge device.

```
vEdge01# config
Entering configuration mode terminal
vEdge01(config)# vpn 0
vEdge01(config-vpn-0)# interface ge0/0
vEdge01(config-interface-ge0/0)# tunnel-interface
vEdge01(config-tunnel-interface)# allow-service sshd
vEdge01(config-tunnel-interface)#
vEdge01(config-tunnel-interface)# commit and-quit
Commit complete.
vEdge01#
```

Upload the certificate from the Linux device:

```
scp CA.crt admin@10.1.1.5:
```

Then install the CA certificate:

```
vEdge01# request root-cert-chain install /home/admin/CA.crt
Uploading root-ca-cert-chain via VPN 0
Copying ... /home/admin/CA.crt via VPN 0
Updating the root certificate chain..
Successfully installed the root certificate chain
vEdge01#
```

Assuming all goes well, we should see the edge device listed in vManage (Figure 7-4).

***Figure 7-4.*** *Our edge device showing in vManage*

If we look at our network now (*Monitor* ➤ *Network*), we should see the edge device (Figure 7-5).

| Hostname | System IP | Device Model | Chassis Number/ID | State | Reachability | Site ID | BFD | Control |
|---|---|---|---|---|---|---|---|---|
| vManage01 | 100.100.1.2 | vManage | 713d0c64-cd24-40f8-b7... | | reachable | 100 | -- | 2 |
| vSmart01 | 100.100.1.4 | vSmart | 5931fdfa-6406-4c85-b6e... | | reachable | 100 | -- | 2 |
| vBond01 | 100.100.1.3 | vEdge Cloud (vBond) | 0b4e8edb-754b-4bf6-ac... | | reachable | 100 | -- | -- |
| vEdge01 | 100.100.1.5 | vEdge Cloud | 567f7a4b-0720-fa13-855... | | reachable | 100 | 0 | 2 |

***Figure 7-5.*** *The network monitoring page*

It will also be visible in our WAN Edge List (Figure 7-6).

| State | Device Model | Chassis Number | Serial No./Token | Hostname | System IP | Site ID | Mode | Device Status | Validity |
|---|---|---|---|---|---|---|---|---|---|
| | CSR1000v | CSR-0502AB1A-20E0-45AE-8AB1-775B... | Token - 588167eb48b6d4fa4a448e1e43e9... | -- | -- | -- | CLI | | valid |
| | CSR1000v | CSR-1782A7B8-852A-7186-8C94-27361... | Token - e04c806c0bb69ebbe6971e42911... | -- | -- | -- | CLI | | valid |
| | CSR1000v | CSR-ED477D6F-23B0-1508-0857-819E... | Token - 875f1a4de898e67eeb217dee857... | -- | -- | -- | CLI | | valid |
| | CSR1000v | CSR-F1C70091-3AF3-4A45-4098-831F... | Token - 36aa9738233a5e58974de0f8d59... | -- | -- | -- | CLI | | valid |
| | CSR1000v | CSR-E5C0F059-E2C8-D2F7-AEB0-3D32... | Token - 0d04f0f3c428f4a218b507bb64a74... | -- | -- | -- | CLI | | valid |
| | vEdge Cloud | 567f7a4b-0720-fa13-8556-f6dceecc9dd7 | 69EEF982 | vEdge01 | 100.100.1.5 | 100 | CLI | In Sync | valid |
| | vEdge Cloud | b0ea0f50-99ac-8bee-463d-91a89cdf4115 | Token - 21x89426de7ba5f4ef1166d86490... | -- | -- | -- | CLI | | valid |

***Figure 7-6.*** *The edge list*

We can look at the vSmart controller and see the OMP connections:

```
vSmart01# show omp summary
oper-state               UP
admin-state              UP
personality              vsmart
omp-uptime               4:20:06:20
routes-received          0
routes-installed         0
routes-sent              0
tlocs-received           1
tlocs-installed          1
tlocs-sent               0
services-received        0
services-installed       0
services-sent            0
mcast-routes-received    0
mcast-routes-installed   0
mcast-routes-sent        0
hello-sent               5
hello-received           6
handshake-sent           1
handshake-received       1
alert-sent               0
alert-received           0
inform-sent              3
inform-received          3
update-sent              0
update-received          1
policy-sent              0
policy-received          0
total-packets-sent       9
```

```
total-packets-received 11
vsmart-peers           0
vedge-peers            1
vSmart01#
```

Note that we have received (and installed) a TLOC, but have not received any routes yet. So, let's add a route on our edge router and see what happens. This will become VPN 1. We can support a huge amount of VPNs, from 1 to 511 and then from 513 to 65527! That said, the vEdge devices can support a total of 64 concurrent VPNs.[1]

```
vEdge01# config
Entering configuration mode terminal
vEdge01(config)# vpn ?
This line doesn't have a valid range expression
Possible completions:
  Allowed values on vedge: <0..65527>
  Allowed values on vsmart/vmanage/vcontainer: <0 and 512>
  0
  512
vEdge01(config)#
vEdge01(config)# vpn 1
vEdge01(config-vpn-1)# interface loopback1
vEdge01(config-interface-loopback1)# ip address 172.16.10.1/24
vEdge01(config-interface-loopback1)# no shut
vEdge01(config-interface-loopback1)# end
Uncommitted changes found, commit them? [yes/no/CANCEL] yes
Commit complete.
vEdge01#
```

---

[1] www.slideshare.net/CiscoCanada/understanding-cisco-next-generation-sdwan-solution

Now if we look at the vSmart controller again, we can see that we have received an additional route:

```
vSmart01# show omp summary
oper-state             UP
admin-state            UP
personality            vsmart
omp-uptime             4:20:59:09
routes-received        1
routes-installed       0
routes-sent            0
tlocs-received         1
tlocs-installed        1
tlocs-sent             0
services-received      1
services-installed     1
services-sent          0
mcast-routes-received  0
mcast-routes-installed 0
mcast-routes-sent      0
hello-sent             164
hello-received         166
handshake-sent         1
handshake-received     1
alert-sent             0
alert-received         0
inform-sent            7
inform-received        7
update-sent            0
update-received        3
policy-sent            0
policy-received        0
```

```
total-packets-sent      172
total-packets-received 177
vsmart-peers            0
vedge-peers             1
vSmart01#
```

We can use the "show omp routes" command to look at the routes we have received. Note that the tloc color (blue) matches what we configured on the vEdge01 device when we set it up:

```
vSmart01# show omp routes

---------------------------------------------------
omp route entries for vpn 1 route 172.16.10.0/24
---------------------------------------------------
                RECEIVED FROM:
peer            100.100.1.5
path-id         74
label           1003
status          C,R
loss-reason     not set
lost-to-peer    not set
lost-to-path-id not set
    Attributes:
    originator      100.100.1.5
    type            installed
    tloc            100.100.1.5, blue, ipsec
    ultimate-tloc   not set
    domain-id       not set
    overlay-id      1
    site-id         100
    preference      not set
```

```
    tag             not set
    origin-proto    connected
    origin-metric   0
    as-path         not set
    unknown-attr-len not set
vSmart01#
```

Let's add vEdge02, following the configuration given here:

```
vedge# config
Entering configuration mode terminal
vedge(config)# system
vedge(config-system)# host-name vEdge02
vedge(config-system)# site-id 100
vedge(config-system)# system-ip 60.100.100.1
vedge(config-system)# vbond 10.1.1.3
vedge(config-system)# organization-name Learning_SD-WAN
vedge(config-system)# vpn 0
vedge(config-vpn-0)# no interface ge0/0
vedge(config-vpn-0)# ip route 0.0.0.0/0 50.11.11.254
vedge(config-vpn-0)# interface ge0/1
vedge(config-interface-ge0/1)# ip address 50.11.11.1/24
vedge(config-interface-ge0/1)# no shut
vedge(config-interface-ge0/1)# tunnel-interface
vedge(config-tunnel-interface)# encapsulation ipsec
vEdge02(config-tunnel-interface)# allow-service sshd
vedge(config-tunnel-interface)# color red
vedge(config-tunnel-interface)# commit and-quit
Commit complete.
vEdge02#
```

**Note**   I have placed it into site 100, instead of site 200 as shown in the topology in Chapter 2. This is on purpose and will be explained in the next chapter.

Before moving on, we should check our connectivity, first by pinging ISP-R, and then vBond:

```
vEdge02# ping 50.11.11.254
Ping in VPN 0
PING 50.11.11.254 (50.11.11.254) 56(84) bytes of data.
64 bytes from 50.11.11.254: icmp_seq=1 ttl=64 time=0.900 ms
64 bytes from 50.11.11.254: icmp_seq=2 ttl=64 time=0.521 ms
^C
--- 50.11.11.254 ping statistics ---
2 packets transmitted, 2 received, 0% packet loss, time 1000ms
rtt min/avg/max/mdev = 0.521/0.710/0.900/0.191 ms
vEdge02#
vEdge02# ping 10.1.1.3
Ping in VPN 0
PING 10.1.1.3 (10.1.1.3) 56(84) bytes of data.
64 bytes from 10.1.1.3: icmp_seq=1 ttl=62 time=25.8 ms
64 bytes from 10.1.1.3: icmp_seq=2 ttl=62 time=27.0 ms
^C
--- 10.1.1.3 ping statistics ---
2 packets transmitted, 2 received, 0% packet loss, time 1001ms
rtt min/avg/max/mdev = 25.814/26.456/27.099/0.662 ms
vEdge02#
```

Next, we can copy the CA.crt over to vEdge02 (from the Linux server):

```
scp CA.crt admin@50.11.11.1:
```

Then, install the certificate:

```
vEdge02# request root-cert-chain install /home/admin/CA.crt
Uploading root-ca-cert-chain via VPN 0
Copying ... /home/admin/CA.crt via VPN 0
Updating the root certificate chain..
Successfully installed the root certificate chain
vEdge02#
```

On vManage, we can navigate to *Configuration* ➤ *Devices* and generate the bootstrap code for the second vEdge Cloud device on the list and activate it:

```
vEdge02# request vedge-cloud activate chassis-
number b0ea9f50-99ac-8bee-4fdd-91a83cdf41f5 token
a2d1493536d8f4b2aebdc7f845d416
vEdge02#
```

We should now see that the device list has been updated (Figure 7-7).

| State | Device Model | Chassis Number | Serial No./Token | Hostname | System IP | Site ID | Mode | Device Status |
|---|---|---|---|---|---|---|---|---|
| | CSR1000v | CSR-0502AB1A-7DED-... | Token - 553f67a845b6... | .. | .. | .. | CLI | |
| | CSR1000v | CSR-17B237B8-852A-7... | Token - e04cf06c0bb69... | .. | .. | .. | CLI | |
| | CSR1000v | CSR-ED477D6F-238C-1... | Token - b7681adde388... | .. | .. | .. | CLI | |
| | CSR1000v | CSR-F1C7D091-3AF3-4... | Token - 86ac8798259a... | .. | .. | .. | CLI | |
| | CSR1000v | CSR-ESC01068-E2C8-D... | Token - 0d04f5ffc4281... | .. | .. | .. | CLI | |
| | vEdge Cloud | 567f7a4b-0720-fa13-8... | 68EFF562 | vEdge01 | 100.100.1.5 | 100 | CLI | In Sync |
| | vEdge Cloud | b0ea9f50-99ac-8bee-4... | 5A096571 | vEdge02 | 60.100.100.1 | 100 | CLI | In Sync |
| | vEdge Cloud | 00b6b5dd-15fb-f9e3-7... | Token - 42b9821f61efb... | .. | .. | .. | CLI | |

***Figure 7-7.*** *The WAN edge device list*

Similarly, our list of network devices has also been updated (Figure 7-8).

| Hostname | System IP | Device Model | Chassis Number/ID | State | Reachability | Site ID | BFD | Control |
|---|---|---|---|---|---|---|---|---|
| vManage01 | 100.100.1.2 | vManage | 713d0c64-cd2A-40f8-b7... | | reachable | 100 | -- | 3 |
| vSmart01 | 100.100.1.4 | vSmart | 5931fdfa-6406-4c85-b6e... | | reachable | 100 | -- | 3 |
| vBond01 | 100.100.1.3 | vEdge Cloud (vBond) | 9b4e8edb-754b-4bf6-ac... | | reachable | 100 | -- | -- |
| vEdge01 | 100.100.1.5 | vEdge Cloud | 567f7a4b-0720-fa13-855... | | reachable | 100 | 0 | 2 |
| vEdge02 | 60.100.100.1 | vEdge Cloud | b0ea9f50-99ac-8bee-4fd... | | reachable | 100 | 0 | 2 |

***Figure 7-8.*** *The Network monitor window (again)*

Let's test OMP by creating a new VPN on vEdge02 (as we did on vEdge01):

```
vEdge02# config
Entering configuration mode terminal
vEdge02(config)# vpn 1
vEdge02(config-vpn-1)# interface loopback1
vEdge02(config-interface-loopback1)# ip address 172.16.20.1/24
vEdge02(config-interface-loopback1)# no shutdown
vEdge02(config-interface-loopback1)# end
Uncommitted changes found, commit them? [yes/no/CANCEL] yes
Commit complete.
vEdge02#
```

We can confirm that we can see both of the routes using the command "show omp routes received":

```
vEdge02# show omp routes received

-------------------------------------------------------
omp route entries for vpn 1 route 172.16.10.0/24
-------------------------------------------------------
              RECEIVED FROM:
peer              100.100.1.4
path-id           1
label             1003
status            Inv,U
loss-reason       not set
lost-to-peer      not set
lost-to-path-id not set
    Attributes:
     originator        100.100.1.5
     type              installed
     tloc              100.100.1.5, blue, ipsec
     ultimate-tloc     not set
```

```
domain-id          not set
overlay-id         1
site-id            100
preference         not set
tag                not set
origin-proto       connected
origin-metric      0
as-path            not set
unknown-attr-len   not set

-------------------------------------------------------
omp route entries for vpn 1 route 172.16.20.0/24
-------------------------------------------------------
             RECEIVED FROM:
peer            0.0.0.0
path-id         72
label           1003
status          C,Red,R
loss-reason     not set
lost-to-peer    not set
lost-to-path-id not set
    Attributes:
      originator       60.100.100.1
      type             installed
      tloc             60.100.100.1, red, ipsec
      ultimate-tloc    not set
      domain-id        not set
      overlay-id       1
      site-id          100
      preference       not set
      tag              not set
```

```
    origin-proto      connected
    origin-metric     0
    as-path           not set
    unknown-attr-len  not set
vEdge02#
```

So far, so good. In the final part of our topology configuration, we will set up the CSR1000V.

# CSR1000v

The commands used by the CSR1000v differ (slightly) from the other configurations we have encountered so far, as you might expect coming from a different vendor.

We start as usual, by logging in using admin/admin as the username and password and then setting a new password when prompted:

```
User Access Verification

Username: admin
Password:

Default admin password needs to be changed.

Enter new password:
Confirm password:
System status solid green (reason: All daemons up)
Router>
Router>
Successfully set new admin password
Router>
```

From here on, things get a bit different:

```
Router>en
Router#config
This command is not supported

Router#configure terminal
This command is not supported

Router#
```

We can no longer use the "config" command. Instead, we need to use the "config-transaction" command:

```
Router#config-transaction

admin connected from 127.0.0.1 using console on Router
Router(config)#
```

Now we are progressing. The hostname command is not configured under the system options (unlike the vEdges); instead, it is set at the top level of the configuration:

```
Router(config)# hostname CSR-1
```

The SD-WAN parameters are under the system command, though:

```
Router(config)# system
Router(config-system)# site-id 100
Router(config-system)# organization-name Learning_SD-WAN
Router(config-system)# vbond 10.1.1.3
Router(config-system)# system-ip 70.100.100.1
Router(config-system)#

Router(config-system)# commit
Commit complete.
CSR-1(config-system)#
```

The way we configure VPN 0 is also different:

```
CSR-1(config-system)# vpn 0
----------------------^
syntax error: unknown command
CSR-1(config-system)#
```

We have to jump around the console to get the SD-WAN tunnel prepared, starting by configuring the interface:

```
CSR-1(config-system)# exit
CSR-1(config)#
CSR-1(config)# interface GigabitEthernet 1
CSR-1(config-if)#
CSR-1(config-if)# ip address 50.10.10.1 255.255.255.0
CSR-1(config-if)# no shut
CSR-1(config-if)# ip route 0.0.0.0 0.0.0.0 50.10.10.254
CSR-1(config)# commit
Commit complete.
CSR-1(config)# end
```

We can test connectivity now to both our default gateway (ISP-R) and the vBond controller:

```
CSR-1#ping 50.10.10.254
Type escape sequence to abort.
Sending 5, 100-byte ICMP Echos to 50.10.10.254, timeout is 2
seconds:
!!!!!
Success rate is 100 percent (5/5), round-trip min/avg/max =
1/5/22 ms
CSR-1#ping 10.1.1.3
Type escape sequence to abort.
```

Sending 5, 100-byte ICMP Echos to 10.1.1.3, timeout is 2
seconds:
!!!!!
Success rate is 100 percent (5/5), round-trip min/avg/max =
20/27/30 ms
CSR-1#

Next, we create a tunnel interface, which is a hidden option, so make
sure you don't put a space between "tunnel" and "1"; otherwise, the
command will fail. Start with a "show interface summary" so you can
copy and paste easily later on (I have truncated the output for formatting).
We also need to set the tunnel mode to "sdwan."

CSR-1#show interface summary

| Interface | IHQ | IQD | OHQ | OQD | RXBS | RXPS | TXBS |
|-----------|-----|-----|-----|-----|------|------|------|
| * GigabitEthernet1 | 0 | 0 | 0 | 0 | 0 | 0 | 0 |
| * GigabitEthernet2 | 0 | 0 | 0 | 0 | 0 | 0 | 0 |
| * GigabitEthernet3 | 0 | 0 | 0 | 0 | 0 | 0 | 0 |
| * GigabitEthernet4 | 0 | 0 | 0 | 0 | 0 | 0 | 0 |
| * Loopback65528 | 0 | 0 | 0 | 0 | 0 | 0 | 0 |

CSR-1#
CSR-1#config-transaction
CSR-1(config)# interface ?
Possible completions:
  ATM                     ATM-ACR
  AppGigabitEthernet      AppNav-Compress
  AppNav-UnCompress       BD-VIF
  BDI                     CEM
  CEM-ACR                 Cellular
  Dialer                  Embedded-Service-Engine
  Ethernet                Ethernet-Internal

```
 FastEthernet           FiveGigabitEthernet
 FortyGigabitEthernet   GMPLS
 GigabitEthernet        Group-Async
 HundredGigE            LISP
 Loopback               Multilink
 Port-channel           SM
 Serial                 Service-Engine
 TenGigabitEthernet     Tunnel
 TwentyFiveGigE         TwentyFiveGigabitEthernet
 TwoGigabitEthernet     Vif
 Virtual-PPP            Virtual-Template
 VirtualPortGroup       Vlan
 Wlan-GigabitEthernet   nat64
 nat66                  nve
 ospfv3                 overlay
 pseudowire             ucse
 vasileft               vasiright
CSR-1(config)# interface Tunnel1
CSR-1(config-if)# ip unnumbered GigabitEthernet1
CSR-1(config-if)# tunnel source GigabitEthernet1
CSR-1(config-if)# tunnel mode sdwan
CSR-1(config-if)# no shutdown
CSR-1(config-if)#
CSR-1(config-if)# commit
Commit complete.
CSR-1(config-if)#
*Apr  7 19:35:34.704: %LINEPROTO-5-UPDOWN: Line protocol on
Interface Tunnel1, changed state to down
CSR-1(config-if)#
```

Next, we configure the SD-WAN commands, setting the physical interface, the encapsulation, and the color:

```
CSR-1(config)# sdwan
CSR-1(config-sdwan)# interface GigabitEthernet1
CSR-1(config-interface-GigabitEthernet1)# tunnel-interface
CSR-1(config-tunnel-interface)# encapsulation ipsec
CSR-1(config-tunnel-interface)# color biz-internet
CSR-1(config-tunnel-interface)# commit
Commit complete.
CSR-1(config-tunnel-interface)#
*Apr  7 19:40:45.596: %LINEPROTO-5-UPDOWN: Line protocol on
Interface Tunnel1, changed state to up
CSR-1(config-tunnel-interface)#
```

Whatever you do, don't be tempted to shorten the interface name to Gi1 (as most engineers would); the IOS XE CLI is *very* picky, and the interface name you use in the tunnel declaration and the SDWAN configuration has to match the output of "show interface summary".

Select the three dots next to the first CSR1000v device under *Configuration* ➤ *Devices*, and select the Generate Bootstrap Configuration option from the drop-down, selecting Cloud-Init when prompted. Save the file, and open it in a text editor (again so that we can grab the UUID and OTP).

Enable SSHD on the router, so that we can SCP the file across, and we might as well enable NETCONF, while we are there:

```
CSR-1(config-tunnel-interface)# allow-service sshd
CSR-1(config-tunnel-interface)# allow-service netconf
CSR-1(config-tunnel-interface)# commit
CSR-1(config-tunnel-interface)# end
```

Copy the certificate over from the Linux server, the command for which is slightly different for this device:

```
scp CA.crt admin@50.10.10.1:bootflash:/CA.crt
```

Check that the file has been copied over:

```
CSR-1#dir | i CA
   21  -rw-   1363   Apr 9 2020 08:56:49 +00:00  CA.crt
CSR-1#
```

SSH onto the router from the Linux machine, and then enter the following, copying and pasting the chassis number and OTP into the appropriate places:

```
CSR-1# request platform software sdwan vedge_cloud activate
chassis-number <uuid> token <otp>
```

Note how different the command is compared to the vEdge devices we set up previously:

```
vEdge02# request vedge-cloud activate chassis-number <uuid>
token <otp>
vEdge02#
```

With the cEdge, we need to install the new image and activate it; this is why we specify the "platform software sdwan".

Install the CA certificate, and watch the magic happen!

```
CSR-1#request platform software sdwan root-cert-chain install
bootflash:CA.crt
Uploading root-ca-cert-chain via VPN 0
Copying ... /bootflash/CA.crt via VPN 0
Updating the root certificate chain..
Successfully installed the root certificate chain
CSR-1#
```

We can now see the CSR-1 router under devices (Figure 7-9).

***Figure 7-9.*** *Our CSR-1 device*

It has also increased the edge device count on our dashboard (Figure 7-10).

***Figure 7-10.*** *Our updated dashboard*

Now we will turn our attention to what happens behind the scenes when we add an edge device onto the network.

# vEdge Authentication

When we deploy vEdge routers, they need to connect to the vManage server so it may receive the configuration and to the vSmart controller so it can become part of the overlay network.

Before the vEdge router can talk to the vManage or vSmart devices, it builds a connection to the vBond, and once this has been completed, the vBond sends the IP addresses of vManage and vSmart to the vEdge.

The vEdge starts by initiating a DTLS connection to the IP address of the vBond device that is set in its configuration. This is secured through RSA private and public keys.

The vBond then works out whether the vEdge is behind a NAT device and, if it is, maps the public IP address and port to the private IP address. Now that the DTLS tunnel has been established, the two devices can authenticate against each other.

171

Firstly, vBond sends the root CA-signed certificate to the vEdge router. The organization name is extracted from the certificate, and vEdge compares the one in the certificate to the one locally configured. If the names match, then vEdge checks that the vBond certificate is signed by the root CA. If the organization name and the certificate pass the check, then vBond has authenticated to vEdge. If either of these two checks fails, the DTLS tunnel is torn down and periodically retried. You can see a Wireshark capture of this traffic in Chapter 14.

Now, vEdge must authenticate to vBond.

vBond starts by sending A 256-bit challenge (a random value), and in return, vEdge sends the following to vBond:

- The serial number

- The chassis number

- The board ID certificate (located on a chip inside the router)

- A 256-bit random value signed with the vEdge's private key

Once the vBond has received these, it compares the serial number and chassis number to the list it has been sent by vManage. If these are found in the list, vBond then checks the 256-bit random value to check that it has been correctly signed using the vEdge's public key, which is gained from the board ID certificate. If this is correctly signed, then vBond uses the root CA chain to validate the board ID certificate.

If the board ID certificate is valid, then the authentication of vEdge to vBond is also complete. vBond now sends two messages. The first message is sent to the vEdge, and this contains the IP addresses and the serial number of the vManage and vSmart controllers in the network. The second message is sent to the vSmart controllers and contains a message announcing a new vEdge router in the network and a request for the vSmart to set up a session with the new router.

With this done, vEdge terminates the DTLS tunnel to vBond and starts a DTLS tunnel to vManage.

vManage sends its trusted root CA-signed certificate to vEdge, which vEdge uses to check the organization name. If this matches, then vEdge uses its own CA certificate to check that the certificate is valid. If both pass, then vManage has authenticated to vEdge.

If this is starting to sound familiar, it is because it is. The process then follows with vManage sending a 256-bit random value challenge to vEdge, and vEdge sends the same details that it sent to vBond, to vManage. vManage then performs the same checks against this, checking the serial and chassis numbers, uses vEdge's board ID certificate to extract vEdge's public certificate, and checks the board ID certificate using the CA certificate. If these pass, then vEdge has authenticated to vEdge.

The next step is that vManage then sends the configuration file to the vEdge router (if one exists). Once received, this is activated, and vEdge starts advertising its prefixes to vSmart.

This kicks off another set of authentications, of vSmart to vEdge and vice versa, which once completed switches the temporary DTLS tunnel used for authentication to a permanent tunnel over which OMP sessions will run.

# Alternative vEdge Deployments

As the vEdge device is the same as vBond, refer back to that chapter for the installation steps on KVM and VMWare.

## vEdge in the Cloud

Viptela edge devices are also offered by several cloud providers, such as AWS and Azure, and in this step, we will look at how to deploy vEdge in AWS.

Start by navigating to the AWS Console (`https://aws.amazon.com/console/`), and then select the option for EC2. Select the Launch instance option in the main window (Figure 7-11).

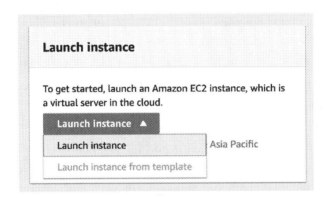

**Figure 7-11.** *Launching a vEdge EC2 instance*

In the net window, search for "vEdge," and select the AWS Marketplace option (Figure 7-12).

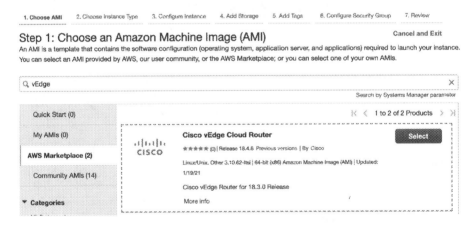

**Figure 7-12.** *The AWS marketplace*

Select the Cisco vEdge Cloud Router option, review the pricing details, and select Continue (Figure 7-13).

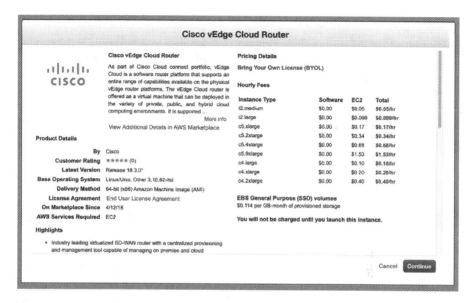

**Figure 7-13.** *Many different size options*

Choose your instance type, some of which are eligible for "free tier" (Figure 7-14).

1. Choose AMI    **2. Choose Instance Type**    3. Configure Instance    4. Add Storage    5. Add Tags    6 Configure Security Group    7. Review

## Step 2: Choose an Instance Type

Amazon EC2 provides a wide selection of instance types optimized to fit different use cases. Instances are virtual servers that can run applications. They have varying combinations of CPU, memory, storage, and networking capacity, and give you the flexibility to choose the appropriate mix of resources for your applications. Learn more about instance types and how they can meet your computing needs.

Filter by:    t2 ▾    All generations ▾    Show/Hide Columns

Currently selected: t2.medium (- ECUs, 2 vCPUs, 2.3 GHz, -, 4 GiB memory, EBS only)

Note: The vendor recommends using a **c3.large** instance (or larger) for the best experience with this product.

| | Family | Type | vCPUs ⓘ | Memory (GiB) | Instance Storage (GB) ⓘ |
|---|---|---|---|---|---|
| ⊘ | t2 | t2.nano | 1 | 0.5 | EBS only |
| ⊘ | t2 | t2.micro<br>Free tier eligible | 1 | 1 | EBS only |
| ⊘ | t2 | t2.small | 1 | 2 | EBS only |
| ▣ | t2 | t2.medium | 2 | 4 | EBS only |
| ◯ | t2 | t2.large | 2 | 8 | EBS only |
| ⊘ | t2 | t2.xlarge | 4 | 16 | EBS only |
| ⊘ | t2 | t2.2xlarge | 8 | 32 | EBS only |

**Figure 7-14.** *Choosing the AWS instance type*

Review and launch (Figure 7-15).

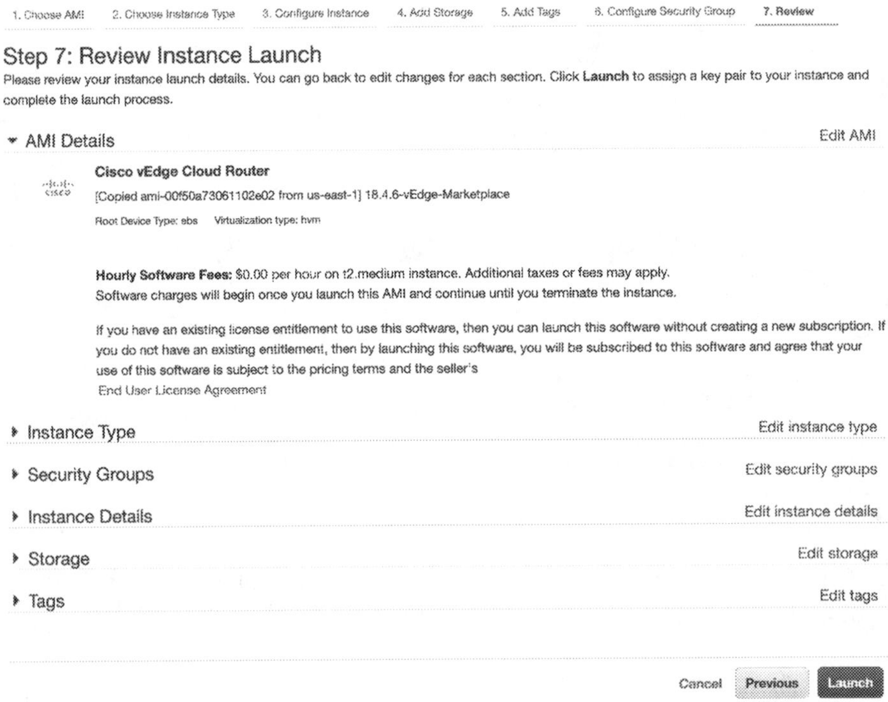

*Figure 7-15.  Reviewing before launch*

Select an existing key pair, or create a new key pair (Figure 7-16). You do need to do this, even though some (older) documentation specifies to not use a key pair. If you are creating a new key pair, download it and keep it safe.

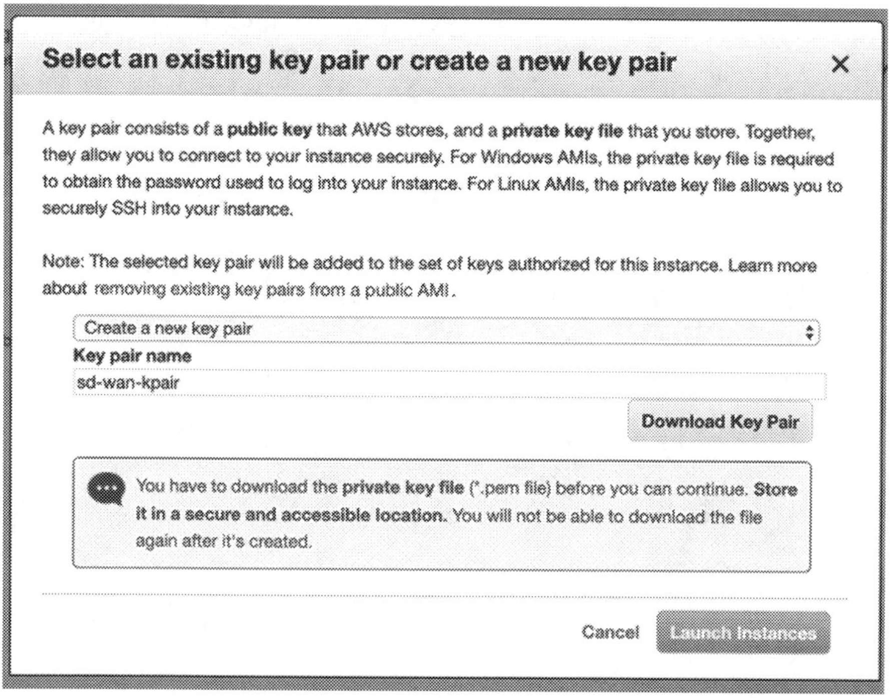

**Select an existing key pair or create a new key pair**                    ✕

A key pair consists of a **public key** that AWS stores, and a **private key file** that you store. Together, they allow you to connect to your instance securely. For Windows AMIs, the private key file is required to obtain the password used to log into your instance. For Linux AMIs, the private key file allows you to securely SSH into your instance.

Note: The selected key pair will be added to the set of keys authorized for this instance. Learn more about removing existing key pairs from a public AMI.

Create a new key pair                                                         ⇕
**Key pair name**
sd-wan-kpair

                                                        **Download Key Pair**

💬  You have to download the **private key file** (*.pem file) before you can continue. **Store it in a secure and accessible location.** You will not be able to download the file again after it's created.

                                        Cancel    **Launch Instances**

***Figure 7-16.*** *The AWS key pair*

Click Launch Instances, which will start the build process (Figure 7-17).

Launch Status

Initiating Instance Launches
Please do not close your browser while this is loading

Creating security groups... Successful
Authorizing inbound rules.... Successful
**Subscribing to Product...**

***Figure 7-17.*** *Initiating the instance*

After a few moments, the instance will be ready for you to connect (Figure 7-18).

**Figure 7-18.** *The launched instance*

Once it is in a "running" state, click Connect (Figure 7-19).

**Figure 7-19.** *Connecting to the instance*

The next window will explain how to connect to your instance (Figure 7-20).

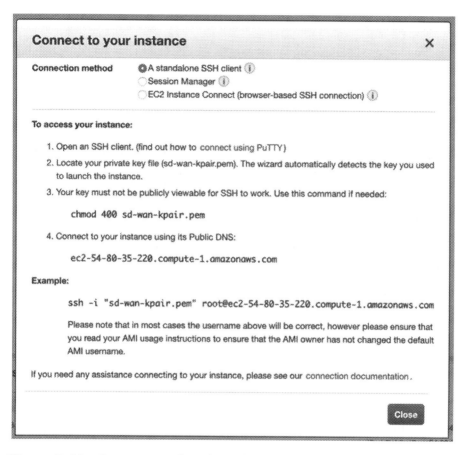

*Figure 7-20.*  *Connection details*

Note, though, that we need to connect with the "admin" username, rather than "root," as shown:

```
iMac:Docs sfordham$ chmod 400 sd-wan-kpair.pem
iMac:Docs sfordham$ ssh -i "sd-wan-kpair.pem" root@ec2-54-
80-35-220.compute-1.amazonaws.com
The authenticity of host 'ec2-54-80-35-220.compute-1.amazonaws.
com (54.80.35.220)' can't be established.
ECDSA key fingerprint is SHA256:wzOA5ECpcg5v7eeVSMIOWmmBL2rqlF8
kmFXOXgh6tmc.
```

```
Are you sure you want to continue connecting (yes/no)? yes
Warning: Permanently added 'ec2-54-80-35-220.compute-1.
amazonaws.com,54.80.35.220' (ECDSA) to the list of known hosts.
viptela 18.3.0
```

```
Please login as the user "admin" rather than the user "root".
```

```
Connection to ec2-54-80-35-220.compute-1.amazonaws.com closed.
iMac:Docs sfordham$ ssh -i "sd-wan-kpair.pem" admin@ec2-54-
80-35-220.compute-1.amazonaws.com
viptela 18.3.0
```

```
Last login: Wed Oct 16 21:58:25 2019 from 54.185.130.54
Welcome to Viptela CLI
admin connected from 18.175.30.183 using ssh on vedge
vedge#
vedge# exit
Connection to ec2-54-80-35-220.compute-1.amazonaws.com closed.
iMac:Docs sfordham$
```

From there, the configuration is exactly as we have performed earlier in the chapter, and if your vBond is publicly accessible, the AWS vEdge will connect to it.

# Preparing vEdge for ZTP

ZTP stands for zero-touch provisioning and allows us to configure vEdge devices to join the overlay just by powering them up! OK, so the process isn't *quite* that simple; we do need to make sure we have things set up already:

1.  The site the new router is on must have access to vtp. viptela.com, and this must be reachable via public DNS servers (Cisco recommends using Google's DNS servers 8.8.8.8 and 8.8.4.4).

2. The correct ZTP interface must be connected. For vEdge 1000, this is ge0/0; for vEdge 2000, the interface to use is g2/0; and for the 100 series routers, it is ge0/4.

The process of zero-touch provisioning is as follows:

3. The router boots up.

4. The router tries to get an IP address from DHCP. With vEdge routers, if there is no DHCP server, then the router initiates an automatic IP address detection, by examining ARP packets on the network and using a free IP address in the range to assign to the ZTP interface. For the IOS XE routers, if there is no DHCP server available, then the ZTP process stops.[2]

5. The router sends a DNS request for `ztp.viptela.com`.

6. The vEdge connects to the ZTP server, which then verifies the router and sends it the IP address of the vBond orchestrator.

7. The vEdge router sends the chassis ID and serial number to the vBond orchestrator. Once the vBond has verified the chassis ID and serial number, it sends the vEdge router the IP address for the vManage NMS.

8. The router connects to and is verified by the vManage NMS, which then sends it back its system IP.

---

[2] `www.cisco.com/c/en/us/td/docs/routers/sdwan/configuration/sdwan-xe-gs-book/cisco-sd-wan-overlay-network-bringup.html`

9. Now that the new vEdge router has a system IP, it reconnects to the vBond orchestrator using its new system IP.

10. The vEdge router also re-establishes a connection to the vManage NMS, and, if necessary and enforced, the NMS pushes a software image to the router, whereupon the router will install this and reboot.

11. After the reboot, the router re-establishes the connection to the vBond orchestrator and the vManage NMS. The vManage then pushes the full configuration to the router.

12. Now that the router has the full configuration, it joins the overlay network.

For this process to work, the vManage NMS requires device configuration templates for the ZTP routers; otherwise, the process will fail. While we cannot, in our lab environment, test out ZTP fully, in the next chapter, we are going to start creating and applying some templates and correct some of the "misconfigurations" created in this chapter.

# Summary

In this chapter, we set up our three edge devices and started to advertise some routes into our network. We also looked at cloud deployment and zero-touch provisioning.

# CHAPTER 8

# Templates

In this chapter, we are going to look at, create, and apply templates to our devices. Using templates, the edge device configurations will, for the most part, be the same, leaving us just to fill in the parts that are unique (such as IP addresses).

We are going to start this by putting things right which once went wrong. Just like Doctor Samuel Beckett.

We start with vEdge02 which, according to the topology, should be in site 200, so let's put this into the correct site:

```
vEdge02# config
Entering configuration mode terminal
vEdge02(config)# system
vEdge02(config-system)# site-id 200
vEdge02(config-system)# commit and-quit
Commit complete.
vEdge02#
```

We can see that the overlay network updates quickly to reflect the change:

```
vBond01# show orchestrator connections
```

© Stuart Fordham 2021
S. Fordham, *Learning SD-WAN with Cisco*, https://doi.org/10.1007/978-1-4842-7347-0_8

|          | PEER    | PEER     | PEER        | SITE | DOMAIN |
|----------|---------|----------|-------------|------|--------|
| INSTANCE | TYPE    | PROTOCOL | SYSTEM IP   | ID   | ID IP  |
| 0        | vedge   | dtls     | 100.100.1.5 | 100  | 1      |
| 0        | vedge   | dtls     | 70.100.100.1| 100  | 1      |
| 0        | vedge   | dtls     | 60.100.100.1| 200  | 1      |
| 0        | vsmart  | dtls     | 100.100.1.4 | 100  | 1      |
| 0        | vsmart  | dtls     | 100.100.1.4 | 100  | 1      |
| 0        | vmanage | dtls     | 100.100.1.2 | 100  | 0      |
| 0        | vmanage | dtls     | 100.100.1.2 | 100  | 0      |
| 0        | vmanage | dtls     | 100.100.1.2 | 100  | 0      |
| 0        | vmanage | dtls     | 100.100.1.2 | 100  | 0      |

vBond01#

Now let's try the same with CSR-1, which should be in site 300:

```
CSR-1#config-transaction

admin connected from 127.0.0.1 using console on CSR-1
CSR-1(config)# sdwan
CSR-1(config)# system
CSR-1(config-system)# site-id 300
CSR-1(config-system)# commit
Aborted: 'system is-vmanaged': This device is being managed by
the vManage. Configuration through the CLI is not allowed.
CSR-1(config-system)#
```

Now, this is why we made the "misconfigurations" in the last chapter, so we can see what kind of issues we might run into. With this in mind, we are going to look at templates and the caveats that come with them.

Templates work well, but they can also completely hose your configurations if implemented incorrectly.

The example here is that I created a basic template that included a new user. I assigned it to the CSR-1, which was then downloaded and applied to the router. So far, so good, I thought.

I then lost connectivity between the new router and vSmart, and I could see this on the router console:

```
OMPD: vSmart peer 100.100.1.4 state changed to Init
OMPD: vSmart peer 100.100.1.4 state changed to Handshake
OMPD: vSmart peer 100.100.1.4 state changed to Up
OMPD: Number of vSmarts connected : 1
Line protocol on Interface Tunnel1, changed state to down
Line protocol on Interface Tunnel1, changed state to up
Configured from NETCONF/RESTCONF by vmanage-admin, transaction-id 591
Line protocol on Interface NVIO, changed state to up
OMPD: vSmart peer 100.100.1.4 state changed to Init
OMPD: Number of vSmarts connected : 0
OMPD: Operational state changed to DOWN
OMPD: Operational state changed to UP
OMPD: vSmart peer 100.100.1.4 state changed to Init
OMPD: vSmart peer 100.100.1.4 state changed to Handshake
OMPD: vSmart peer 100.100.1.4 state changed to Up
OMPD: Number of vSmarts connected : 1
Line protocol on Interface Tunnel1, changed state to down
Line protocol on Interface Tunnel1, changed state to up
Configured from NETCONF/RESTCONF by system, transaction-id 627
OMPD: vSmart peer 100.100.1.4 state changed to Init
OMPD: Number of vSmarts connected : 0
OMPD: Using empty policy from peer 100.100.1.4
```

I have truncated the output, but you should be able to see that initially we connect to vSmart, we receive a new configuration, courtesy of NETCONF, and then lose our vSmart connection.

So, what went wrong?

Programmatically, nothing went wrong. The overlay did exactly as it was told. It applied the template as it was instructed. From an operator standpoint, everything went wrong. The template had several defaults left in it, one of which was this:

```
interface GigabitEthernet1
 no shutdown
 arp timeout 1200
 ip address dhcp client-id GigabitEthernet1
 ip redirects
 ip dhcp client default-router distance 1
 ip mtu     1500
 mtu 1500
 negotiation auto
exit
```

Instead of the IP address I set in the previous chapter, the interface was now set for DHCP, and the admin password had changed (again, according to the template default).

Taking into account the ease with which you can turn a working network into a non-working network through applying badly configured templates, we are going to tread very lightly!

# Creating Templates

The basic process of templating is that we create a template and attach a device (or devices) to that template and then vManage pushes it out to the respective endpoints.

We can create two types of templates: device and feature. Device templates are assigned to devices, and feature templates target specific areas of the configuration, such as AAA, but are also for specific devices. Don't worry, this will make more sense as we move forward.

Device templates are essentially an amalgamation of different feature templates. We do not cover CLI templates here, but these allow us to create the templates by typing (or pasting) the configuration directly in the browser.

We start by navigating to *Configuration* ➤ *Templates* (Figure 8-1).

*Figure 8-1.*   *Creating our first template*

The choices here are Device or Feature. Let's start by creating some feature templates. Select the Feature option at the top of the page, and then click "Add Template."

We won't see the available options until we select a device model, or models (Figure 8-2).

*Figure 8-2.*   *Select a device*

We can select multiple models as some templates will be more generic than others, and having the same code-base or command structure means that one template can span multiple different devices. Our first feature template will be for local users. However, as we will see, sometimes it's not easy to create one template for everything.

Start by searching for "cloud" and selecting the vEdge Cloud device (Figure 8-3).

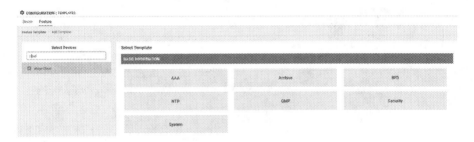

***Figure 8-3.** vEdge Cloud templates*

You will see that we now have some options, including AAA, which is what we need. Now search for CSR, and select the CSR1000v device (Figure 8-4).

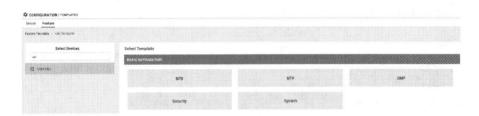

***Figure 8-4.** CSR1000v templates*

Notice that we have now lost AAA, as well as Archive. This is because we cannot use the same code for creating the same user. On the vEdge routers, the command syntax would be

```
vEdge01# config
Entering configuration mode terminal
vEdge01(config)# system
vEdge01(config-system)# aaa
vEdge01(config-aaa)# user test
vEdge01(config-user-test)# exit
vEdge01(config-aaa)#
```

Or simply

```
vEdge01(config)# system aaa user test
vEdge01(config-user-test)#
```

But for the CSR router, we do not need to use such a long command to achieve the same result:

```
CSR-1#config-transaction
CSR-1(config)# user test
CSR-1(config-user-test)# exit
CSR-1(config)#
```

Therefore, we will have to create two templates, one for each of our router types. Deselect the CSR router from the left-hand side, so that we are left with just the vEdge Cloud ticked. Select AAA from the options under Basic Information when it reappears. Call the new template "v-AAA" (the "v" is for vEdge), and give it a description (Figure 8-5).

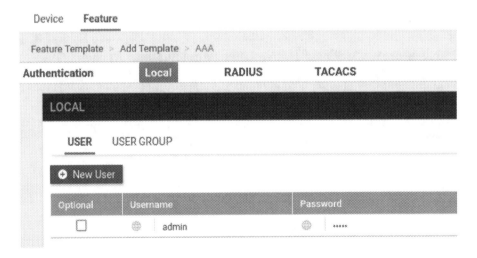

**Figure 8-5.** *v-AAA template*

By default, the "admin" user has a password of "admin" (Figure 8-6). If we apply the template as it currently stands, then it will overwrite the password set when the router was set up, so let's start by changing the default.

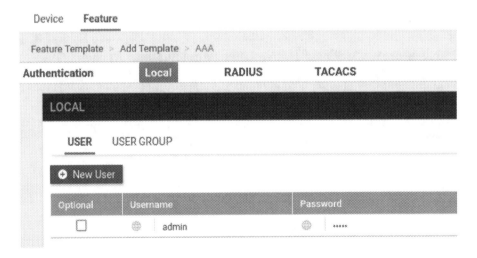

**Figure 8-6.** *The default admin user*

Click the action icon at the right-hand side to bring up the user properties window. Change the password to something you prefer, and click "Save Changes" (Figure 8-7).

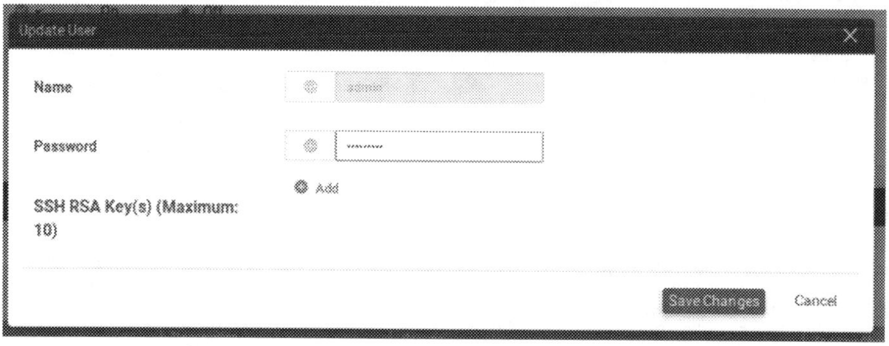

***Figure 8-7.*** *Editing the admin user*

Now click "New User," and create a user called "net-ops" making them a member of the Operators group (Figure 8-8).

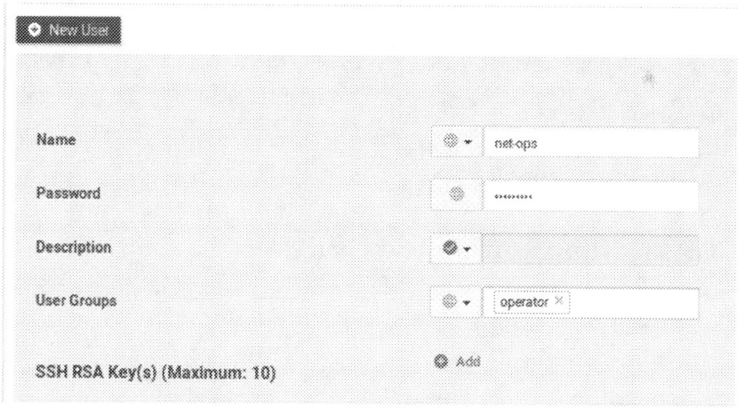

***Figure 8-8.*** *Creating a new user*

Click "Add" at the bottom right-hand side of the window. The new user should appear in our user list (Figure 8-9).

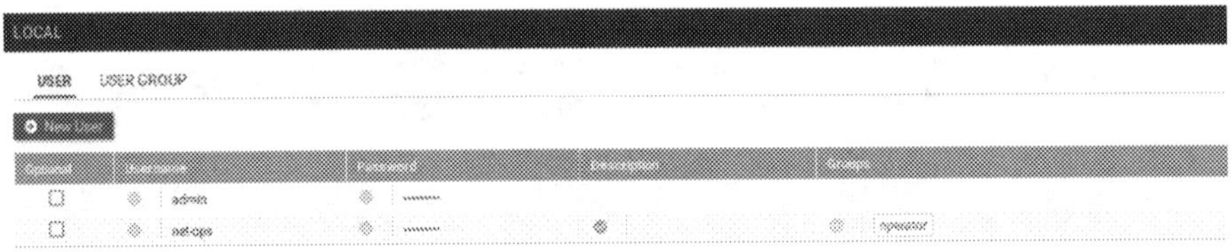

***Figure 8-9.*** *Our vEdge users*

We are not going to add any more under AAA, so scroll to the end of the page and click "Save."

Our first template should show up under our feature template list.

Repeat the process, this time selecting the CSR1000v router and the AAA-Cisco template, naming the template "c-AAA" (the "c" is for Cisco). The net-ops user will have to have privilege 1 (Figure 8-10).

***Figure 8-10.*** *Our cEdge users*

Scroll down to the end of the page, and select the ServerGroups priority order, which is the authentication order, and select the "local" option. Click "Save" (Figure 8-11).

***Figure 8-11.*** *AAA authentication order*

You should end up with this (Figure 8-12).

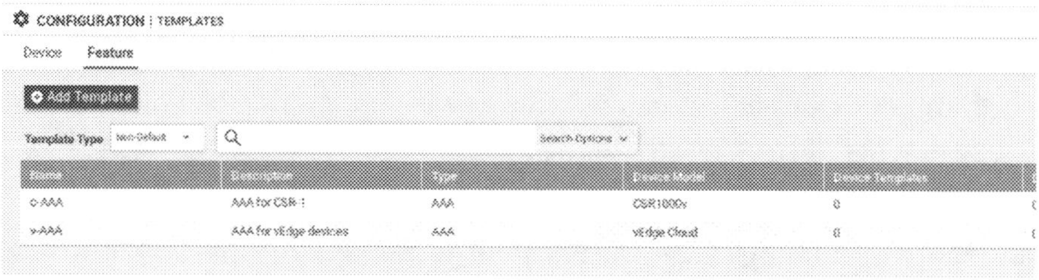

**Figure 8-12.** *Our AAA feature templates*

We have our first two device-specific templates. Let's add a template that we can use across both devices, something nice and simple, like a banner.

Click Add Template, and then select the CSR1000v and vEdge Cloud devices. From the "Other Templates" section, select Banner. Call the banner "c-v-Banner," and set a useful description.

There are two types of banners: login and MOTD (message of the day). Select the drop-down next to Login Banner (Figure 8-13).

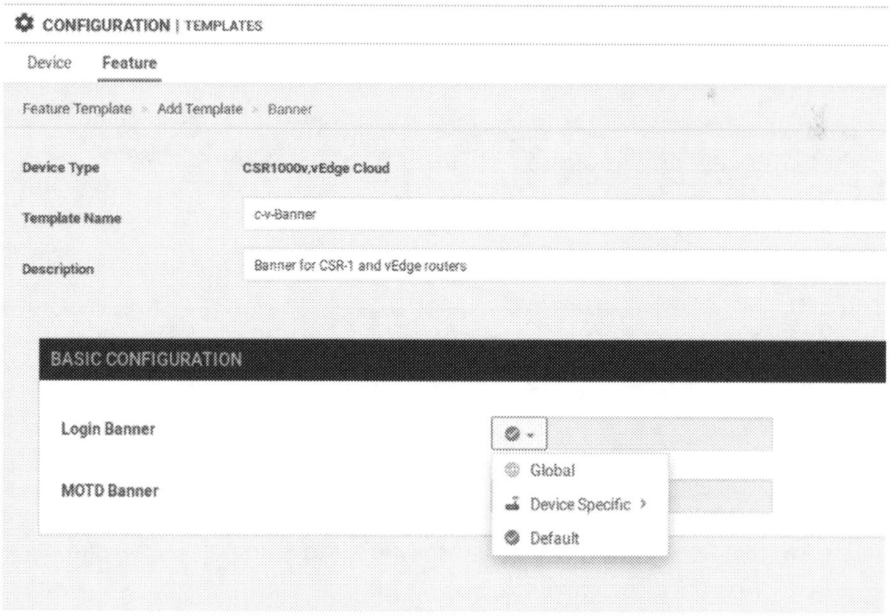

**Figure 8-13.** *A login banner template*

We have three options: Global, Device Specific, and Default. The Default option will always be the one selected when creating templates (because, you know, it's the default). For banners, the Default option is that there is no banner (we can tell this as we would have seen one when connecting to our devices already).

Global will apply to all devices, so we could use this to set the same banner across all the devices the template is applied to. This is what we want to go for at the moment, so select that and enter a suitable banner in the box (Figure 8-14).

*Figure 8-14.* *A global banner for all our devices*

Click Save at the bottom of the page. We should now have three templates (Figure 8-15).

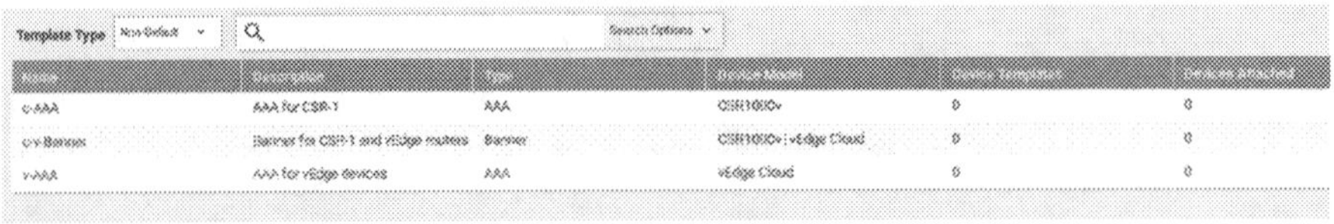

*Figure 8-15.* *Three templates*

Let's now create a template that is a little less generic to our deployment.

The "Device Specific" option allows us to customize the template on a per-device basis. This can either be manual, whereby the vManage NMS will prompt us for the values when we attach it to a device, or we can use a CSV file to read values and insert them into our templates on a device-by-device basis. So we can have one template that says to assign a site ID, but each site ID is matched to a device and can be unique (or as unique as you need depending on your network). In a large deployment, the CSV file is the preferred option, but for smaller-scale deployments, like ours, we can use the manual option. We are going to use both types for fun.

Create a new template, selecting both the device types in our network and select System. Name the template "c-v-System," and give it a description (Figure 8-16).

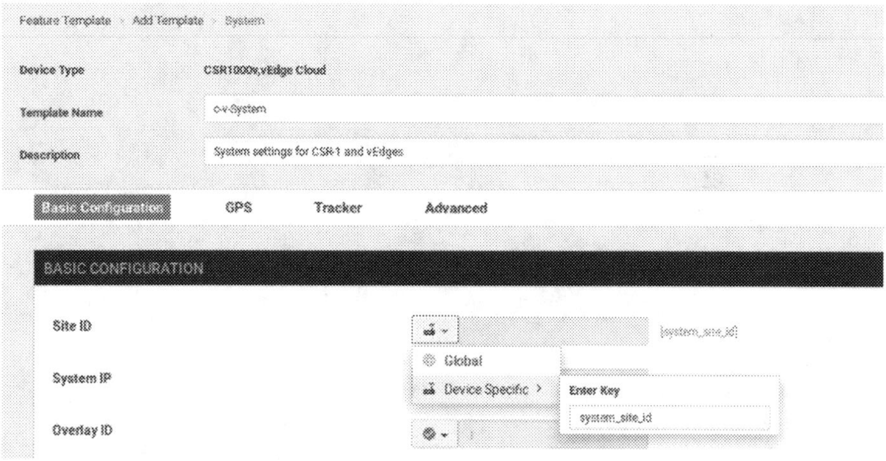

*Figure 8-16.* *The System template*

Many of the fields are already set as Device Specific, and there is nothing there to change.

Moving down the template, set the Location and the Console Baud Rate (bps) (Figure 8-17).

---

**TIP**    You have to set the baud rate; otherwise, you'll get an error.

---

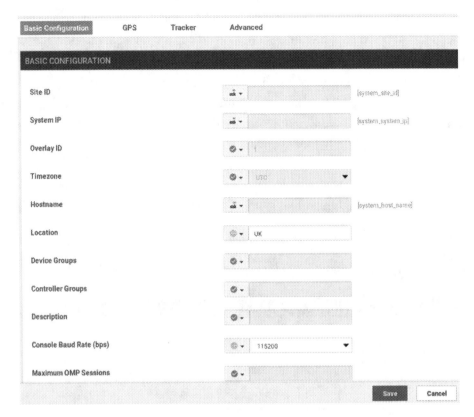

***Figure 8-17.***   *Setting the location and baud rate*

Once you click Save, we should have our fourth template (Figure 8-18).

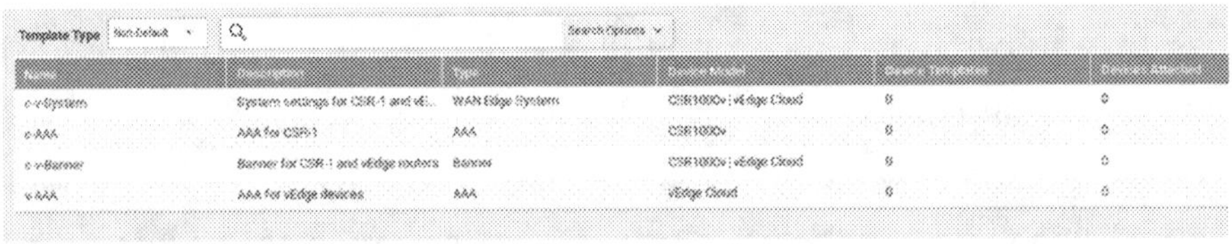

***Figure 8-18.***   *Four templates*

Let's move on to the network settings. By default, the interface templates are set for DHCP, and if we start to apply templates now, that is what we will inherit and we'll lose connection to our devices.

> **Note**   With the vEdge templates, we can implement a rollback timer, which will allow a vEdge device to roll back its configuration if it is unable to start after a preconfigured time.[1]

We are going to take a slightly different approach to this next template and create it as part of our CSR1000v device template.

# cEdge Templates

Click Device and then select *Create Template ➤ From Feature Template* (Figure 8-19).

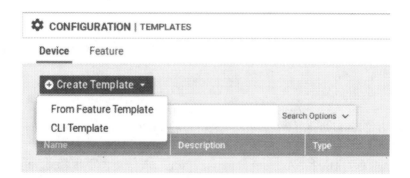

*Figure 8-19.*  *From Feature Template*

Select CSR1000v from the drop-down list, name the template "t-CSR1000v" (the "t" being short for template), and set a description (Figure 8-20).

---

[1] https://sdwan-docs.cisco.com/Product_Documentation/vManage_Help/
Release_18.3/Configuration/Templates#Change_the_Device_Rollback_Timer

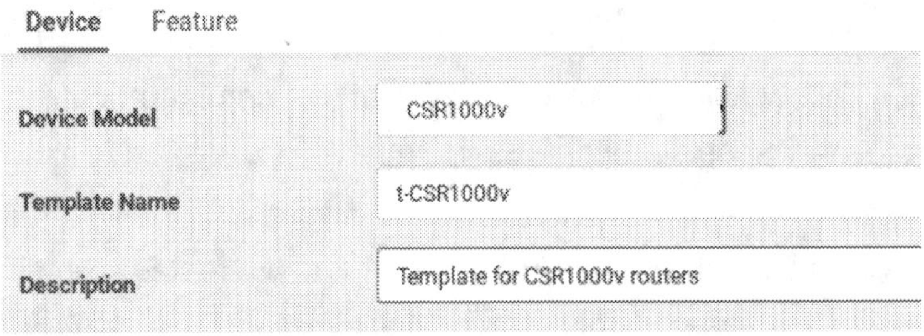

Device    Feature

| Device Model | CSR1000v |
| Template Name | t-CSR1000v |
| Description | Template for CSR1000v routers |

*Figure 8-20.* *The t-CSR1000v template*

In the Basic Information section, select the c-v-System template we created earlier (Figure 8-21).

**Basic Information**

| System * | c-v-System |
| Logging* | Factory_Default_Logging_Template |

*Figure 8-21.* *Using the system template in our feature template*

Next, select the c-AAA template we created in the AAA-Cisco field (Figure 8-22).

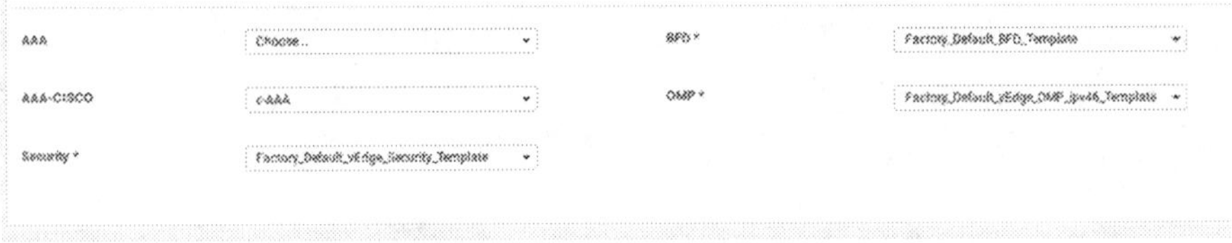

*Figure 8-22.* *Select the c-AAA template*

Scroll down to "Additional Templates," and select the c-v-Banner we created (Figure 8-23).

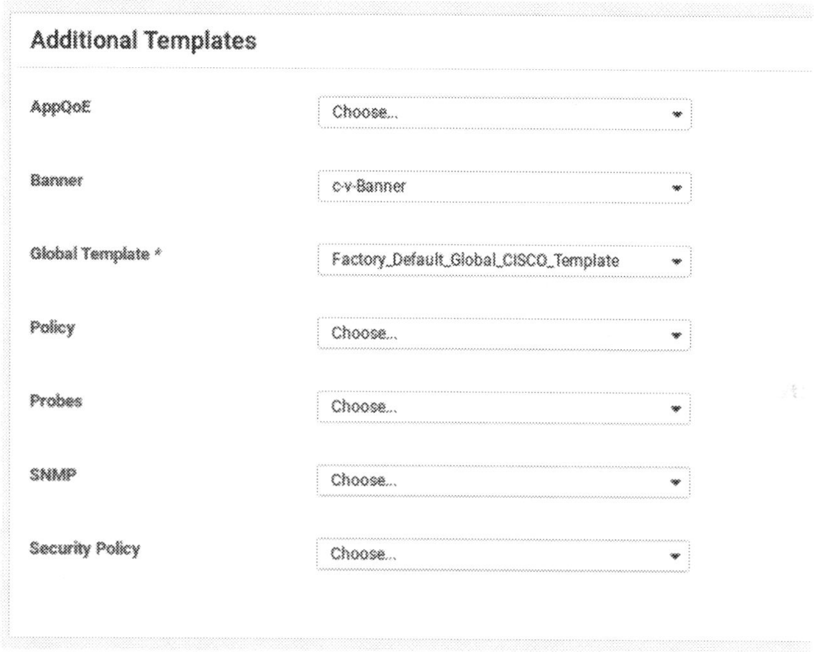

## Additional Templates

| | |
|---|---|
| AppQoE | Choose... ▾ |
| Banner | c-v-Banner ▾ |
| Global Template * | Factory_Default_Global_CISCO_Template ▾ |
| Policy | Choose... ▾ |
| Probes | Choose... ▾ |
| SNMP | Choose... ▾ |
| Security Policy | Choose... ▾ |

*Figure 8-23.* *Select the c-v-Banner template*

We now need to start adding our VPN information to the template. Head back up to the Transport & Management VPN section. Click the drop-down for the VPN Interface section, and click "Create Template" (Figure 8-24).

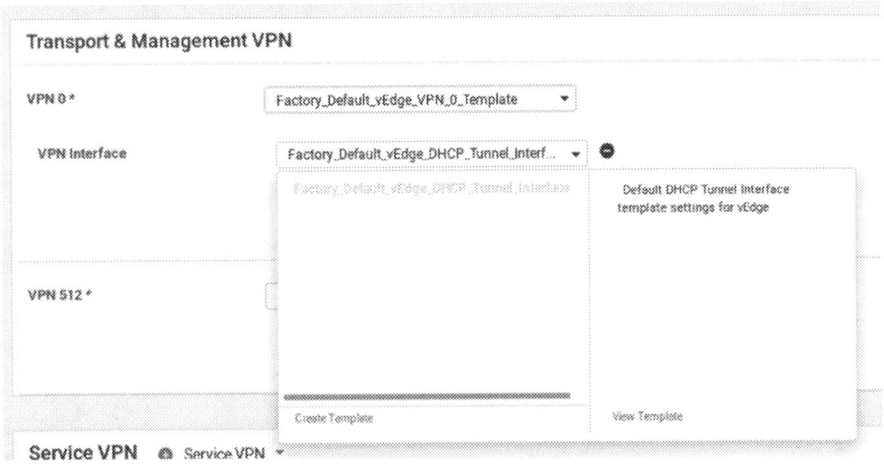

**Figure 8-24.** *Creating a VPN interface template*

In the new window, we can set up our interface. By default, the interface is in a shutdown state (Figure 8-25).

**Figure 8-25.** *Default interface template settings*

Change the setting to Global, and click the "No" radio button where it says "Shutdown," so that the interface will be enabled. Set the interface name, which must match the interface name on the device. In our case, this is "GigabitEthernet1" (Figure 8-26).

**BASIC CONFIGURATION**

| | | |
|---|---|---|
| Shutdown | ⊕ ▾ | ◯ Yes     ◉ No |
| Interface Name | ⊕ ▾ | GigabitEthernet1 |
| Description | ✓ ▾ | |

***Figure 8-26.*** *Setting the interface details*

Scroll down, and under the IPv4 settings, set the IPv4 address to "Device Specific" (Figure 8-27).

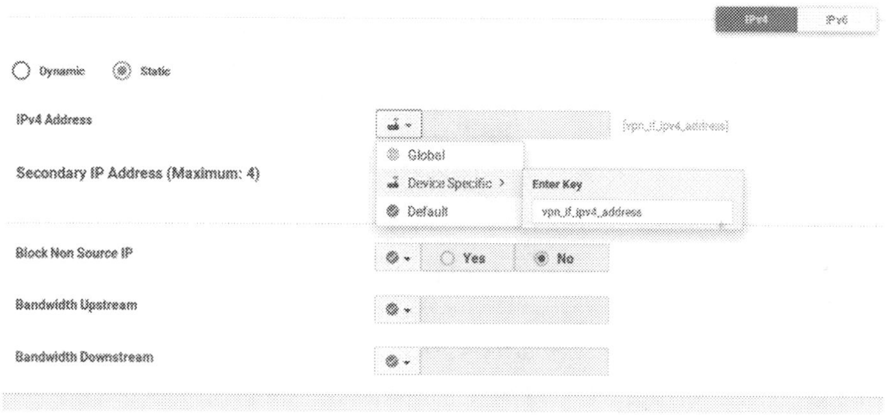

| | | |
|---|---|---|
| | | IPv4    IPv6 |
| ◯ Dynamic   ◉ Static | | |
| IPv4 Address | ▾ | {vpn_if_ipv4_address} |
| Secondary IP Address (Maximum: 4) | ⊗ Global<br>▣ Device Specific ›   Enter Key<br>✓ Default    vpn_if_ipv4_address | |
| Block Non Source IP | ✓ ▾ | ◯ Yes    ◉ No |
| Bandwidth Upstream | ✓ ▾ | |
| Bandwidth Downstream | ✓ ▾ | |

***Figure 8-27.*** *Setting the IP address to Device Specific*

Save the template. The new template will appear in our template list (Figure 8-28).

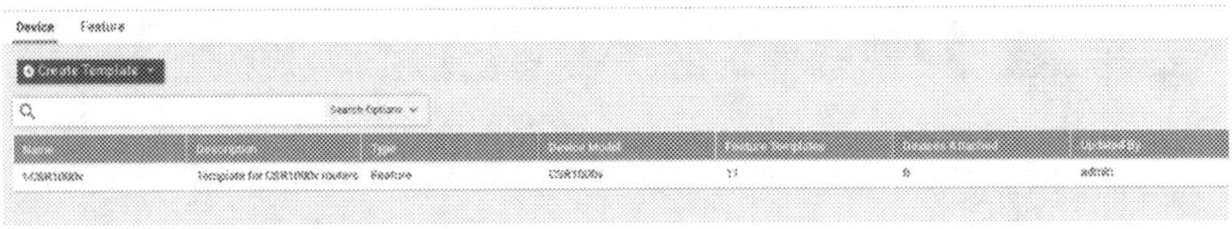

*Figure 8-28.*  *Our device template list*

On the same line, click the triple dots, and select "Export CSV" (Figure 8-29).

**Figure 8-29.**  *Exporting the CSV file*

Save and open the downloaded CSV file. At the top of the file will be our template values, and each line under that can be for one of our devices (Figure 8-30).

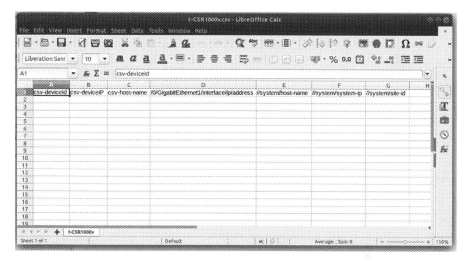

***Figure 8-30.*** *The basic CSV file*

Now we just need to edit our CSV file adding in the device-specific details. If you switch over to the Network details in vManage, then you can copy and paste the UUID of the device, and this goes into the csv-deviceid field (Figure 8-31), and then fill in the rest of the details for CSR-1.

***Figure 8-31.*** *The CSV for CSR-1*

Save the file, making sure that you keep the CSV format. Before we see the CSV upload in action, we should look at manually setting the details. We start by attaching a device to a template. To attach the CSR-1 router to this template, head back over to the template page, and click the triple dots and select "Attach Devices" (Figure 8-32).

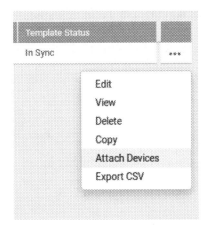

***Figure 8-32.*** *Attaching CSR-1 to our template*

In the window that pops up, select our CSR-1 router (Figure 8-33).

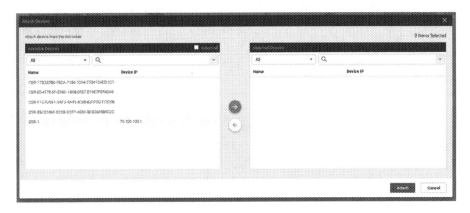

***Figure 8-33.*** *Select CSR-1*

Click the arrow to move it over to the Selected Devices list, and click "Attach" (Figure 8-34).

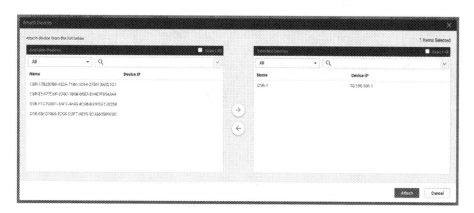

***Figure 8-34.*** *Click the arrow to select the device*

We now get a new window, where we can double-click in any empty field and enter the details manually (Figure 8-35).

***Figure 8-35.*** *Manually entering device details*

Enter the IPv4 address of 50.10.10.1/24 and tab into the next field (Figure 8-36).

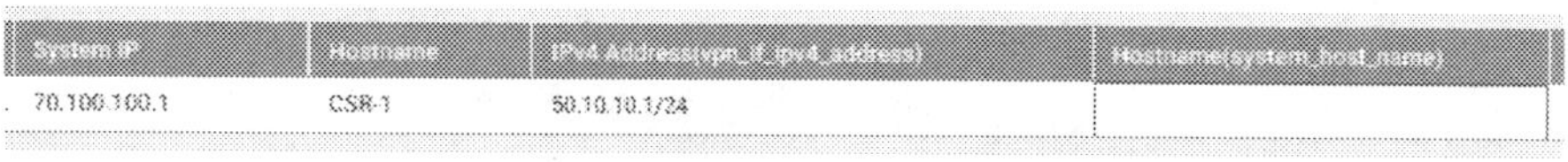

| System IP | Hostname | IPv4 Address(vpn_if_ipv4_address) | Hostname(system_host_name) |
|---|---|---|---|
| 70.100.100.1 | CSR-1 | 50.10.10.1/24 | |

***Figure 8-36.*** *Manually entering the details*

If the horizontal view is awkward, then click the three-dot menu, and select "Change Device Template" to switch to a vertical view. We could carry on like this, entering all the information manually, or we can upload the CSV file we created, by clicking the upload icon (Figure 8-37).

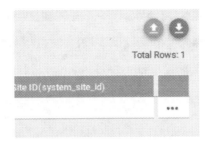

***Figure 8-37.*** *Uploading the CSV file*

Browse to and select the CSV file we edited earlier, and then click Upload (Figure 8-38).

***Figure 8-38.*** *Select the t-CSRV1000v.csv file*

Et voila! All our fields are populated (Figure 8-39).

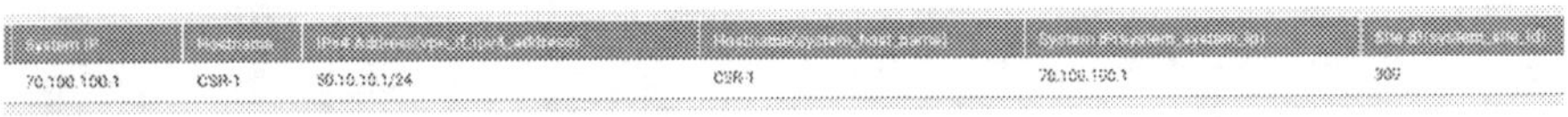

***Figure 8-39.*** *Populated by CSV!*

There is a slightly easier way to fill out the CSV file, and that is to download it from the same window in which we upload the CSV. If we choose this option, then the CSV file will be prepopulated with the device IDs of the devices we are trying to configure. It's a little easier than typing in the long UUID each time.

Click the "Next" button at the bottom of the window. Now we have to apply the template, which will configure the devices. Click the device in the left-hand column (Figure 8-40).

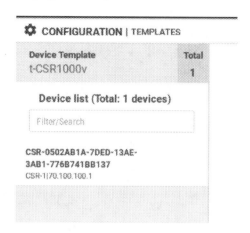

***Figure 8-40.*** *Select the device you are configuring*

The main window will then change to show us the configuration preview (Figure 8-41).

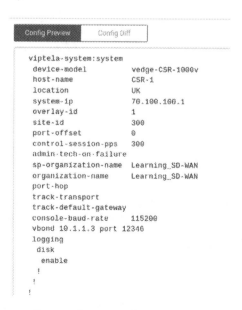

***Figure 8-41.*** *The configuration preview*

We can also compare the current configuration with the one that will be applied (Figure 8-42).

| | | Local Configuration vs. New Configuration |
|---|---|---|
| 1 | 1 | viptela-system:system |
| 2 | | personality           vedge |
| 3 | 2 | device-model          vedge-CSR-1000v |
| 4 | | chassis-number        CSR-0502AB1A-7DED-13AE-3AB1-7768741BB137 |
| 5 | 3 | host-name             CSR-1 |
| | 4 | location              UK |
| 6 | 5 | system-ip             70.100.100.1 |
| 7 | 6 | overlay-id            1 |
| 8 | | site-id               100 |
| | 7 | site-id               300 |
| 9 | 8 | port-offset           0 |
| 10 | 9 | control-session-pps   300 |
| 11 | 10 | admin-tech-on-failure |
| 12 | 11 | sp-organization-name  Learning_SD-WAN |
| 13 | 12 | organization-name     Learning_SD-WAN |
| 14 | 13 | port-hop |
| 15 | 14 | track-transport |
| 16 | 15 | track-default-gateway |
| 17 | | console-baud-rate     9600 |
| 18 | | config-template-name  CSR-1 |
| | 16 | console-baud-rate     115200 |
| 19 | 17 | vbond 10.1.1.3 port 12346 |
| 20 | 18 | logging |

*Figure 8-42.*  *The configuration differences*

The lines highlighted in green are the new lines to be added, and the ones in red are the ones that will be removed. If you have ever used a program such as RANCID or SolarWinds, then this should be familiar.

So far, it looks OK. We gain a location of "UK," and the site ID will be corrected. The console-baud-rate will also change, which is not a big deal in our environment, though you should check the documentation for the devices to make sure that the baud rate is supported. Scrolling down though, we appear to lose our SD-WAN configuration (Figure 8-43).

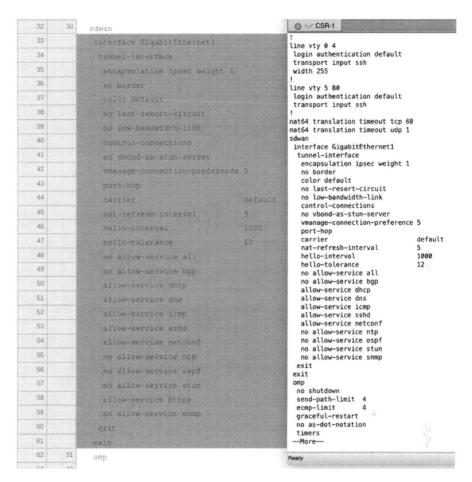

***Figure 8-43.*** *We are going to lose our SD-WAN configuration!*

More drastically, we lose our default route (Figure 8-44).

209

| 112 | 82 | no ip dhcp use class |
| 113 | | ip route 0.0.0.0 0.0.0.0 50.10.10.254 |
| 114 | | no ip source-route |
| | 83 | ip multicast route-limit 2147483647 |
| 115 | 84 | no ip http ctc authentication |
| 116 | 85 | no ip igmp ssm-map query dns |
| 117 | 86 | interface GigabitEthernet1 |
| 118 | 87 | no shutdown |
| 119 | 88 | arp timeout 1200 |
| 120 | 89 | ip address 50.10.10.1 255.255.255.0 |
| 121 | 90 | ip redirects |
| 122 | | ip dhcp client default-router distance 1 |
| 123 | 91 | ip mtu    1500 |
| 124 | 92 | mtu 1500 |
| 125 | 93 | negotiation auto |
| 126 | | exit |

***Figure 8-44.*** *And our default route*

This would mean that if we needed to correct our device, vManage would not be able to contact it!

We can temporarily overwrite such issues, but we would see this kind of warning:

```
CSR-1#config-transaction
CSR-1(config)# interface GigabitEthernet1
CSR-1(config-if)#
CSR-1(config-if)# ip address 50.10.10.1 255.255.255.0
CSR-1(config-if)# ip route 0.0.0.0 0.0.0.0 50.10.10.254
CSR-1(config-if)# commit
The following warnings were generated:
  'system is-vmanaged': This device is being managed by the
  vManage. Any configuration changes to this device will be
  overwritten by the vManage after the control connection to
  the vManage comes back up.
```

```
Proceed? [yes,no] yes
Commit complete.
CSR-1(config-if)#
```

In this case, if you had pushed the template to the device, manually adding the default route may allow vManage to push down the corrected configuration to the device.

Thankfully, we have a big "Cancel" button at the bottom of the screen. Click it (Figure 8-45).

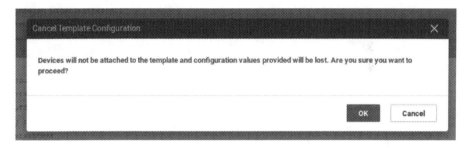

***Figure 8-45.** Cancel before we do some damage!*

Click "OK" on the dialog box, and head back over to templates and into Feature templates.

Somewhat annoyingly, when we create feature templates from the device template screen, you are dropped straight into the basic configuration setting, so it is easy to miss the naming section. The new feature template gets the same name as the device template, so go to the feature templates and select the "t-CSR1000v" template and edit it using the drop-down options after you click the three dots.

Click Tunnel, then set it to Global, and select "On" (Figure 8-46).

***Figure 8-46.*** *Turn on the tunnel interface*

Under "Allow Service," make sure that NETCONF and SSH are set to "On" (Figure 8-47).

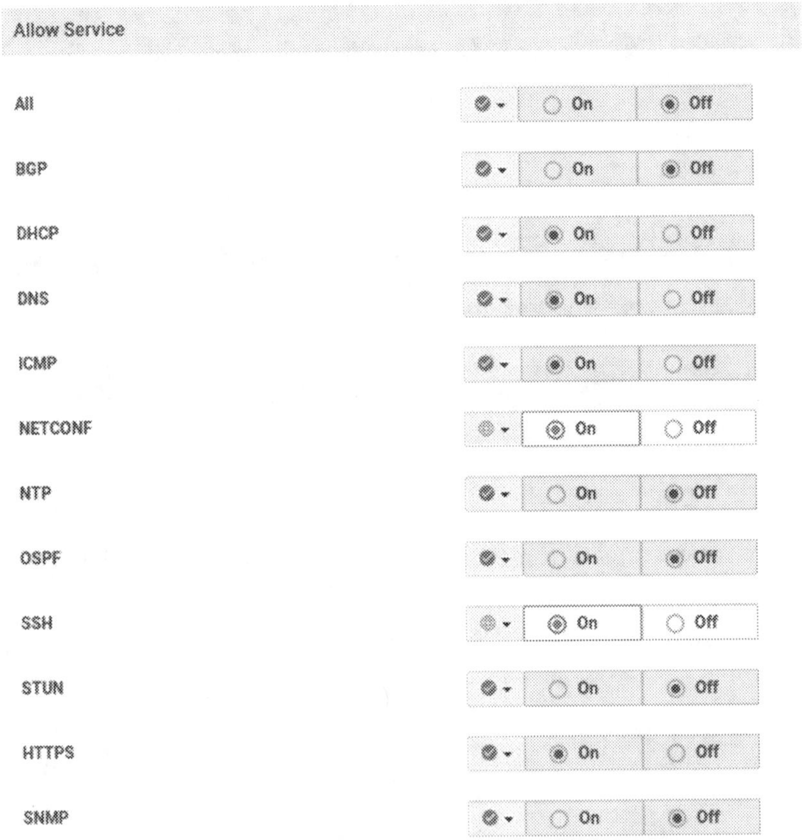

***Figure 8-47.*** *Enabling NETCONF and SSH in templates*

Click "Update" to update the template. But what about the default route? For this, we need to create a new VPN template. Name the template "c-VPN0," and set a description (Figure 8-48).

*Figure 8-48.* *The new VPN template*

Scroll down to "IPv4 Route," or click the menu item to be taken straight to that section (Figure 8-49).

*Figure 8-49.* *IPv4 routes*

Click "New IPv4 Route" and enter 0.0.0.0/0 in the Prefix field. Leave the gateway as "next hop," and click "Add Next Hop" (Figure 8-50).

***Figure 8-50.*** *Adding a next hop*

As we could have several devices, each with a unique next hop, we are going to use the device-specific option (Figure 8-51).

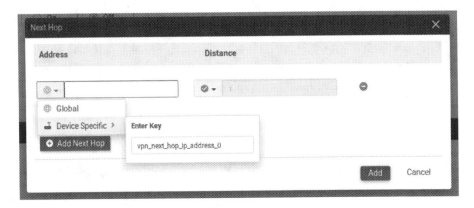

***Figure 8-51.*** *Device Specific Options*

Click "Add," and then make sure you click "Add" again, so it shows in the route section (Figure 8-52):

***Figure 8-52.*** *Our default route*

Save the template. Now we should have another template in our list (Figure 8-53).

***Figure 8-53.*** *our c-VPN0 template*

Head back to device templates, and edit the t-CSR1000v template. Scroll down to Transport & Management VPN, and select c-VPN0 from the list (Figure 8-54).

**Transport & Management VPN**

| | |
|---|---|
| VPN 0 * | Factory_Default_vEdge_VPN_0_Template ▾ |
| VPN Interface | Factory_Default_vEdge_VPN_0_Template |
| | c-VPN0 |

VPN 0 template for CSR-1

***Figure 8-54.*** *Select the c-VPN0 template*

We should see both templates applied now (Figure 8-55).

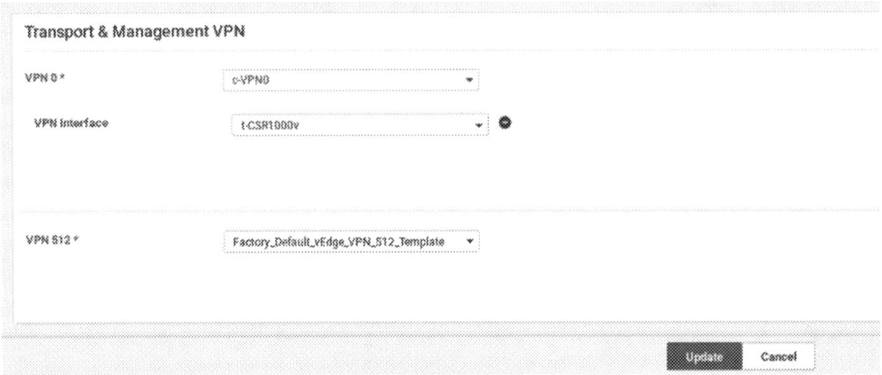

**Figure 8-55.**  *Both VPN templates applied*

Click Update. Repeat the process of attaching the CSR device and uploading the CSV file to fill in the blanks, as well as the new field for the next hop, which will be 50.10.10.254 (Figure 8-56).

| System IP | Hostname | Address(vpn_next_hop_ip_address_0) | IPv4 Address(vpn_if_ipv4_address) |
|---|---|---|---|
| 70.100.100.1 | CSR-1 | 50.10.10.254 | 50.10.10.1/24 |

**Figure 8-56.**  *Add the next hop*

Click Next and look at the config diff (Figure 8-57); it should be much cleaner, and, more critically, the default route should still be present (albeit with a distance attached, which we previously did not have).

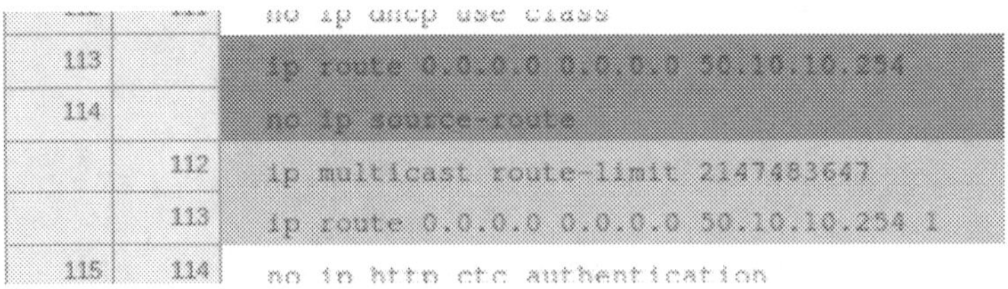

**Figure 8-57.**  *We have a default route (again)*

If you are happy with the results, click "Configure Devices" (Figure 8-58).

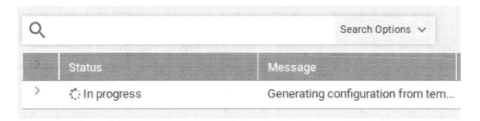

***Figure 8-58.*** *Configuring the CSR*

We will see the progress in the next window (Figure 8-59).

| Status | Message | Chassis Number |
|---|---|---|
| ⟳ In progress | Pushing configuration to device | CSR-0502AB1A-7DED-13AE-3AB1-... |

```
[22-Apr-2020 13:36:22 UTC] Configuring device with feature template: t-CSR1000v
[22-Apr-2020 13:36:22 UTC] Generating configuration from template
[22-Apr-2020 13:36:27 UTC] Checking and creating device in vManage
[22-Apr-2020 13:36:29 UTC] Device is online
[22-Apr-2020 13:36:29 UTC] Updating device configuration in vManage
[22-Apr-2020 13:36:35 UTC] Pushing configuration to device
```

***Figure 8-59.*** *The configuration in action*

During this process, vManage performs syntax checks for the variables entered. If any are incorrect, then the template will not be attached. For example, if the variable has the incorrect syntax (as in a text string is put into a field requiring an IP address), this will be picked up on. An incorrect IP address will not be picked up during this check, and if there are no other issues causing the checks to fail, then the template will be attached.

On the CSR routers, we can watch everything happening on the console:

```
%SYS-5-CONFIG_P: Configured programmatically by process iosp_
vty_100001_dmi_nesd from console as NETCONF on vty32131
%DMI-5-CONFIG_I: R0/0: nesd: Configured from NETCONF/RESTCONF
by vmanage-admin, transaction-id 45215
%Cisco-SDWAN-RP_0-OMPD-3-ERRO-400002: R0/0: OMPD: vSmart peer
100.100.1.4 state changed to Init
%Cisco-SDWAN-RP_0-OMPD-6-INFO-400005: R0/0: OMPD: Number of
vSmarts connected : 0
%Cisco-SDWAN-RP_0-OMPD-3-ERRO-400003: R0/0: OMPD: Operational
state changed to DOWN
%Cisco-SDWAN-RP_0-OMPD-5-NTCE-400003: R0/0: OMPD: Operational
state changed to UP
%Cisco-SDWAN-RP_0-OMPD-3-ERRO-400002: R0/0: OMPD: vSmart peer
100.100.1.4 state changed to Init
%DMI-5-AUTH_PASSED: R0/0: dmiauthd: User 'vmanage-admin'
authenticated successfully from 100.100.1.2:54107 and was
authorized for netconf over ssh. External groups:
%Cisco-SDWAN-RP_0-OMPD-6-INFO-400002: R0/0: OMPD: vSmart peer
100.100.1.4 state changed to Handshake
%Cisco-SDWAN-RP_0-OMPD-5-NTCE-400002: R0/0: OMPD: vSmart peer
100.100.1.4 state changed to Up
%Cisco-SDWAN-RP_0-OMPD-6-INFO-400005: R0/0: OMPD: Number of
vSmarts connected : 1
%Cisco-SDWAN-RP_0-VDAEMON-2-CRIT-500010: R0/0: VDAEMON: CDB
snapshotted after vmanage connection establishedHands off my
SD-WAN!

User Access Verification

Username:
```

Now we can find out if we mistyped the password in the template, and check that we have a banner (just in case you missed it in the previous output):

```
Username: admin
Password:

CSR-1>en
CSR-1#
CSR-1#sh run | i banner
banner login ^CHands off my SD-WAN!^C
CSR-1#
```

Back in vManage, we can see that the site ID has updated (Figure 8-60).

| Hostname | System IP | Device Model | Chassis Number ID | State | Reachability | Site ID |
|---|---|---|---|---|---|---|
| vManage01 | 100.100.1.2 | vManage | a9e8cabb-8259-478a-bcbe-16447753a8f3e | | reachable | 100 |
| vManage02 | 100.100.1.22 | vManage | c085d89d-bfbb-4757-b752-ddea9402bd6c | | reachable | 100 |
| vSmart01 | 100.100.1.4 | vSmart | 611a5b84-b2n5-4c71-961b-a91c93520063 | | reachable | 100 |
| vBond01 | 100.100.1.3 | vEdge Cloud (vBond) | 87563514-cc06-47a9-85ea-03d4cf2e0a2A | | reachable | 100 |
| CSR-1 | 70.100.100.1 | CSR1000v | CSR-0502AB1A-7DED-13AE-3AB1-7768741BB137 | | reachable | 300 |
| vEdge01 | 100.100.1.5 | vEdge Cloud | 567f7e4b-0720-fa13-8556-f66dece9dd77 | | reachable | 100 |
| vEdge02 | 60.100.100.1 | vEdge Cloud | b0ea9f50-99ac-8bee-4fdd-91a83cdf41f5 | | reachable | 200 |

***Figure 8-60.*** *CSR-1 now has a corrected site ID*

# vEdge Templates

Let's go ahead and create the same set of templates for our vEdge devices. I won't be using screenshots in this next section; instead, we'll just run through the steps to create the templates we need.

> *Feature Template* ➤ *Add Template* ➤ *VPN*
>
> Name: v-VPN0
>
> Basic Configuration:
>
> VPN: 0

IPv4 route:

0.0.0.0/0 to device-specific next hop

*Feature Template* ➤ *Add Template* ➤ *VPN Interface Ethernet*

Name: v-VPN-Interface

Basic Configuration:

Shutdown: Global/No

Interface name: Device Specific

IPv4 Address: Device Specific

Tunnel Interface:

Global, On

Allow Services:

NETFCONF & SSH: On

*Feature Template* ➤ *Add Template* ➤ *VPN*

Name: v-VPN512

Basic Configuration:

VPN: 512

*Feature Template* ➤ *Add Template* ➤ *VPN Interface Ethernet*

Name: v-VPN512-Interface

Basic Configuration:

Shutdown: Global/No

Interface Name: eth0

Dynamic

You should end up with a list of templates that looks like Figure 8-61.

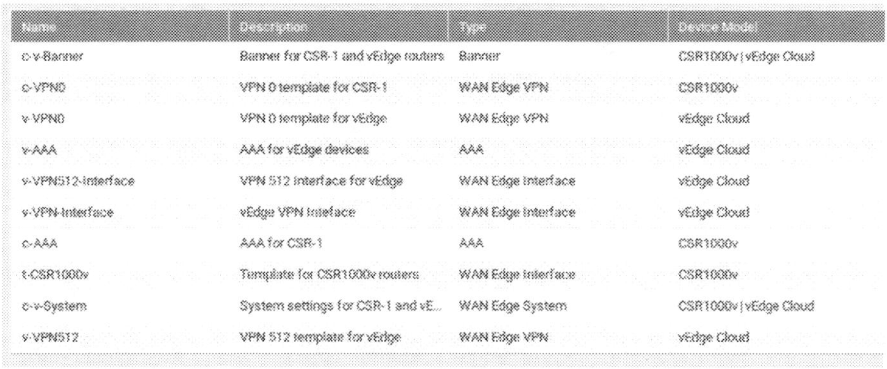

| Name | Description | Type | Device Model |
|------|-------------|------|--------------|
| c-v-Banner | Banner for CSR-1 and vEdge routers | Banner | CSR1000v \| vEdge Cloud |
| c-VPN0 | VPN 0 template for CSR-1 | WAN Edge VPN | CSR1000v |
| v-VPN0 | VPN 0 template for vEdge | WAN Edge VPN | vEdge Cloud |
| v-AAA | AAA for vEdge devices | AAA | vEdge Cloud |
| v-VPN512-interface | VPN 512 interface for vEdge | WAN Edge Interface | vEdge Cloud |
| v-VPN-Interface | vEdge VPN Inteface | WAN Edge Interface | vEdge Cloud |
| c-AAA | AAA for CSR-1 | AAA | CSR1000v |
| t-CSR1000v | Template for CSR1000v routers | WAN Edge Interface | CSR1000v |
| c-v-System | System settings for CSR-1 and vE... | WAN Edge System | CSR1000v \| vEdge Cloud |
| v-VPN512 | VPN 512 template for vEdge | WAN Edge VPN | vEdge Cloud |

***Figure 8-61.*** *Our long list of templates*

Head back to Device, and create the main device template, selecting vEdge Cloud as the device model, calling it "t-vEdge" (Figure 8-62).

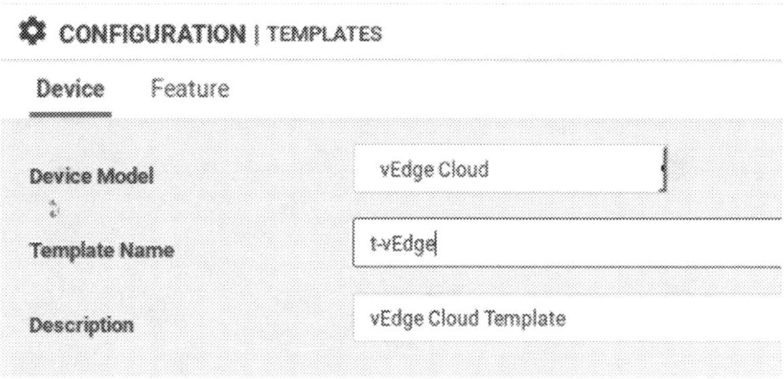

***Figure 8-62.*** *Our t-vEdge template*

Select the generic c-v-System template we created earlier, as well as the device-specific v-AAA template (Figure 8-63).

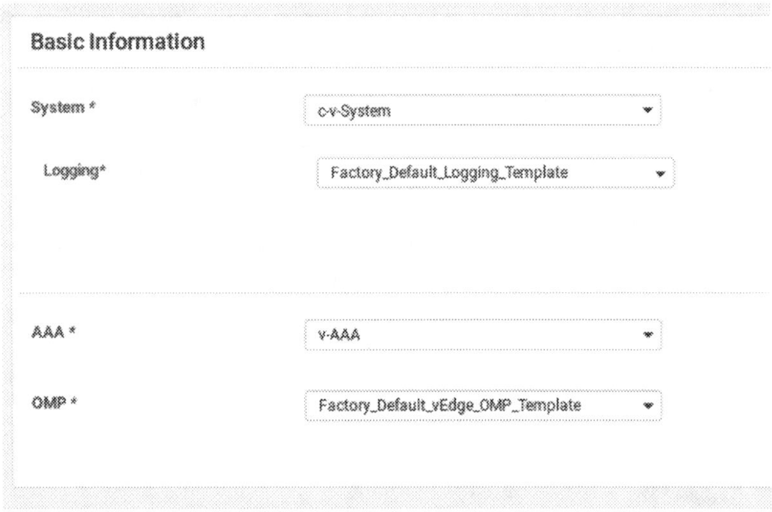

**Figure 8-63.** *Adding our existing templates*

Under Transport & Management VPN, select v-VPN0, and v-VPN-Interface for VPN 0, and v-VPN512 and v-VPN512-Interface for VPN 512 (Figure 8-64).

**Figure 8-64.** *Setting the VPN templates*

To set the VPN interface for VPN 512, you need to click the plus sign next to "VPN Interface" under "Additional VPN 512 Templates." Set the banner under "Additional Templates" (Figure 8-65).

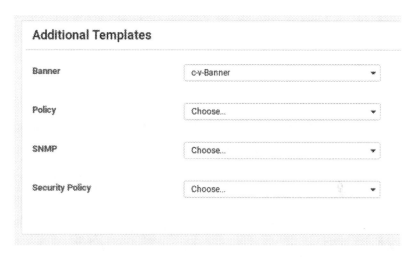

*Figure 8-65.* *Setting the banner*

Save the template. We now have two device templates (Figure 8-66).

| Name | Description | Type | Device Model | Feature Templates | Devices Attached |
|---|---|---|---|---|---|
| t-CSR1000v | Template for CSR1000v routers | Feature | CSR1000v | 11 | 1 |
| t-vEdge | vEdge Cloud Template | Feature | vEdge Cloud | 11 | 0 |

*Figure 8-66.* *Our device templates*

Assign the two vEdge Cloud devices by clicking the three dots next to our new template and selecting "Attach Devices." Move them from the available devices column to the selected devices column (Figure 8-67).

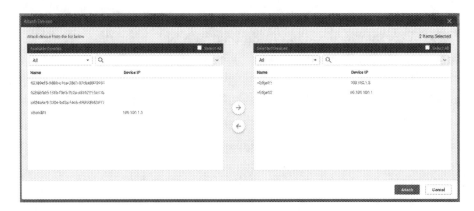

***Figure 8-67.*** *Select the vEdge devices*

We will see the familiar window where we need to add the device-specific variables (Figure 8-68).

| System IP | Hostname | Prefix(vpn_ipv4_ip_prefix) | Address(vpn_next_hop_ip_address_0) | Interface Name(vpn_if_name_v-VPN-interface) |
|---|---|---|---|---|
| 60.100.100.1 | vEdge02 | | | |
| 100.100.1.5 | vEdge01 | | | |

***Figure 8-68.*** *Add the details for the vEdge devices*

Either fill in the details manually or download the CSV, edit it, and reupload it. Once all the details have been entered, you will see green ticks under the Status column (Figure 8-69).

| S. | Chassis Number | System IP | Hostname | Prefix(vpn_ipv4_ip_prefix) | Address(vpn_next_hop_ip_address_0) |
|---|---|---|---|---|---|
| ✅ | b0ea9f50-99ac-8bee-4fdd... | 60.100.100.1 | vEdge02 | 0.0.0.0/0 | 50.11.11.254 |
| ✅ | 567f7a4b-0720-fa13-8556... | 100.100.1.5 | vEdge01 | 0.0.0.0/0 | 10.1.1.1 |

***Figure 8-69.*** *Completed vEdge details*

Once we have the green, we can click Next. Check the config diff window, and make sure all is OK to proceed.

Because of our template, we are going to lose our VPN 1 configuration, but we will recreate it shortly. If all else is OK, then click Configure Devices and acknowledge the prompt (Figure 8-70).

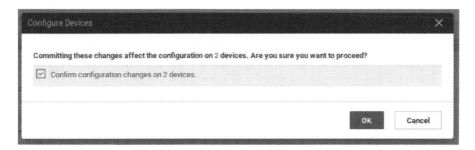

*Figure 8-70.* *Committing the vEdge templates*

Watch the progress to check everything is proceeding as planned.

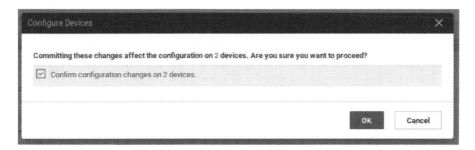

*Figure 8-71.* *Our final configuration push*

We can check if the template has worked in a couple of ways; the quickest is to see if we can log in and have a banner:

```
vEdge01#
*** IDLE TIMEOUT ***

viptela 19.2.1
```

```
vEdge01 login:
Hands off my SD-WAN!
vEdge01 login: admin
Password:
Welcome to Viptela CLI
admin connected from 127.0.0.1 using console on vEdge01
vEdge01#
```

We do. We are good to move on to the next chapter!

## Summary

Wow! This has been a long chapter, and we have had some major wins and some minor losses (the VPN 1s we configured on our vEdge devices, for example).

In the next chapter, we will be adding those back as we look at routing.

# CHAPTER 9

# Routing

In this chapter, we are going to use templates to set up routing in our network. Cisco's SD-WAN supports dynamic routing by way of OSPF, BGP in vEdge, and the IOS XE cEdge. The latter also supports EIGRP, IS-IS, and LISP. We are not going to go through all of them; instead, we will use the "public" Internet for OSPF and our "MPLS" link for BGP. The reason we are not going to do the others is that OSPF and BGP redistribute nicely into OMP, whereas the others don't.

## OSPF

Our OSPF network is going to look like Figure 9-1.

© Stuart Fordham 2021
S. Fordham, *Learning SD-WAN with Cisco*, https://doi.org/10.1007/978-1-4842-7347-0_9

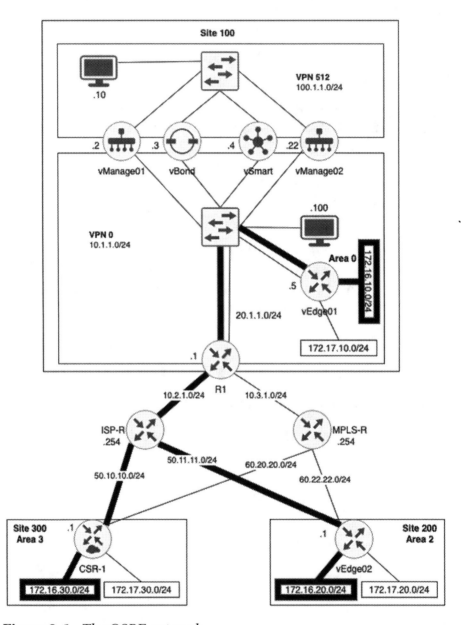

*Figure 9-1.*  *The OSPF network*

As you will recall, we lost our VPN 1s when we applied our templates in the previous chapter, not that they were doing much anyway. We are going to use templates to set them up again, from scratch. The process is similar to how we set up our VPN 0s in the last chapter. There will be a couple of hurdles along the way as you will see.

The first step is to tell each router that we want to redistribute OSPF routes into OMP. This way, we can leave our overlay network to do all the hard work for us.

We can do this with a joint template for both CSR-1 and the vEdge, so head over to feature templates and create a new OMP template (Figure 9-2).

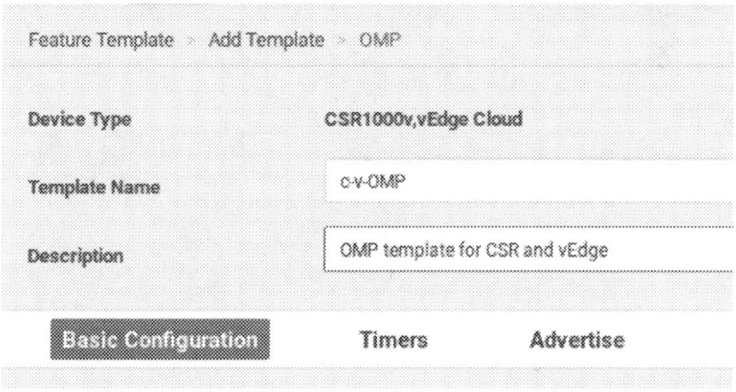

***Figure 9-2.*** *Our OMP template*

Click "Advertise" and select OSPF External and save the template (Figure 9-3).

***Figure 9-3.*** *Advertising OSPF into OMP*

Next, we can create the loopback interface (loopback1), which is a WAN Edge interface and can be created for both router types (Figure 9-4).

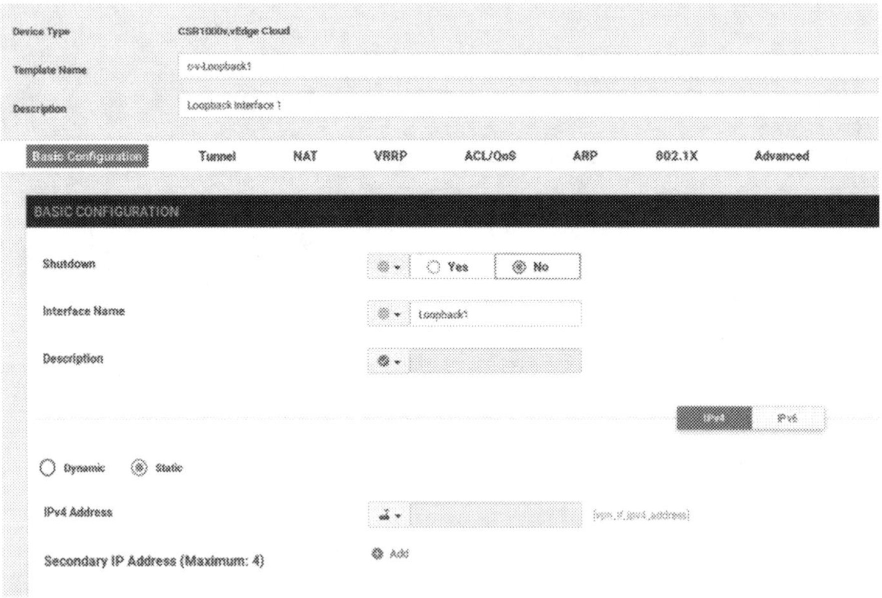

***Figure 9-4.*** *Loopback1 interface*

The IP address will be device specific, and we will fill in the details when we apply the template to our devices. Now create a new VPN interface template for VPN 1 (Figure 9-5).

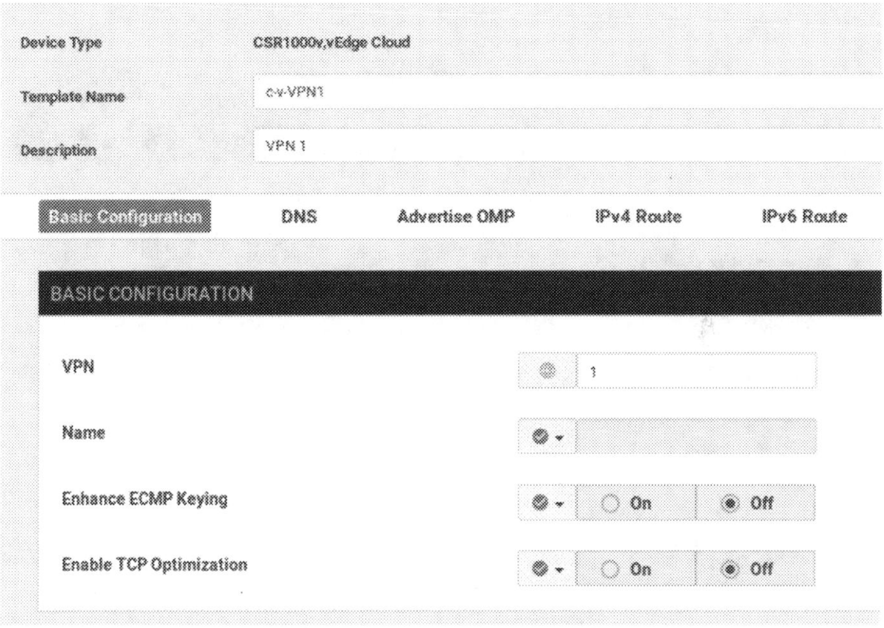

| Device Type | CSR1000v,vEdge Cloud |
|---|---|
| Template Name | c-v-VPN1 |
| Description | VPN 1 |

**Basic Configuration**    DNS    Advertise OMP    IPv4 Route    IPv6 Route

**BASIC CONFIGURATION**

| VPN | ⊕ | 1 |
|---|---|---|
| Name | ⊘ ▾ | |
| Enhance ECMP Keying | ⊘ ▾ | ○ On    ● Off |
| Enable TCP Optimization | ⊘ ▾ | ○ On    ● Off |

*Figure 9-5.*  *VPN 1 interface*

Lastly, we set up OSPF, using a joint template for both router types. We are going to manually add the router ID. Although the router ID will, by default, inherit the system IP of the router, router IDs for routing protocols should be hard coded (Figure 9-6).

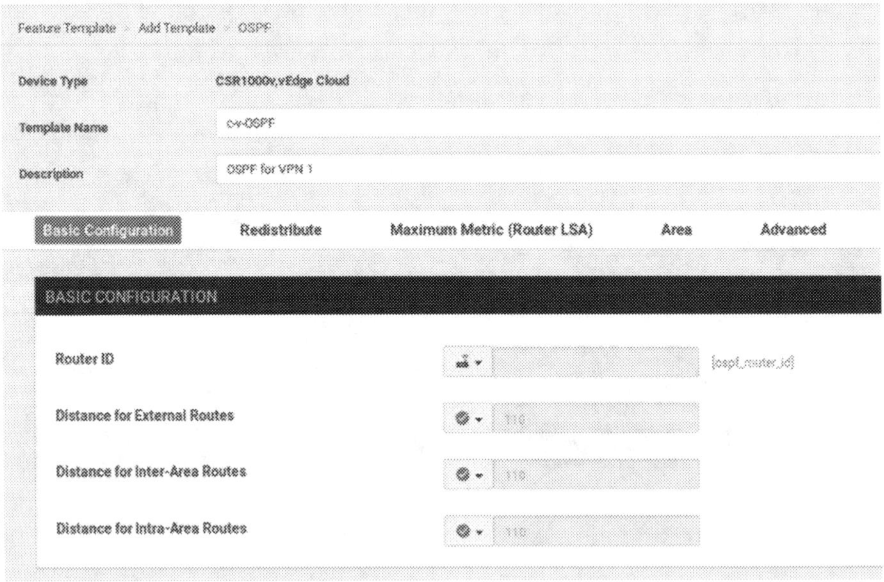

**Figure 9-6.** *OSPF template*

The area ID will also be individual to each router. This will be interesting as none of our routers will have interfaces in the same area, so we are going against how OSPF operates here (Figure 9-7).

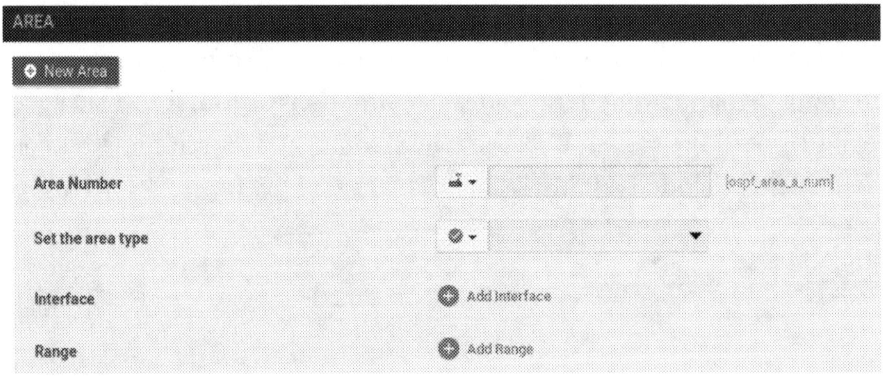

**Figure 9-7.** *The OSPF area*

We now need something to advertise into OSPF, so click "Add Interface" (Figure 9-8).

***Figure 9-8.*** *Adding an interface to OSPF*

Click "Add Interface" again, and when the new window pops up, enter Loopback1, and then click "Add" (Figure 9-9).

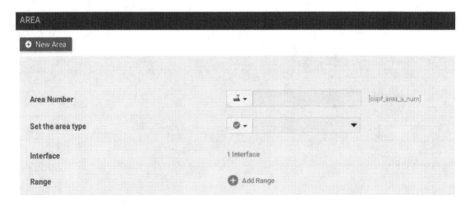

*Figure 9-9.* *Advertising the Loopback 1 network*

Click "Add" again so that the interface is added to the template (Figure 9-10).

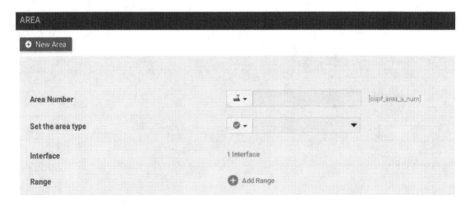

*Figure 9-10.* *Loopback 1 added to OSPF*

The template should now show the area details (Figure 9-11).

**AREA**

⊕ New Area

| Optional | Number | Area Type |
|---|---|---|
| ☐ | ⚏ [ospf_area_a_nu..] | ⊘ |

***Figure 9-11.*** *The OSPF area*

Save the template, and then head back to device templates, and edit
the t-CSR1000v template. Under Basic Information, set the OMP template
to be the c-v-OMP feature template (Figure 9-12).

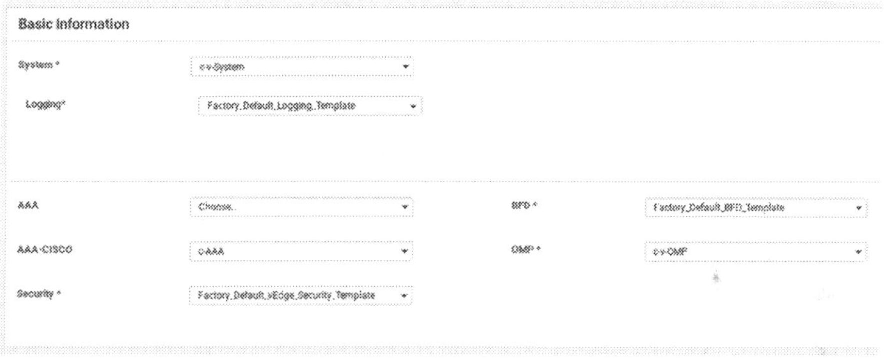

***Figure 9-12.*** *Adding the OMP template*

Scroll down to Service VPN, and click the plus sign and add one service
VPN. The number in the box that comes up just means how many you
want to add, rather than the service VPN number (Figure 9-13).

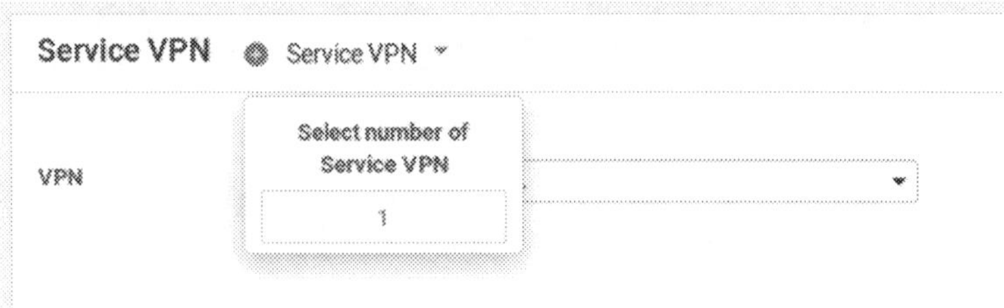

**Figure 9-13.**  *Adding a service VPN*

In the VPN box, select c-v-VPN1. Click the plus sign next to OSPF on the right-hand side, and select c-v-OSPF in the drop-down box. Lastly, click the plus sign next to VPN Interface and select c-v-Loopback1. You should end up with the same settings as Figure 9-14.

**Figure 9-14.**  *The service VPN settings*

Click "Update" at the bottom of the page to update the device template, and on the next page, enter the OSPF details for CSR-1, which are the network to advertise (172.16.30.1/24), the router ID (3.3.3.3), and the area number (3) (Figure 9-15).

| System IP | Hostname | IPv4 Address(vpn_if_ipv4_address) | Router ID(ospf_router_id) | Area Number(ospf_area_a_num) |
|---|---|---|---|---|
| 70.100.100.1 | CSR-1 | 172.16.30.1/24 | 3.3.3.3 | 3 |

**Figure 9-15.**  *Adding the OSPF details for CSR-1*

Click Next. We can see the new lines in the config diff, and these look correct as we are advertising OSPF via OMP up to the vSmart controller (Figure 9-16).

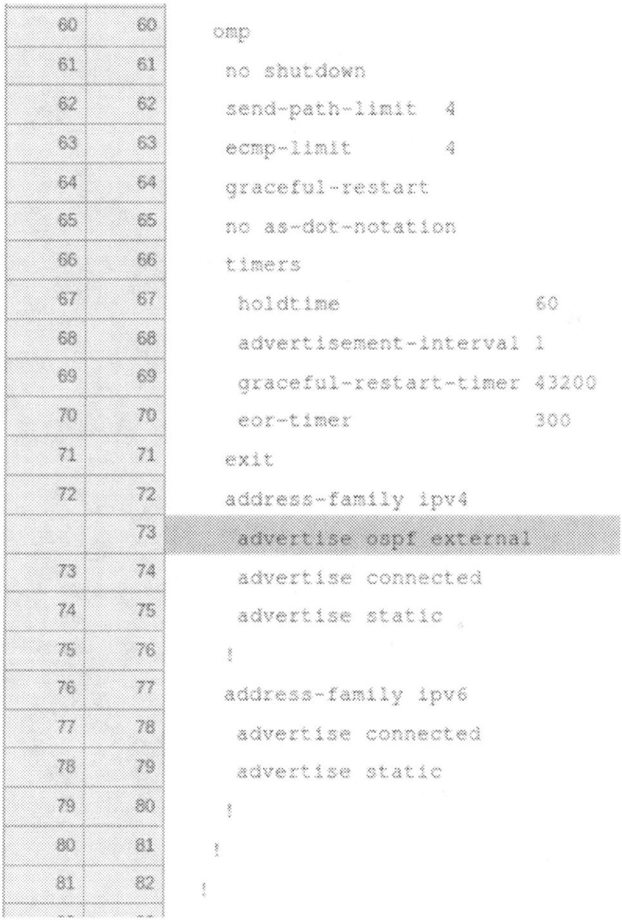

| | | |
|---|---|---|
| 60 | 60 | omp |
| 61 | 61 | no shutdown |
| 62 | 62 | send-path-limit   4 |
| 63 | 63 | ecmp-limit        4 |
| 64 | 64 | graceful-restart |
| 65 | 65 | no as-dot-notation |
| 66 | 66 | timers |
| 67 | 67 | holdtime                60 |
| 68 | 68 | advertisement-interval 1 |
| 69 | 69 | graceful-restart-timer 43200 |
| 70 | 70 | eor-timer              300 |
| 71 | 71 | exit |
| 72 | 72 | address-family ipv4 |
| | 73 | advertise ospf external |
| 73 | 74 | advertise connected |
| 74 | 75 | advertise static |
| 75 | 76 | ! |
| 76 | 77 | address-family ipv6 |
| 77 | 78 | advertise connected |
| 78 | 79 | advertise static |
| 79 | 80 | ! |
| 80 | 81 | ! |
| 81 | 82 | ! |

*Figure 9-16.* *Advertising OSPF into OMP*

Our loopback interface is getting created and is OSPF enabled (Figure 9-17).

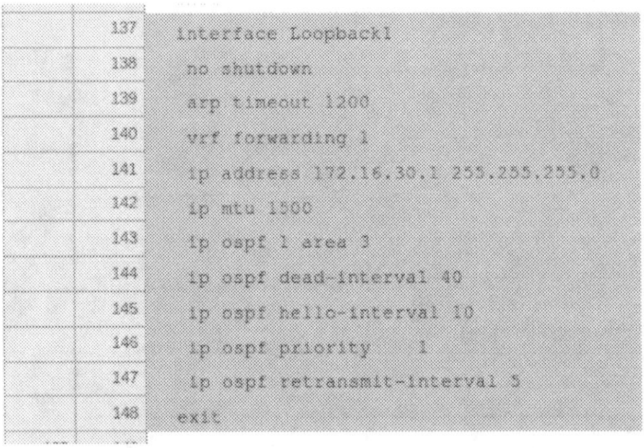

```
137   interface Loopback1
138   no shutdown
139   arp timeout 1200
140   vrf forwarding 1
141   ip address 172.16.30.1 255.255.255.0
142   ip mtu 1500
143   ip ospf 1 area 3
144   ip ospf dead-interval 40
145   ip ospf hello-interval 10
146   ip ospf priority    1
147   ip ospf retransmit-interval 5
148   exit
```

*Figure 9-17. CSR-1's loopback interface configuration*

We also have the OSPF routing declarations (Figure 9-18).

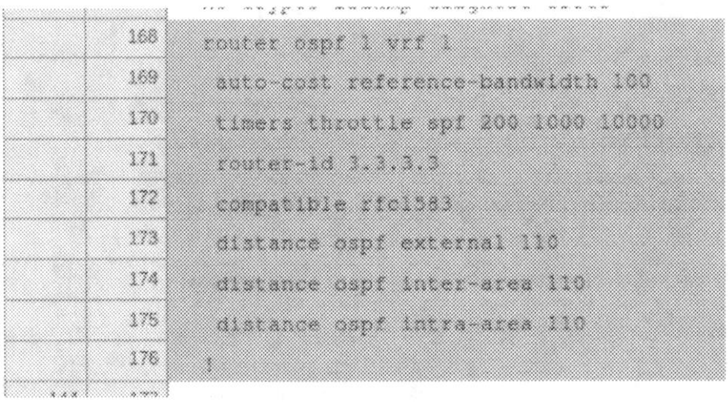

```
168   router ospf 1 vrf 1
169   auto-cost reference-bandwidth 100
170   timers throttle spf 200 1000 10000
171   router-id 3.3.3.3
172   compatible rfc1583
173   distance ospf external 110
174   distance ospf inter-area 110
175   distance ospf intra-area 110
176   !
```

*Figure 9-18. CSR-1's OSPF configuration*

There is also a VRF (virtual routing and forwarding) definition, but this is not pictured. Click Configure Devices to apply the template changes, and we should have a success (Figure 9-19).

| | Status | Message | Chassis Number |
|---|---|---|---|
| ∨ | ✅ Success | Done - Push Feature Template Con... | CSR-0502AB1A-7DE... |

```
[23-Apr-2020 11:42:09 UTC] Generating configuration from template
[23-Apr-2020 11:42:14 UTC] Checking and creating device in vManage
[23-Apr-2020 11:42:17 UTC] Device is online
[23-Apr-2020 11:42:17 UTC] Updating device configuration in vManage
[23-Apr-2020 11:42:22 UTC] Pushing configuration to device
[23-Apr-2020 11:43:01 UTC] Template successfully attached to device
```

***Figure 9-19.*** *Successful configuration*

We can confirm the changes on the router by looking at the interfaces:

```
CSR-1#sh ip int bri
Interface        IP-Address   OK? Method Status  Protocol
GigabitEthernet1 50.10.10.1   YES other  up      up
GigabitEthernet2 unassigned   YES unset  up      up
GigabitEthernet3 unassigned   YES unset  up      up
GigabitEthernet4 unassigned   YES unset  up      up
Loopback1        172.16.30.1  YES other  up      up
Loopback65528    192.168.1.1  YES other  up      up
NVI0             unassigned   YES unset  up      up
Tunnel1          50.10.10.1   YES TFTP   up      up
CSR-1#
```

Let's try and get the vEdges talking as well, and you will see why I use the word "try."

Because we created templates covering both the CSR1000v and the vEdge Cloud devices, we can reuse them here. Start by editing the t-Vedge template and setting the OMP template to c-v-OMP (Figure 9-20).

**Basic Information**

| System * | c-v-System ▾ |
| Logging* | Factory_Default_Logging_Template ▾ |
| AAA * | v-AAA ▾ |
| OMP * | c-v-OMP ▾ |

***Figure 9-20.*** *Editing the vEdge template*

Create another service VPN template (Figure 9-21).

**Service VPN** ⊕ Service VPN ▾

| VPN | c-v-VPN1 ▾ |
| OSPF | c-v-OSPF ▾ ⊖ |
| VPN Interface | c-v-Loopback1 ▾ ⊖    ⊕ Sub-Templates ▾ |

***Figure 9-21.*** *A new VPN template*

Click Update and fill in the details (Figure 9-22).

| System IP | Hostname | IPv4 Address(vpn_if_ipv4_address) | Router ID(ospf_router_id) | Area Number(ospf_area_a_num) |
|---|---|---|---|---|
| 100.100.1.5 | vEdge01 | 172.16.10.1/24 | 1.1.1.1 | 0 |
| 60.100.100.1 | vEdge02 | 172.16.20.1/24 | 2.2.2.2 | 2 |

***Figure 9-22.*** *The OSPF details for the vEdge devices*

Click Next. Now, instead of being able to compare the current configuration to the new template (as we could with the CSR template), we get an IPv6 error (Figure 9-23).

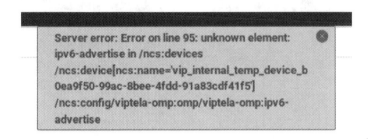

**Server error: Error on line 95: unknown element: ipv6-advertise in /ncs:devices /ncs:device[ncs:name='vip_internal_temp_device_b 0ea9f50-99ac-8bee-4fdd-91a83cdf41f5'] /ncs:config/viptela-omp:omp/viptela-omp:ipv6-advertise**

***Figure 9-23.***  *IPv6 error!*

The reason for this is that the template is shared between the vEdge and cEdge devices, and we need to disable IPv6 advertisement on the vEdges if we are not using it. To resolve this, we need to cancel the current task and return to our feature templates. Click the three dots for the c-v-OMP template, and click "Copy." Give the copy a new name (v-OMP), and click "Copy" (Figure 9-24).

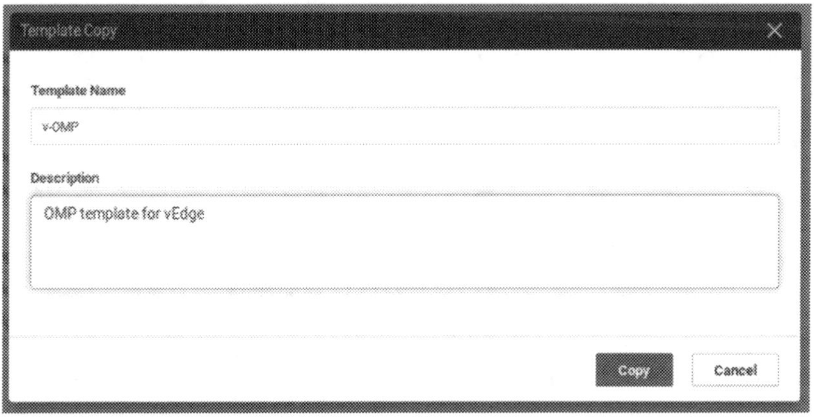

Template Copy

Template Name

v-OMP

Description

OMP template for vEdge

Copy     Cancel

***Figure 9-24.***  *Copying the c-v-OMP template*

Edit the new template, and click IPv6 under the "Advertise" section. Disable all the entries, and click "Update" (Figure 9-25).

*Figure 9-25.* *The IPv6 settings*

Update the t-vEdge template to use the new v-OMP template, and set up the service VPN 1 again. Run through the process again, and try to configure the devices.

We get more errors, and this time it is an issue with the loopback interface as the error states "Invalid interface Loopback1" (Figure 9-26).

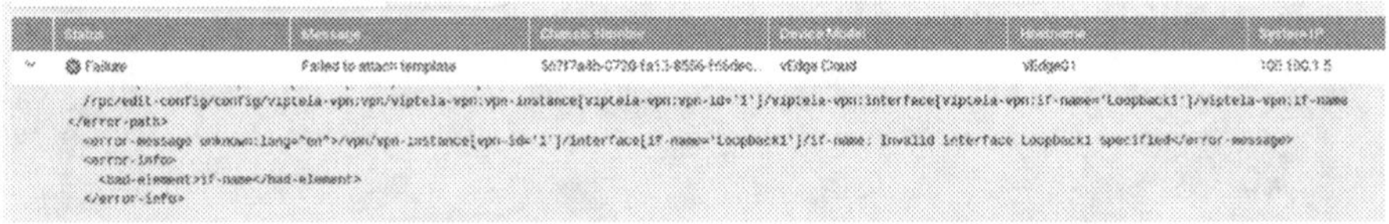

*Figure 9-26.* *Interface naming details*

Remember when I said that the system is very picky about names? Well, it will not go easy on you if there are capitalization errors. Using shared (vEdge and cEdge) templates does lead to issues like this at times.

Copy the c-v-Loopback1 template (naming it "v-Loopback1") and edit it, changing "Loopback1" to "loopback1." Copy and edit the OSPF template as well, changing the interface name to "loopback1" as well (Figure 9-27).

***Figure 9-27.*** *Fixing the interface name*

Save the template, and then set up the device template again, this time using the newly copied and edited templates (Figure 9-28).

***Figure 9-28.*** *The new service VPN*

Push the configuration to the devices (Figure 9-29).

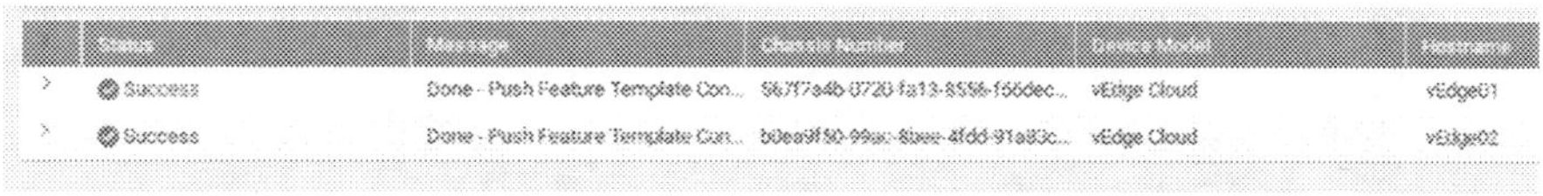

***Figure 9-29.*** *Pushing the OSPF configuration to the vEdge devices*

The routes for 172.16.10.0/24, 172.16.20.0/24, and 172.16.30.0/24 should be visible to the vEdge routers. As you can see, they are showing as OMP routes (Figure 9-30).

```
vEdge01# show ip routes | b VPN
VPN    PREFIX          PROTOCOL      SUB TYPE  IF NAME    ADDR        VPN    TLOC IP        COLOR      ENCAP  STATUS
---------------------------------------------------------------------------------------------------------------------
0      0.0.0.0/0       static        ~         ge0/0      10.1.1.1    ~      ~              ~          ~      F,S
0      10.1.1.0/24     connected     ~         ge0/0      ~           ~      ~              ~          ~      F,S
0      100.100.1.5/32  connected     ~         system     ~           ~      ~              ~          ~      F,S
1      172.16.10.0/24  ospf          IA        loopback1  ~           ~      ~              ~          ~      ~
1      172.16.10.0/24  connected     ~         loopback1  ~           ~      ~              ~          ~      F,S
1      172.16.20.0/24  omp           ~         ~           ~           ~      60.100.100.1   default    ipsec  F,S
1      172.16.30.0/24  omp           ~         ~           ~           ~      70.100.100.1   default    ipsec  F,S

vEdge01#
```

*Figure 9-30.* *Our new OMP routes in vEdge01*

Most importantly, we can ping them:

```
vEdge01# ping vpn 1 172.16.30.1
Ping in VPN 1
PING 172.16.30.1 (172.16.30.1) 56(84) bytes of data.
64 bytes from 172.16.30.1: icmp_seq=1 ttl=255 time=12.1 ms
64 bytes from 172.16.30.1: icmp_seq=2 ttl=255 time=2.60 ms
64 bytes from 172.16.30.1: icmp_seq=3 ttl=255 time=2.80 ms
64 bytes from 172.16.30.1: icmp_seq=4 ttl=255 time=2.78 ms
64 bytes from 172.16.30.1: icmp_seq=5 ttl=255 time=2.35 ms
^C
--- 172.16.30.1 ping statistics ---
5 packets transmitted, 5 received, 0% packet loss, time 4005ms
rtt min/avg/max/mdev = 2.351/4.530/12.116/3.796 ms
vEdge01#
vEdge01# traceroute vpn 1 172.16.30.1
Traceroute  172.16.30.1 in VPN 1
traceroute to 172.16.30.1 (172.16.30.1), 30 hops max, 60 byte
packets
 1  172.16.30.1 (172.16.30.1)  4.764 ms * *
vEdge01#
```

We can also see the vEdge routes on the CSR-1 router:

```
CSR-1#sh sdwan omp routes 172.16.20.0/24
-------------------------------------------------------
omp route entries for vpn 1 route 172.16.20.0/24
-------------------------------------------------------
            RECEIVED FROM:
peer               100.100.1.4
path-id            2
label              1004
status             C,I,R
loss-reason        not set
lost-to-peer       not set
lost-to-path-id not set
    Attributes:
      originator       60.100.100.1
      type             installed
      tloc             60.100.100.1, default, ipsec
      ultimate-tloc    not set
      domain-id        not set
      overlay-id       1
      site-id          200
      preference       not set
      tag              not set
      origin-proto     connected
      origin-metric    0
      as-path          not set
      unknown-attr-len not set

CSR-1#
```

The route has a status of "C,I,R". This means that the paths have chosen (C), and the route has been installed into the routing table (I) and resolved (R), as Table 9-1 shows, along with the other statuses.

***Table 9-1.***  *Route Status codes*

| Status | Meaning |
|--------|---------|
| C | Chosen |
| I | Installed |
| Red | Redistributed |
| Rej | Rejected |
| L | Looped |
| R | Resolved |
| S | State |
| Ext | Extranet |
| Inv | Invalid |
| Stg | Staged |
| U | TLOC Unresolved |

It is slightly different to ping from CSR-1 as you have to specify the VRF (virtual routing and forwarding) number, rather than the VPN:

```
CSR-1#show vrf
   Name          Default RD       Protocols    Interfaces
   1             1:1              ipv4,ipv6    Lo1
   65528         <not set>        ipv4         Lo65528
   Mgmt-intf     1:512            ipv4,ipv6
CSR-1#
```

```
CSR-1#ping vrf 1 172.16.20.1
Type escape sequence to abort.
Sending 5, 100-byte ICMP Echos to 172.16.20.1:
!!!!!
Success rate is 100 percent (5/5), rt min/avg/max = 1/1/3 ms
CSR-1#
```

This is a bit of a mic drop moment, and let's admit, it is cool stuff happening here. We have broken many of the rules of OSPF here; the areas are all different, none of the IPs are in the same subnets, and we have no OSPF adjacencies, but it still works. In fact, it works better than usual, as the overlay is carrying all our OSPF traffic and handling everything for us.

Let's try this with BGP.

# BGP

Our BGP network will look like Figure 9-31.

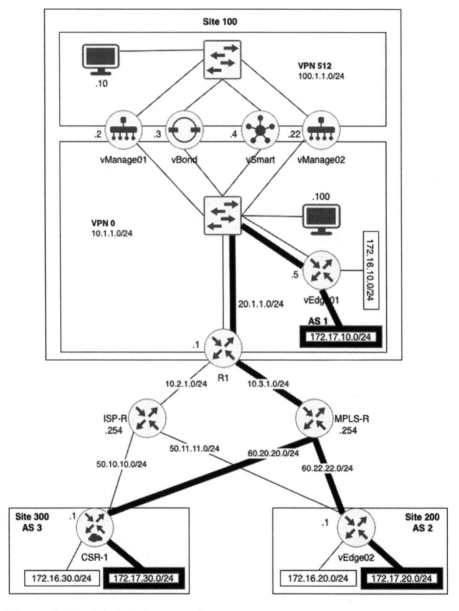

*Figure 9-31.* *The BGP network*

We are going to implement three AS (autonomous systems). Along the way, we will find that we have the same caveats as we did when setting up OSPF, in that the CSR-1 router can have a capitalized loopback interface, but the vEdge routers cannot, and the issue with IPv6 being enabled on OMP (or not as the case was).

The first step is to connect our router's MPLS interfaces. These will need to be separated from our existing interfaces, and this is where colors come into play.

Our first task is to set our existing interfaces to be the same color, which will be "biz-internet."

Within the feature templates, edit the v-VPN-Interface we created in the previous chapter, and set the color to be global and "biz-internet" (Figure 9-32).

***Figure 9-32.*** *Editing the VPN 0 interface*

Click Update, and then Next. Confirm that the changes to be made are correct by checking the config diff screen (Figure 9-33).

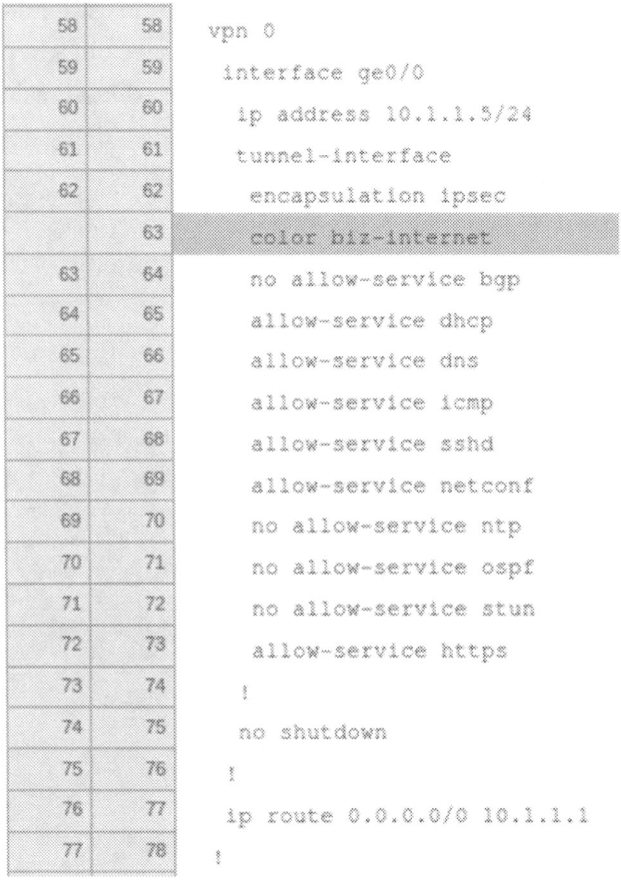

```
 58   58    vpn 0
 59   59      interface ge0/0
 60   60        ip address 10.1.1.5/24
 61   61        tunnel-interface
 62   62          encapsulation ipsec
      63          color biz-internet
 63   64          no allow-service bgp
 64   65          allow-service dhcp
 65   66          allow-service dns
 66   67          allow-service icmp
 67   68          allow-service sshd
 68   69          allow-service netconf
 69   70          no allow-service ntp
 70   71          no allow-service ospf
 71   72          no allow-service stun
 72   73          allow-service https
 73   74        !
 74   75        no shutdown
 75   76      !
 76   77      ip route 0.0.0.0/0 10.1.1.1
 77   78    !
```

***Figure 9-33.*** *Confirming the color changes*

If the changes are correct, then configure the devices. Repeat the process for the t-CSR1000v feature template. The config diff should look like Figure 9-34.

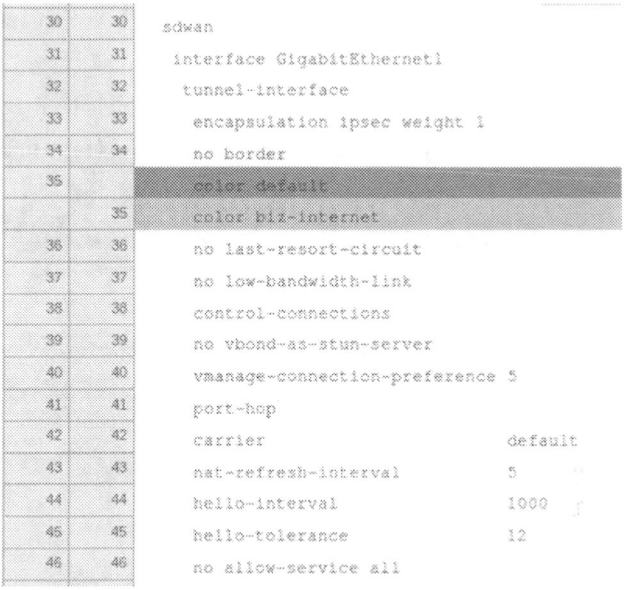

*Figure 9-34.* *The CSR template color changes*

Once all the devices have updated, it's probably a good idea to check we didn't break anything with our OSPF network:

```
vEdge01# ping vpn 1 172.16.30.1
Ping in VPN 1
PING 172.16.30.1 (172.16.30.1) 56(84) bytes of data.
64 bytes from 172.16.30.1: icmp_seq=1 ttl=255 time=2.58 ms
64 bytes from 172.16.30.1: icmp_seq=2 ttl=255 time=2.31 ms
64 bytes from 172.16.30.1: icmp_seq=3 ttl=255 time=3.26 ms
^C
--- 172.16.30.1 ping statistics ---
3 packets transmitted, 3 received, 0% packet loss, time 2001ms
rtt min/avg/max/mdev = 2.318/2.720/3.264/0.403 ms
vEdge01#
```

So far so good. Now we need to create two new VPN interface templates.

Create a new VPN Interface Ethernet called MPLS-Int-vEdge; set both the interface name and IPv4 address to device specific (Figure 9-35).

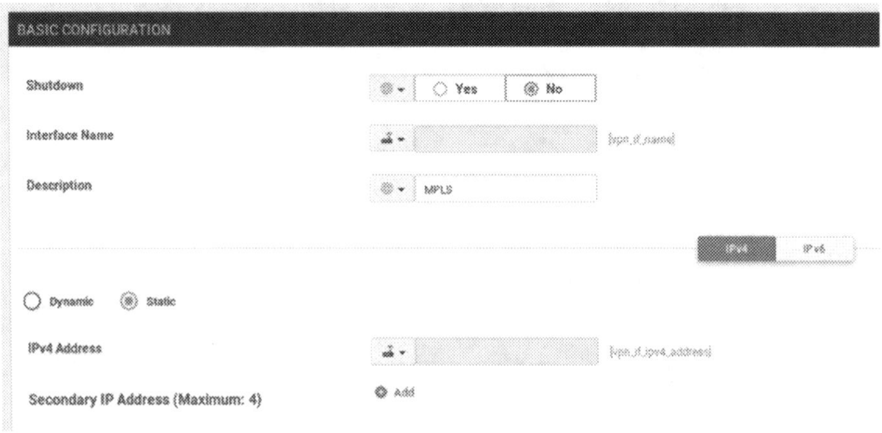

*Figure 9-35.*  *The MPLS-Int-vEdge template*

Enable the tunnel interface, and set the color to "mpls." Set the restrict option to On (Figure 9-36).

*Figure 9-36.*  *The restrict option*

The restrict option controls which remote TLOCs the local TLOC can establish a BFD session with. When we use the "restrict" option, the TLOC on the local router can only establish BFD sessions with TLOCs of the same color.

In the main vEdge device template, create an additional VPN interface under Transport & Management VPN, and select the MPLS-Int-vEdge template (Figure 9-37).

***Figure 9-37.*** *The MPLS interface*

Update the template, and fill in the details when prompted (Figure 9-38).

| System IP | Hostname | (s.0) | Interface Name(vpn_if_name_MPLS-Int-vEdge) | IPv4 Address(vpn_if_ipv4_address) |
|---|---|---|---|---|
| 100.100.1.5 | vEdge03 | | ge0/1 | 20.1.1.5/24 |
| 60.100.100.1 | vEdge02 | | ge0/0 | 60.22.22.1/24 |

***Figure 9-38.*** *Setting the MPLS interface details*

Push the configuration, and check it over (Figure 9-39).

| | |
|---|---|
| 77 | interface ge0/1 |
| 78 | description MPLS |
| 79 | ip address 20.1.1.5/24 |
| 80 | tunnel-interface |
| 81 | encapsulation ipsec |
| 82 | color mpls restrict |
| 83 | no allow-service bgp |
| 84 | allow-service dhcp |
| 85 | allow-service dns |
| 86 | allow-service icmp |
| 87 | no allow-service sshd |
| 88 | no allow-service netconf |
| 89 | no allow-service ntp |
| 90 | no allow-service ospf |
| 91 | no allow-service stun |
| 92 | allow-service https |
| 93 | ! |
| 94 | no shutdown |
| 95 | ! |

**Figure 9-39.** *The MPLS configuration*

Once the configuration has been pushed to the devices, we can check the results on the device:

```
vEdge01# show interface ge0/1
interface vpn 0 interface ge0/1 af-type ipv4
 ip-address        20.1.1.5/24
 if-admin-status   Up
 if-oper-status    Up
 if-tracker-status NA
 encap-type        null
```

```
port-type           transport
mtu                 1500
hwaddr              50:00:00:06:00:02
speed-mbps          1000
duplex              full
tcp-mss-adjust      1416
uptime              0:00:03:10
rx-packets          100
tx-packets          13
vEdge01#
vEdge01# ping 20.1.1.1 count 3
Ping in VPN 0
PING 20.1.1.1 (20.1.1.1) 56(84) bytes of data.
64 bytes from 20.1.1.1: icmp_seq=1 ttl=255 time=1.37 ms
64 bytes from 20.1.1.1: icmp_seq=2 ttl=255 time=1.66 ms
64 bytes from 20.1.1.1: icmp_seq=3 ttl=255 time=1.43 ms

--- 20.1.1.1 ping statistics ---
3 packets transmitted, 3 received, 0% packet loss, time 2001ms
rtt min/avg/max/mdev = 1.377/1.491/1.664/0.128 ms
vEdge01#

vEdge02# ping 60.22.22.254 count 3
Ping in VPN 0
PING 60.22.22.254 (60.22.22.254) 56(84) bytes of data.
64 bytes from 60.22.22.254: icmp_seq=1 ttl=255 time=0.583 ms
64 bytes from 60.22.22.254: icmp_seq=2 ttl=255 time=0.668 ms
64 bytes from 60.22.22.254: icmp_seq=3 ttl=255 time=0.736 ms

--- 60.22.22.254 ping statistics ---
3 packets transmitted, 3 received, 0% packet loss, time 2000ms
rtt min/avg/max/mdev = 0.583/0.662/0.736/0.066 ms
vEdge02#
```

Looks good, right? We have the connectivity we need. However, when we look at the vManage dashboard, we can see that now we only have partial control (Figure 9-40).

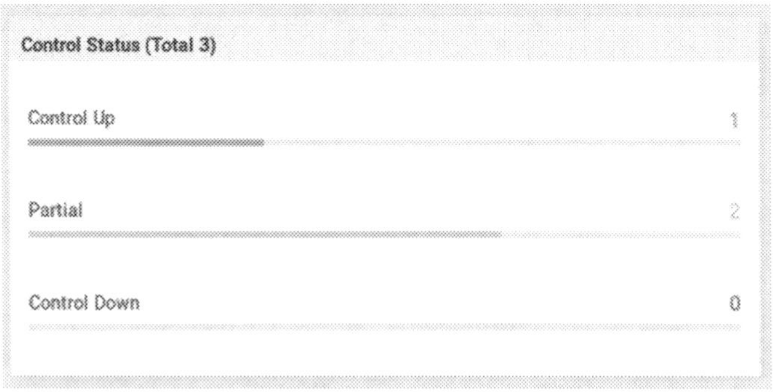

Control Status (Total 3)

Control Up                                                          1

Partial                                                            2

Control Down                                                       0

***Figure 9-40.***  *Partial control*

This is a routing issue: since we pushed the new interface configuration, we lost the control because the edge devices cannot reach the orchestration servers via the new interface. So try to edit the v-VPN0 template, and add a new IPv4 default route, again, with a device-specific next hop.

Unfortunately, as you will see, we cannot have two default routers (Figure 9-41).

Failed to create template: Duplicate value: 0.0.0.0/0

***Figure 9-41.***  *We cannot have two default routes*

The workaround is to set the second default route as device specific (Figure 9-42).

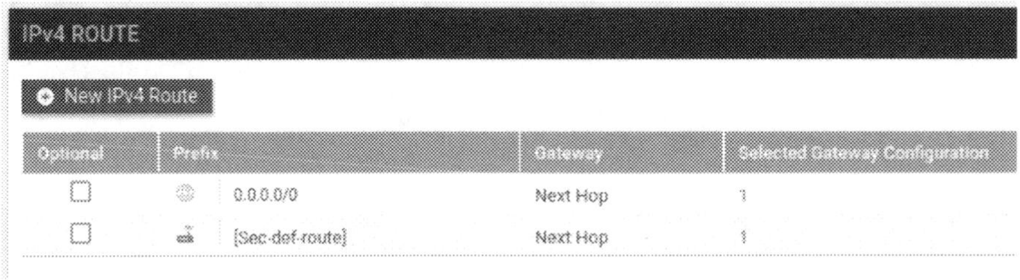

| IPv4 ROUTE | | | |
|---|---|---|---|
| **O** New IPv4 Route | | | |
| Optional | Prefix | Gateway | Selected Gateway Configuration |
| ☐ | ⊕  0.0.0.0/0 | Next Hop | 1 |
| ☐ | 🖻  [Sec-def-route] | Next Hop | 1 |

***Figure 9-42.*** *A second default route*

Update the template, and fill in the details, specifying 0.0.0.0/0 as the destination and 20.1.1.1 and 60.22.22.254 as the next-hop IP addresses for vEdge01 and vEdge02, respectively (Figure 9-43).

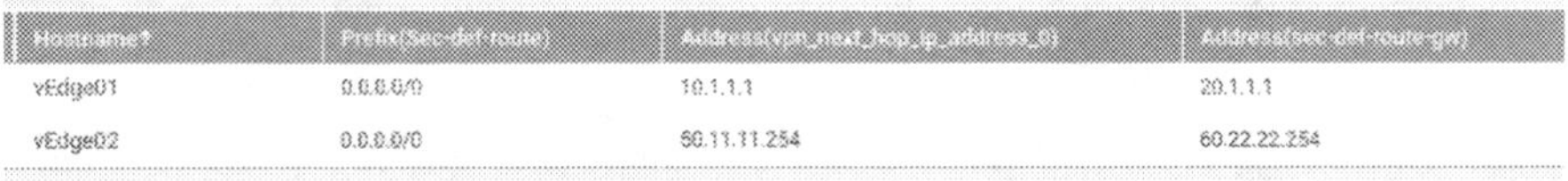

| Hostname↑ | Prefix(Sec-def-route) | Address(vpn_next_hop_ip_address_0) | Address(sec-def-route-gw) |
|---|---|---|---|
| vEdge01 | 0.0.0.0/0 | 10.1.1.1 | 20.1.1.1 |
| vEdge02 | 0.0.0.0/0 | 50.11.11.254 | 60.22.22.254 |

***Figure 9-43.*** *The default route settings*

Once completed, the template will add a second default route:

```
vEdge02# sh run vpn 0 | incl route
 ip route 0.0.0.0/0 50.11.11.254
 ip route 0.0.0.0/0 60.22.22.254
vEdge02#
vEdge02# sh ip route | inc 0.0.0.0 | display xml
    <prefix>0.0.0.0/0</prefix>
    <prefix>0.0.0.0/0</prefix>
vEdge02#
```

Now, back on the dashboard, our control is green again (Figure 9-44).

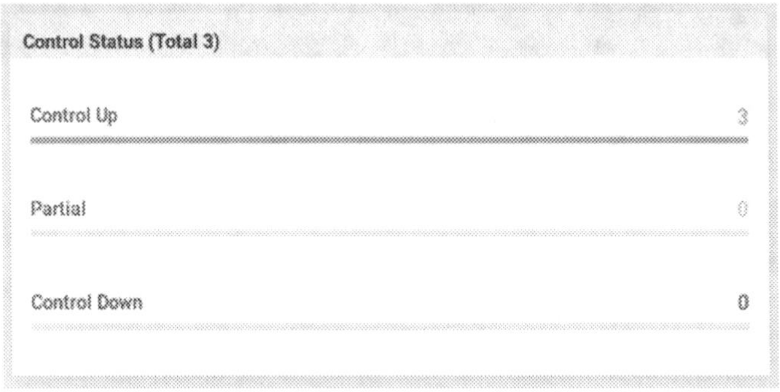

Control Status (Total 3)

Control Up                                                                    3

Partial                                                                       0

Control Down                                                                  0

**Figure 9-44.**  *Control is green again!*

The next step is to advertise BGP into OMP, which we do inside the
OMP template (Figure 9-45).

**Figure 9-45.**  *Advertising BGP into OMP*

Create the loopback2 interface by copying the v-Loopback1 template,
renaming it to v-Loopback2 (Figure 9-46).

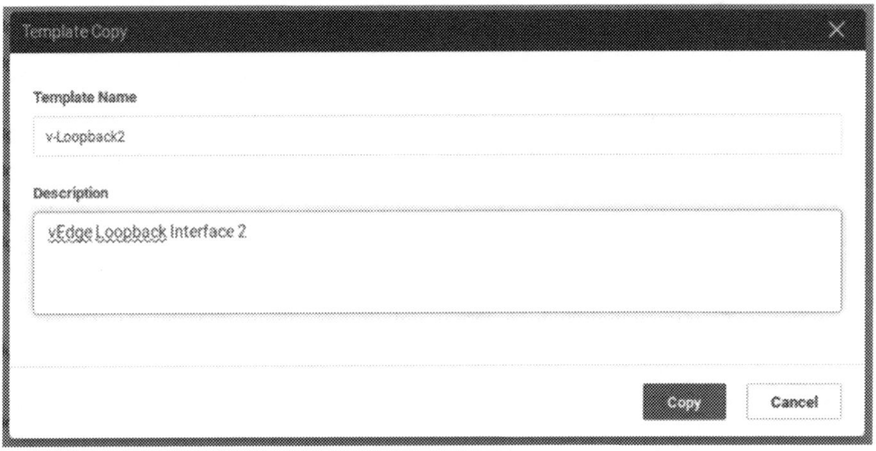

***Figure 9-46.*** *Copying the Loopback template*

Change the interface name (Figure 9-47), remembering that it is lowercase on the vEdge routers!

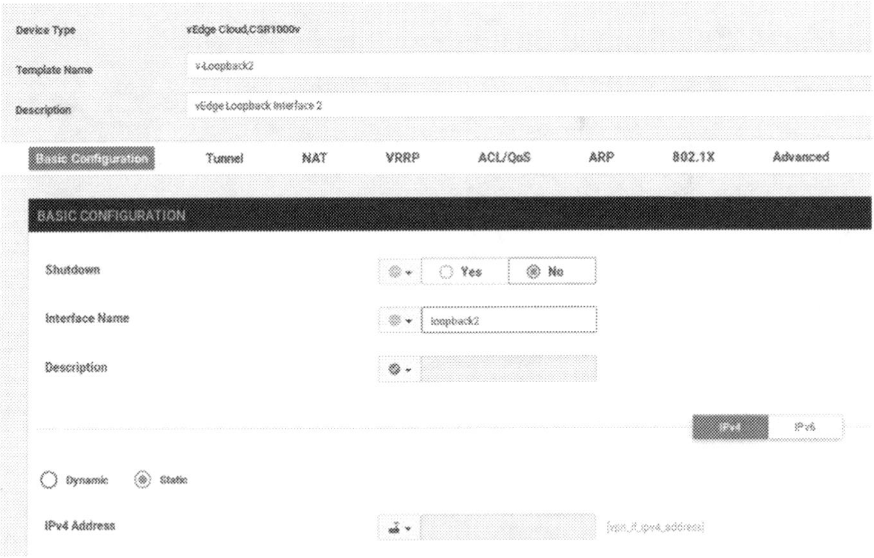

***Figure 9-47.*** *The new Loopback template*

Click Update. Next, create a template for BGP, making sure that the AS number and router ID are both device specific (Figure 9-48).

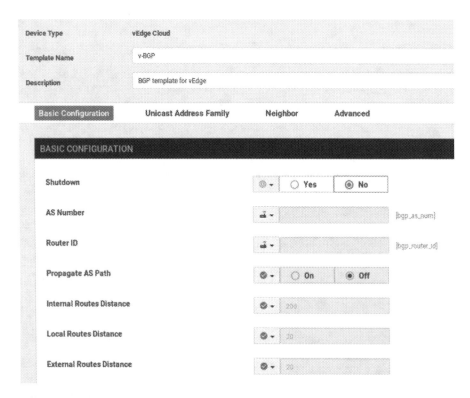

*Figure 9-48.*  *Our BGP template*

To advertise our second loopback network, on the Unicast Address Family section, click Network and add a device-specific network prefix (Figure 9-49).

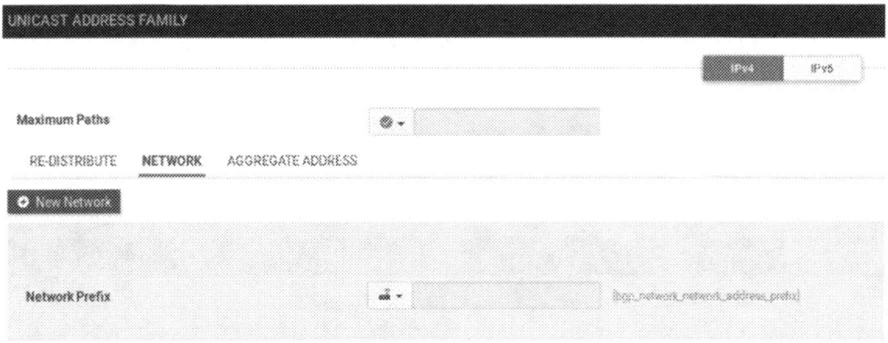

*Figure 9-49.* *The device-specific network prefix*

Click Add to update the template (Figure 9-50).

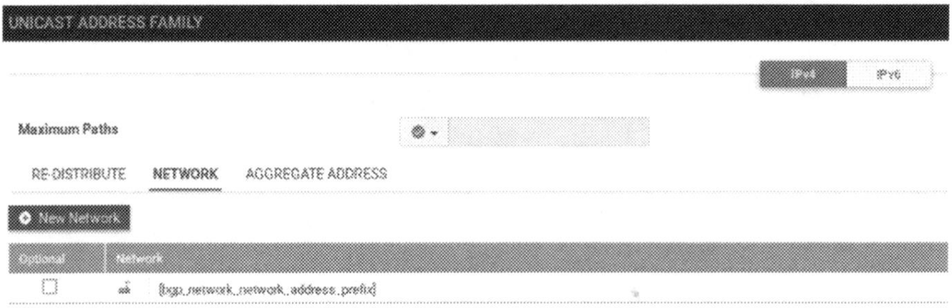

*Figure 9-50.* *The updated BGP template*

Save the template, and create another VPN interface template, called vEdge-VPN2 (Figure 9-51).

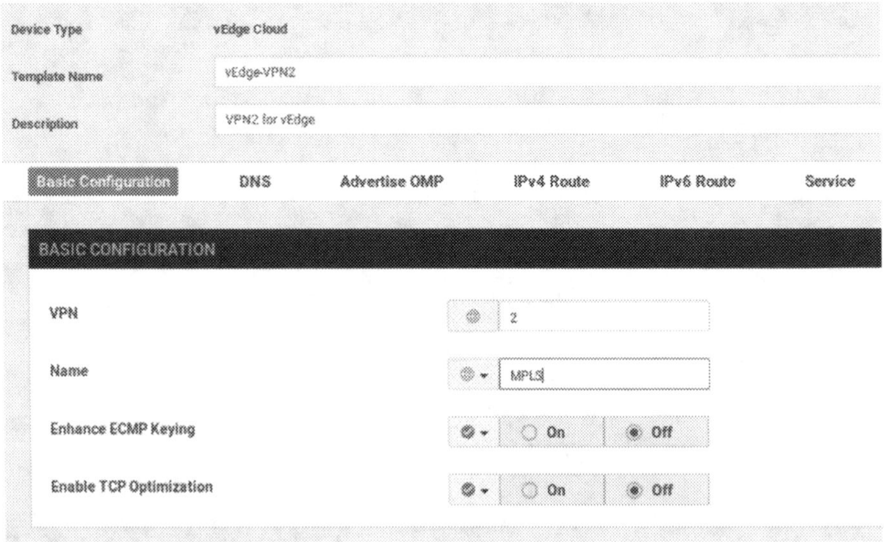

| Device Type | vEdge Cloud | | |
|---|---|---|---|
| Template Name | vEdge-VPN2 | | |
| Description | VPN2 for vEdge | | |

| Basic Configuration | DNS | Advertise OMP | IPv4 Route | IPv6 Route | Service |
|---|---|---|---|---|---|

**BASIC CONFIGURATION**

| VPN | ⊕ | 2 |
|---|---|---|
| Name | ⊕ ▾ | MPLS |
| Enhance ECMP Keying | ⊘ ▾ | ○ On  ● Off |
| Enable TCP Optimization | ⊘ ▾ | ○ On  ● Off |

*Figure 9-51.  vEdge-VPN2*

Now edit the t-vEdge device template, and add a new Service VPN, setting the BGP section to "v-BGP" and the VPN interface to "v-Loopback2" (Figure 9-52).

| VPN | vEdge-VPN2 | ▾ | |
|---|---|---|---|
| BGP | v-BGP | ▾ | ⊖ |
| VPN Interface | v-Loopback2 | ▾ | ⊖  ⊕ Sub-Templates ▾ |

*Figure 9-52.  VPN 2 settings*

Update the template, filling in the device-specific details for the loopback interface IP address, the BGP AS number (1 for vEdge01 and 2 for vEdge02), the router ID (1.1.1.1 and 2.2.2.2, respectively), and the prefix to advertise (172.17.10.0/24 for vEdge01 and 172.17.20.0/24 for vedge02), shown in Figure 9-53.

| Hostname | IPv4 Address (gp_if_ipv4_address) | AS Number (bgp_as_num) | Router ID (bgp_router_id) | Network Prefix (bgp_network_network_address_prefix) |
|---|---|---|---|---|
| vEdge01 | 172.17.10.1/24 | 1 | 1.1.1.1 | 172.17.10.0/24 |
| vEdge02 | 172.17.20.1/24 | 2 | 2.2.2.2 | 172.17.20.0/24 |

***Figure 9-53.*** *The BGP settings*

Check the new configuration over before we push it to the devices (Figure 9-54).

```
116   vpn 2
117    name MPLS
118    router
119     bgp 1
120      no shutdown
121      router-id 1.1.1.1
122      address-family ipv4-unicast
123       network 172.17.10.0/24
124      !
125     !
126    !
127    interface loopback2
128     ip address 172.17.10.1/24
129     no shutdown
130    !
131   !
```

***Figure 9-54.*** *The VPN 2 configuration*

If you are happy with the settings, then push the configuration to the devices.

Our configuration works. Kind of. We have the advertised route from vEdge01 showing in vEdge02, and it is reachable (Figure 9-55).

```
vEdge02# sh ip route | b VPN
VPN    PREFIX              PROTOCOL        SUB TYPE  IF NAME    ADDR          VPN    TLOC IP        COLOR         ENCAP  STATUS
0      0.0.0.0/0           static          ~         ge0/1      50.11.11.254  ~      ~              ~             ~      F,S
0      0.0.0.0/0           static          ~         ge0/0      60.22.22.254  ~      ~              ~             ~      F,S
0      50.11.11.0/24       connected       ~         ge0/1      ~             ~      ~              ~             ~      F,S
0      60.22.22.0/24       connected       ~         ge0/0      ~             ~      ~              ~             ~      F,S
0      60.100.100.1/32     connected       ~         system     ~             ~      ~              ~             ~      F,S
1      172.16.10.0/24      omp             ~         ~          ~             ~      100.100.1.5    biz-internet  ipsec  F,S
1      172.16.20.0/24      ospf            IA        loopback1  ~             ~      ~              ~             ~      F,S
1      172.16.20.0/24      connected       ~         loopback1  ~             ~      ~              ~             ~      F,S
1      172.16.30.0/24      omp             ~         ~          ~             ~      70.100.100.1   biz-internet  ipsec  F,S
2      172.17.10.0/24      omp             ~         ~          ~             ~      100.100.1.5    biz-internet  ipsec  F,S
2      172.17.20.0/24      connected       ~         loopback2  ~             ~      ~              ~             ~      F,S

vEdge02# ping vpn 2 172.17.10.1 count 3
Ping in VPN 2
PING 172.17.10.1 (172.17.10.1) 56(84) bytes of data.
64 bytes from 172.17.10.1: icmp_seq=1 ttl=64 time=2.27 ms
64 bytes from 172.17.10.1: icmp_seq=2 ttl=64 time=2.01 ms
64 bytes from 172.17.10.1: icmp_seq=3 ttl=64 time=1.89 ms

----- 172.17.10.1 ping statistics -----
3 packets transmitted, 3 received, 0% packet loss, time 2002ms
rtt min/avg/max/mdev = 1.896/2.059/2.273/0.166 ms
vEdge02#
```

***Figure 9-55.***  *We have reachability*

We can see the new routes and ping them, but the color is wrong; it should show as "mpls," not "biz-internet." If you head over to the vManage monitoring page and select Network, then select one of the vEdge devices, and choose *WAN ➤ Tunnel*, you can see that the mpls tunnel is down (Figure 9-56).

| Tunnel Endpoints | Protocol | State | Jitter (ms) |
|---|---|---|---|
| ⌄  biz-internet | ~~ | ~~ | |
| ☑  vEdge01:biz-internet-vEdge02:biz-internet | IPSEC | ↑ | 0.00 |
| ☑  vEdge01:biz-internet-CSR-1:biz-internet | IPSEC | ↑ | 0.00 |
| ⌄  mpls | ~~ | ~~ | |
| ☑  vEdge01:mpls-vEdge02:mpls | IPSEC | ↓ | 0.00 |
| ⌄  default | ~~ | ~~ | |
| ☑  vEdge01:default-vEdge02:default | IPSEC | ~ | 0.00 |
| ☑  vEdge01:default-CSR-1:default | IPSEC | ~ | 0.00 |

***Figure 9-56.***  *The mpls vpn is down*

The issue here is that once we start to differentiate our networks and traffic using colors, and especially when we separate them into public and private networks, we introduce issues with the control connections.

# Public and Private

The SD-WAN understands two types of networks: public and private. The public colors are 3g, biz-internet, blue, bronze, custom1, custom2, custom3, default, gold, green, lte, public-internet, red, and silver. The private colors are metro-ethernet, mpls, and the private colors 1 through to 6. There is an expectation, when using private colors, that there is no NAT involved along the way.

When we use private colors, the edge devices will try to build an IPSec tunnel to other edge devices using the private IP address, which makes sense. However, in our case, we are getting issues in bringing up the tunnels. We can see this by running the command "`show control connections-history`" from the edge router; the error is "DCONFAIL."

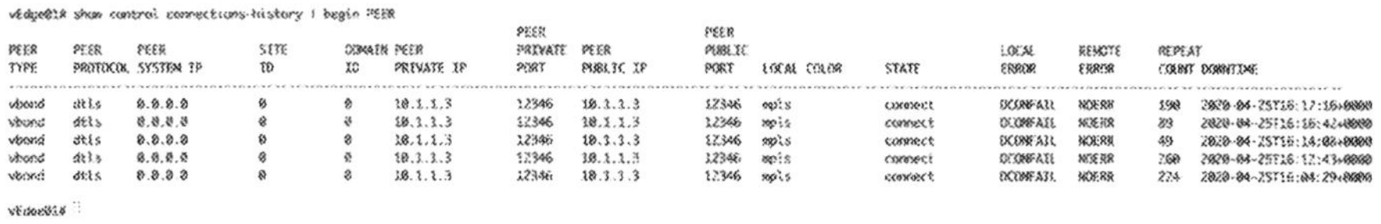

```
vEdge01# show control connections-history | begin PEER
                                                                  PEER                       PEER
PEER    PEER      PEER            SITE        DOMAIN PEER              PRIVATE  PEER             PUBLIC                                   LOCAL      REMOTE     REPEAT
TYPE    PROTOCOL  SYSTEM IP       ID          ID     PRIVATE IP        PORT     PUBLIC IP        PORT    LOCAL COLOR     STATE            ERROR      ERROR      COUNT  DOWNTIME
--------------------------------------------------------------------------------------------------------------------------------------------------------------------------------
vbond   dtls      0.0.0.0         0           0      10.1.1.3          12346    10.1.1.3         12346   mpls            connect          DCONFAIL   NOERR      190    2020-04-25T16:17:16+0000
vbond   dtls      0.0.0.0         0           0      10.1.1.3          12346    10.1.1.3         12346   mpls            connect          DCONFAIL   NOERR      89     2020-04-25T16:16:42+0000
vbond   dtls      0.0.0.0         0           0      10.1.1.3          12346    10.1.1.3         12346   mpls            connect          DCONFAIL   NOERR      49     2020-04-25T16:14:08+0000
vbond   dtls      0.0.0.0         0           0      10.1.1.3          12346    10.1.1.3         12346   mpls            connect          DCONFAIL   NOERR      260    2020-04-25T16:12:43+0000
vbond   dtls      0.0.0.0         0           0      10.1.1.3          12346    10.1.1.3         12346   mpls            connect          DCONFAIL   NOERR      224    2020-04-25T16:04:29+0000

vEdge01#
```

***Figure 9-57.*** *Show control connections-history*

If we jump back on the vManage, we can also see the errors (Figure 9-58).

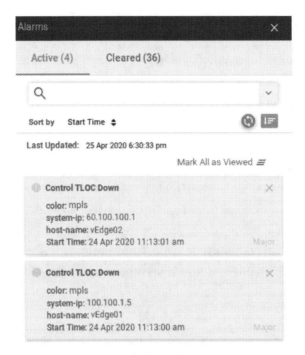

*Figure 9-58.*   *TLOC down*

There are two reasons we are getting this error. The first reason is that a route learned on one interface will never be seen on another interface, even if that route is more specific than an existing one. We have a default route of 0.0.0.0/0 on Ge0/0 on our vEdge1, and that is the way we will get to our management and orchestration servers. Never through ge0/1. This brings us back to the similarity of VRFs, where we gain traffic separation but introduce complexity.

We can reach it if we specify how we reach the vBond when we use options in a ping command to specify the interface, but without manually specifying a VPN, the vEdge will use the default route, naturally.

```
vEdge01# show ip routes vpn 0 10.1.1.3 detail | beg ----
--------------------------------------------
 VPN 0        PREFIX 10.1.1.0/24
--------------------------------------------
 proto            connected
 distance         0
 metric           0
 uptime           0:23:12:20
 nexthop-ifname   ge0/0
 status           F,S

vEdge01#
```

So how do we fix this issue? The answer is to tell the edge device that we do not want to create a control session over the MPLS interface. This is something we should do on all private interfaces, the reason being is, as they are private, there is a very good chance that there will be no Internet breakout on the line (each network is different, granted, but we are taking the word "private" literally here). The command we use to do this is "max-control-connections". Setting this to 0 allows the MPLS TLOC to be advertised up to the vSmart controller over the biz-internet OMP connection, and, once again, the edge devices will bring up the IPSec tunnels to vBond.

We set the Maximum Control Connections to 0 in the Tunnel section of the MPLS-Int-vEdge template and apply the changes (Figure 9-59).

*Figure 9-59.* *Setting the Maximum Control Connections*

Now we start to see routes being advertised with the mpls color
(Figure 9-60).

```
vEdge02# sh ip route | beg VPN
VPN   PREFIX          PROTOCOL      SUB TYPE  IF NAME    ADDR          VPN   TLOC IP        COLOR         ENCAP  STATUS
-------------------------------------------------------------------------------------------------------------------------
0     0.0.0.0/0       static        --        ge0/1      50.11.11.254  --    --             --            --     F,S
0     0.0.0.0/0       static        --        ge0/0      60.22.22.254  --    --             --            --     F,S
0     50.11.11.0/24   connected     --        ge0/1      --            --    --             --            --     F,S
0     60.22.22.0/24   connected     --        ge0/0      --            --    --             --            --     F,S
0     60.100.100.1/32 connected     --        system     --            --    --             --            --     F,S
1     172.16.10.0/24  omp           --        --         --            --    100.100.1.5    mpls          ipsec  F,S
1     172.16.10.0/24  omp           --        --         --            --    100.100.1.5    biz-internet  ipsec  F,S
1     172.16.20.0/24  ospf          IA        loopback1  --            --    --             --            --     --
1     172.16.20.0/24  connected     --        loopback1  --            --    --             --            --     F,S
1     172.16.30.0/24  omp           --        --         --            --    70.100.100.1   biz-internet  ipsec  F,S
2     172.17.10.0/24  omp           --        --         --            --    100.100.1.5    mpls          ipsec  F,S
2     172.17.10.0/24  omp           --        --         --            --    100.100.1.5    biz-internet  ipsec  F,S
2     172.17.20.0/24  connected     --        loopback2  --            --    --             --            --     F,S

vEdge02#
vEdge02# ping vpn 2 172.17.10.1 count 3
Ping in VPN 2
PING 172.17.10.1 (172.17.10.1) 56(84) bytes of data.
64 bytes from 172.17.10.1: icmp_seq=1 ttl=64 time=2.12 ms
64 bytes from 172.17.10.1: icmp_seq=2 ttl=64 time=2.39 ms
64 bytes from 172.17.10.1: icmp_seq=3 ttl=64 time=1.89 ms

--- 172.17.10.1 ping statistics ---
3 packets transmitted, 3 received, 0% packet loss, time 2002ms
rtt min/avg/max/mdev = 1.899/2.140/2.393/0.201 ms
vEdge02#
```

*Figure 9-60.* *MPLS routes*

Our tunnels are also up (Figure 9-61).

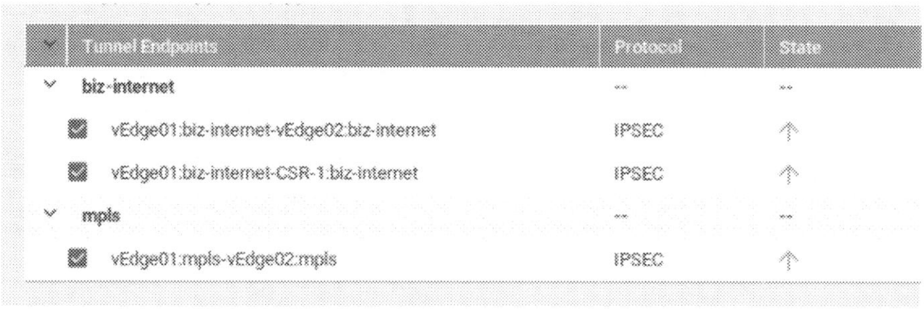

| Tunnel Endpoints | Protocol | State |
|---|---|---|
| ∨   biz-internet | ~~ | ~~ |
| ☑      vEdge01:biz-internet-vEdge02:biz-internet | IPSEC | ↑ |
| ☑      vEdge01:biz-internet-CSR-1:biz-internet | IPSEC | ↑ |
| ∨   mpls | ~~ | ~~ |
| ☑      vEdge01:mpls-vEdge02:mpls | IPSEC | ↑ |

***Figure 9-61.*** *MPLS IPSec tunnels*

Let's move on to configuring CSR-1. Start by editing the c-VPN0 template, and add another device-specific IPv4 route. If you are finding the similar variable names a bit confusing, then you can customize them to make them easier to identify. We can call our new route "secondary_def_route" and the next hop can be called "secondary_dg" (Figure 9-62).

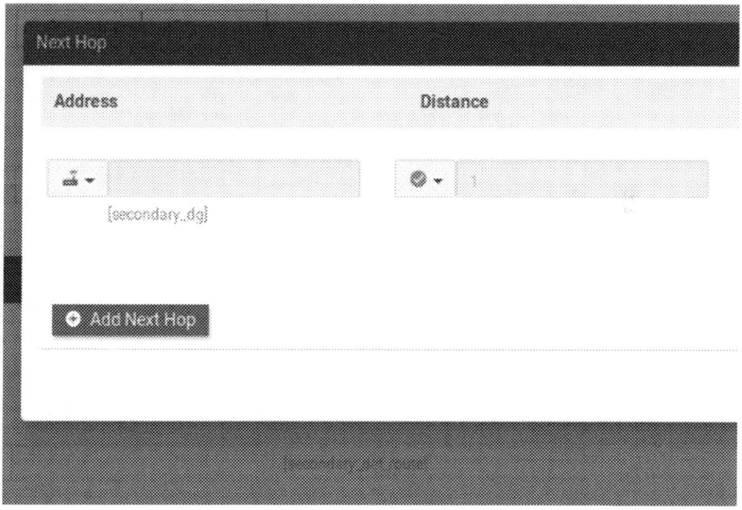

***Figure 9-62.*** *Secondary default gateway on CSR-1*

Add this new route to the template (Figure 9-63).

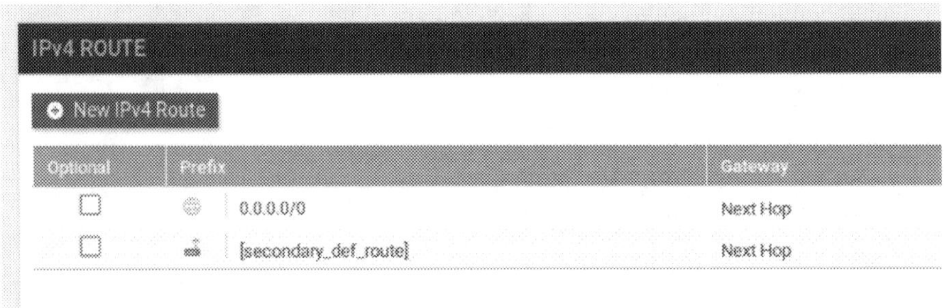

*Figure 9-63.* *The new route is added to the template*

Update the template and update the values with a new default route (secondary_def_route) to 0.0.0.0/0 using the next-hop address – which in the template is referred to as Address(secondary_dg) of 60.20.20.254 (Figure 9-64).

*Figure 9-64.* *Setting the default route variables*

We should now have two default routes:

```
CSR-1#sh run | i ip route
ip route 0.0.0.0 0.0.0.0 50.10.10.254
ip route 0.0.0.0 0.0.0.0 60.20.20.254
CSR-1#
```

Copy the MPLS-Int-vEdge template as MPLS-Int-cEdge, and change the device model (by clicking the three dots at the right-hand side) (Figure 9-65).

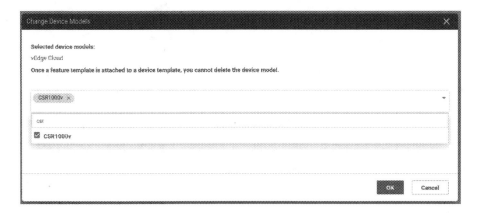

**Figure 9-65.** *Changing the device model*

The other new template copies we need are shown in Table 9-2, but remember to change the device model to CSR1000v on each of the new templates.

**Table 9-2.** *The template changes for CSR-1*

| Template to copy | New template name | Edits |
| --- | --- | --- |
| v-BGP | c-BGP | None |
| v-Loopback2 | c-Loopback2 | Capitalize the interface name |
| vEdge-VPN2 | cEdge-VPN2 | None |

Now edit the t-CSR1000v device template, and set the second VPN interface under VPN 0 (Figure 9-66).

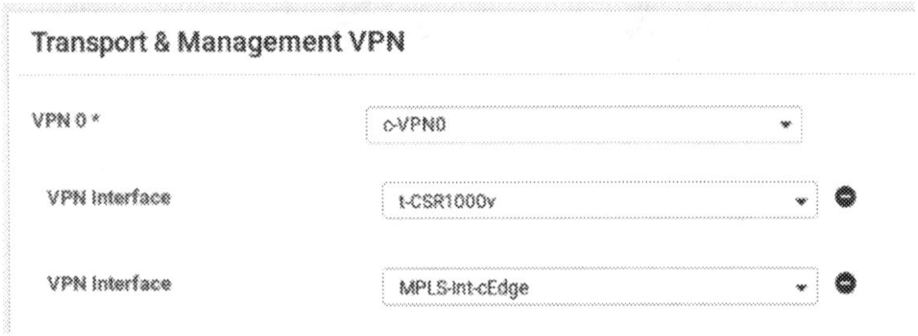

Transport & Management VPN

VPN 0 *                    c-VPN0

    VPN Interface          t-CSR1000v

    VPN Interface          MPLS-Int-cEdge

***Figure 9-66.***  *Adding the second VPN interface*

Then create a new service VPN using our new templates (Figure 9-67).

VPN                        cEdge-VPN2

BGP                        c-BGP

    VPN Interface          c-Loopback2              Sub-Templates ▾

***Figure 9-67.***  *The new service VPN*

Update the template, and push the new configurations, adding the device-specific information, similar to how we did for the vEdges.

Once the configuration has been pushed to the CSR-1, we should have connectivity to it from vEdge01 (Figure 9-68).

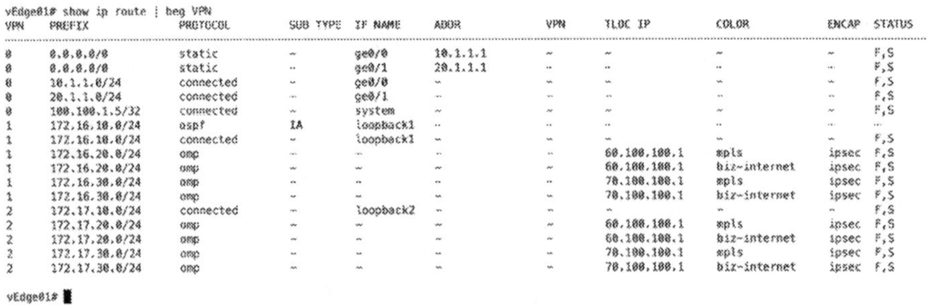

```
vEdge01# show ip route | beg VPN
VPN   PREFIX         PROTOCOL     SUB TYPE  IF NAME    ADDR        VPN   TLOC IP         COLOR         ENCAP  STATUS

0     0.0.0.0/0      static       ~         ge0/0      10.1.1.1    ~     ~               ~             ~      F,S
0     0.0.0.0/0      static       ~         ge0/1      20.1.1.1    ~     ~               ~             ~      F,S
0     10.1.1.0/24    connected    ~         ge0/0      ~           ~     ~               ~             ~      F,S
0     20.1.1.0/24    connected    ~         ge0/1      ~           ~     ~               ~             ~      F,S
0     100.100.1.5/32 connected    ~         system     ~           ~     ~               ~             ~      F,S
1     172.16.10.0/24 ospf         IA        loopback1  ~           ~     ~               ~             ~      ...
1     172.16.10.0/24 connected    ~         loopback1  ~           ~     ~               ~             ~      F,S
1     172.16.20.0/24 omp          ~         ~          ~           ~     60.100.100.1    mpls          ipsec  F,S
1     172.16.20.0/24 omp          ~         ~          ~           ~     60.100.100.1    biz-internet  ipsec  F,S
1     172.16.30.0/24 omp          ~         ~          ~           ~     70.100.100.1    mpls          ipsec  F,S
1     172.16.30.0/24 omp          ~         ~          ~           ~     70.100.100.1    biz-internet  ipsec  F,S
2     172.17.10.0/24 connected    ~         loopback2  ~           ~     ~               ~             ~      F,S
2     172.17.20.0/24 omp          ~         ~          ~           ~     60.100.100.1    mpls          ipsec  F,S
2     172.17.20.0/24 omp          ~         ~          ~           ~     60.100.100.1    biz-internet  ipsec  F,S
2     172.17.30.0/24 omp          ~         ~          ~           ~     70.100.100.1    mpls          ipsec  F,S
2     172.17.30.0/24 omp          ~         ~          ~           ~     70.100.100.1    biz-internet  ipsec  F,S

vEdge01#
```

***Figure 9-68.***  *More routes advertised into OMP*

```
vEdge01# ping vpn 2 172.17.30.1 count 3
Ping in VPN 2
PING 172.17.30.1 (172.17.30.1) 56(84) bytes of data.
64 bytes from 172.17.30.1: icmp_seq=1 ttl=255 time=2.78 ms
64 bytes from 172.17.30.1: icmp_seq=2 ttl=255 time=2.74 ms
64 bytes from 172.17.30.1: icmp_seq=3 ttl=255 time=2.73 ms

--- 172.17.30.1 ping statistics ---
3 packets transmitted, 3 received, 0% packet loss, time 2003ms
rtt min/avg/max/mdev = 2.736/2.754/2.783/0.063 ms
vEdge01#
```

Now we have two routing protocols routing!

While the routing table shows the biz-internet and mpls colors in the other VPNs, it is important to show that they are not reachable. We can test this by pinging vEdge02's second (BGP) loopback from VPN 1 on vEdge01 and by pinging vEdge02's first (OSPF) loopback interface from VPN 2 on vEdge01:

```
vEdge01# ping vpn 1 172.17.20.1 count 3
Ping in VPN 1
PING 172.17.20.1 (172.17.20.1) 56(84) bytes of data.
From 127.1.0.2 icmp_seq=1 Destination Net Unreachable
From 127.1.0.2 icmp_seq=2 Destination Net Unreachable
From 127.1.0.2 icmp_seq=3 Destination Net Unreachable

--- 172.17.20.1 ping statistics ---
3 packets transmitted, 0 received, +3 errors, 100% packet loss

vEdge01# ping vpn 2 172.16.20.1 count 3
Ping in VPN 2
PING 172.16.20.1 (172.16.20.1) 56(84) bytes of data.
From 127.1.0.2 icmp_seq=1 Destination Net Unreachable
```

```
From 127.1.0.2 icmp_seq=2 Destination Net Unreachable
From 127.1.0.2 icmp_seq=3 Destination Net Unreachable

--- 172.16.20.1 ping statistics ---
3 packets transmitted, 0 received, +3 errors, 100% packet loss

vEdge01#
```

Now that we have completed this routing, let's go into the mechanics of SD-WAN routing, by answering the question: "If we receive the same paths for the same route from different peers, then which route will be chosen?"

# SD-WAN Routing Preference

The order of route preference is as follows:

1. Check that the OMP route is valid. Invalid routes will be ignored.

2. Prefer the route with the lowest administrative distance (AD).

3. If the AD values are equal, then prefer the route with the higher preference.

4. If the preference values are equal, then the route with the highest TLOC preference is chosen.

5. If the TLOC preference values match, then the route is selected in the following order:

   Connected

   a. Static

   b. EBGP

   c.   OPSF Intra-area

   d.   OSPF inter-area

   e.   OSPF external

   f.   iBGP

   g.   Unknown

6.   If the origins are the same, then the route with the lower IGP metric is chosen.

7.   Should the origin type an IGP metric, match then the route that comes from the system with the higher router ID.

8.   If the router IDs are equal, then the router with the higher private IP address is chosen.

If all the attributes match, then both the routes are used. By default, we can have up to four equal routes.

# Configuration to Template Overview

Before we leave this chapter and move on to policies, we are going to go through one of the vEdge configurations as they are now and match the configurations to the templates; this is shown in Table 9-3. It will serve as a handy reference if you have any configuration issues and need to locate the correct template.

***Table 9-3.***  *Configurations matched to template*

| Configuration | Template |
|---|---|
| vEdge01# show run | |
| system<br>  host-name vEdge01<br>  location UK<br>  system-ip 100.100.1.5<br>  site-id 100<br>  admin-tech-on-failure<br>  no route-consistency-check | Basic Information/System |
| sp-organization-name<br>Learning_SD-WAN<br>  organization-name<br>Learning_SD-WAN<br>  vbond 10.1.1.3 | These are set during initial device creation |

(*continued*)

***Table 9-3.*** (*continued*)

| Configuration | Template |
|---|---|
| aaa | Basic Information/AAA |

```
aaa
 auth-order local radius tacacs
 usergroup basic
  task system read write
  task interface read write
  !
 usergroup netadmin
  !
 usergroup operator
  task system read
  task interface read
  task policy read
  task routing read
  task security read
  !
 user admin
  password <password>
  !
 user net-ops
  password <password>
  group    operator
  !
 !
```

(*continued*)

**Table 9-3.** (*continued*)

| Configuration | Template |
|---|---|
| logging<br> disk<br>  enable<br>  !<br>  !<br> ! | Other Templates/Logging |
| omp<br>no shutdown<br>graceful-restart<br>advertise bgp<br>advertise ospf external<br>advertise connected<br>advertise static<br>! | Basic Information/OMP |
| security<br>ipsec<br> authentication-type sha1-hmac<br>ah-sha1-hmac<br> !<br> ! | Basic Information/Security |
| banner<br> login "Hands off my SD-WAN!"<br> ! | Other Templates/Banner |
| vpn 0 | VPN/VPN |

(*continued*)

***Table 9-3.*** (*continued*)

| Configuration | Template |
|---|---|
| interface ge0/0<br>ip address 10.1.1.5/24<br>tunnel-interface<br>encapsulation ipsec<br>color biz-internet<br>no allow-service bgp<br>allow-service dhcp<br>allow-service dns<br>allow-service icmp<br>allow-service sshd<br>allow-service netconf<br>no allow-service ntp<br>no allow-service ospf<br>no allow-service stun<br>allow-service https<br>!<br>no shutdown<br>! | VPN/VPN Interface Ethernet |

(*continued*)

***Table 9-3.*** (*continued*)

| Configuration | Template |
|---|---|
| interface ge0/1 | VPN/VPN Interface Ethernet |
| description MPLS | |
| ip address 20.1.1.5/24 | |
| tunnel-interface | |
| encapsulation ipsec | |
| color mpls restrict | |
| max-control-connections 0 | |
| no allow-service bgp | |
| allow-service dhcp | |
| allow-service dns | |
| allow-service icmp | |
| no allow-service sshd | |
| no allow-service netconf | |
| no allow-service ntp | |
| no allow-service ospf | |
| no allow-service stun | |
| allow-service https | |
| ! | |
| no shutdown | |
| ! | |
| ip route 0.0.0.0/0 10.1.1.1 | VPN/VPN |
| ip route 0.0.0.0/0 20.1.1.1 | |
| ! | |
| vpn 1 | VPN/VPN |

(*continued*)

***Table* 9-3.**  (*continued*)

| Configuration | Template |
|---|---|
| router<br> ospf<br>  router-id 1.1.1.1<br>  timers spf 200 1000 10000<br>  area 0<br>   interface loopback1<br>   exit<br>  exit<br>  !<br>  ! | Other Templates/OSPF |
| interface loopback1<br>  ip address 172.16.10.1/24<br>  no shutdown<br>  !<br>  ! | VPN/VPN Interface Ethernet |
| vpn 2<br> name MPLS | VPN/VPN |
| router<br>  bgp 1<br>   router-id 1.1.1.1<br>   address-family ipv4-unicast<br>   network 172.17.10.0/24<br>   !<br>   !<br>   ! | Other Templates/BGP |

(*continued*)

***Table 9-3.*** (*continued*)

| Configuration | Template |
|---|---|
| `interface loopback2`<br>`  ip address 172.17.10.1/24`<br>`  no shutdown`<br>`  !`<br>`!` | VPN/VPN Interface Ethernet |
| `vpn 512` | VPN/VPN |
| `interface eth0`<br>`  ip dhcp-client`<br>`  no shutdown`<br>`  !`<br>`!` | VPN/VPN Interface Ethernet |
| `vEdge01#` | |

# Summary

In this chapter, we focused on OSPF and BGP routing within our network and saw how easy it is to leverage OMP to do all the hard work for us. We looked at the use of "colors" to differentiate our routing domains and the effects this can have on our network. We then looked at routing preference and finally at what parts of the different templates we have created so far correspond to which parts of a router's configuration.

In the next chapter, we are going to look at policies and quality of service.

# CHAPTER 10

# Policies and Quality of Service

In this chapter, we are going to look at how we can implement policies
in our SD-WAN network and use them to change a route metric and
implement a couple of simple quality of service policies.

The Cisco SD-WAN solution provides two types of policies, centralized
and localized (which will be explained later), and we can configure these
policies in two ways, via the vSmart CLI or through vManage. We are going
to use the latter, but to do this, we need to get vSmart in vManage mode,
rather than the CLI mode which it is in now. If we don't, then we will see
this error when we try to activate our policies (Figure 10-1).

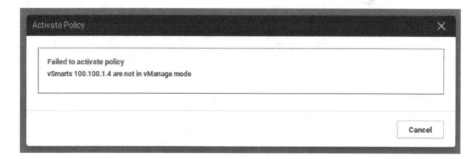

*Figure 10-1. vSmart mode error*

© Stuart Fordham 2021

S. Fordham, *Learning SD-WAN with Cisco*, https://doi.org/10.1007/978-1-4842-7347-0_10

To start, we need to head to *Configuration* ➤ *Devices* ➤ *Controllers* (Figure 10-2).

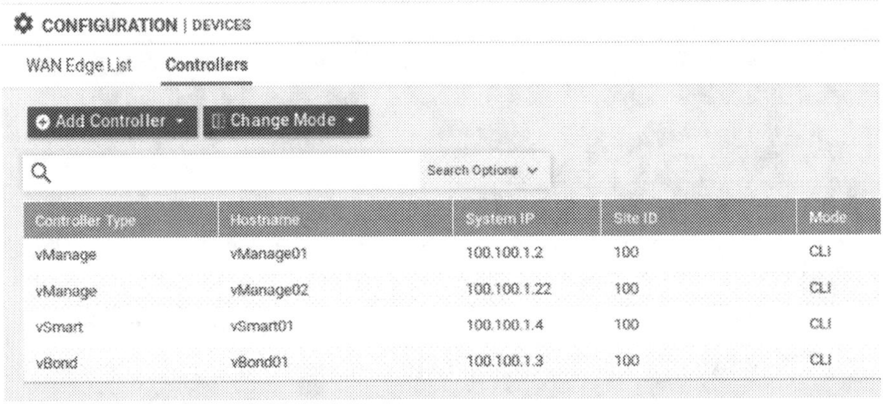

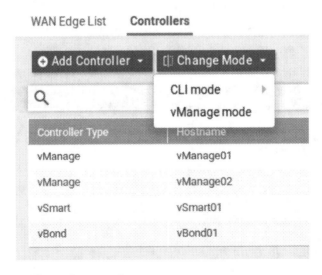

*Figure 10-2.* *The controllers menu*

Select vSmart01 and then click the Change Mode button (Figure 10-3).

*Figure 10-3.* *Changing modes*

Select "vManage Mode." We are told that we need to create a template first (Figure 10-4).

***Figure 10-4.***  *Changing vManage mode on vSmart01*

Navigate to *Configuration* ➤ *Templates* ➤ *Device,* and select the "Create Template" option, and then click "From Feature Template."

Whereas our edge device templates have been quite long, the vSmart template is much shorter. Select vSmart from the drop-down, and give it a name (such as "t-vSmart01") and description.

We can create a new system template, taking the default options. Under AAA, remember that the password will default to "admin," so change this to what you want it to be.

We need to create two new interface templates, as well as templates for VPN0 and VPN512. None of the configurations of our vSmart should change in the new template (unless you have a burning desire to do so), but the interface IP addresses should definitely remain the same. Save the template and attach it to the vSmart01 controller.

Fill in the details when prompted and check the config diff, making sure all is going to work; if not, then fix the templates, making sure there are no issues such as the ones in Figure 10-5.

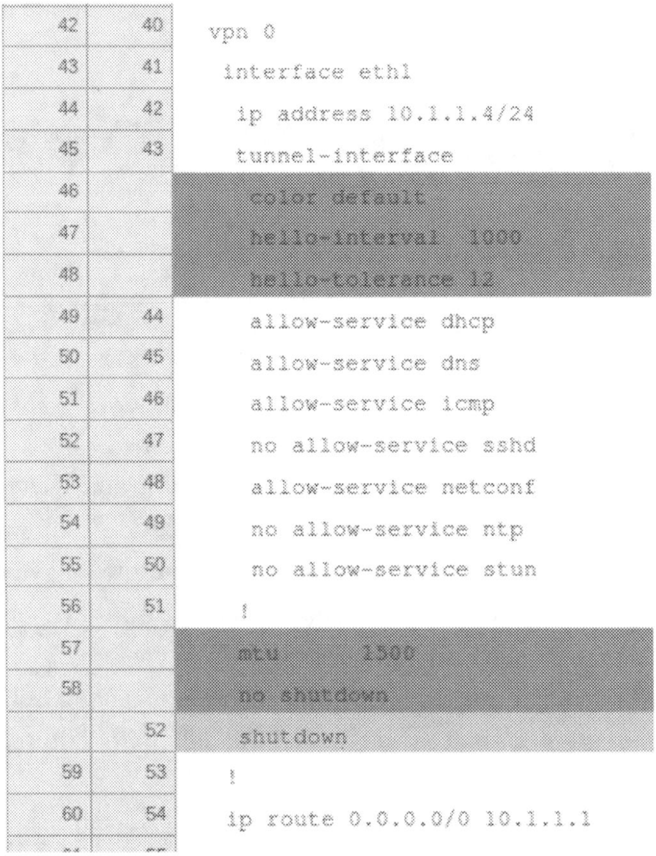

```
42   40   vpn 0
43   41     interface eth1
44   42       ip address 10.1.1.4/24
45   43       tunnel-interface
46              color default
47              hello-interval 1000
48              hello-tolerance 12
49   44         allow-service dhcp
50   45         allow-service dns
51   46         allow-service icmp
52   47         no allow-service sshd
53   48         allow-service netconf
54   49         no allow-service ntp
55   50         no allow-service stun
56   51       !
57            mtu        1500
58            no shutdown
     52       shutdown
59   53     !
60   54     ip route 0.0.0.0/0 10.1.1.1
```

*Figure 10-5.  Errors to avoid!*

If your template is good, then push the configuration onto vSmart01.

Once this has been completed, we should see that vSmart is now in vManage mode (Figure 10-6).

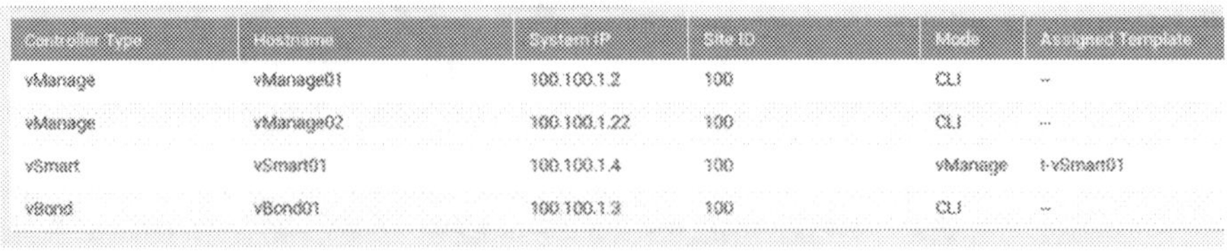

| Controller Type | Hostname | System IP | Site ID | Mode | Assigned Template |
|---|---|---|---|---|---|
| vManage | vManage01 | 100.100.1.2 | 100 | CLI | -- |
| vManage | vManage02 | 100.100.1.22 | 100 | CLI | ... |
| vSmart | vSmart01 | 100.100.1.4 | 100 | vManage | t-vSmart01 |
| vBond | vBond01 | 100.100.1.3 | 100 | CLI | -- |

*Figure 10-6.  vSmart is now in vManage mode*

Now that we have done this, we can use the vManage NMS GUI to create our policies, and then the vSmart can push them to our edge devices.

# Configuring Policies Through vManage

The first policy we are going to create is a local one.

## Localized Policies

Localized control policies affect the local site. This means anything behind the edge device (i.e., the local LAN) and not, for example, routes passed up and into the overlay network.

To show this, we need to turn off CSR-1, and add a vIOS router called "R300," connecting the GigabitEthernet3 interface of CSR-1 to Gi0/0 of the new router. Turn on both devices once they are created.

The new topology for site 300 should look like Figure 10-7.

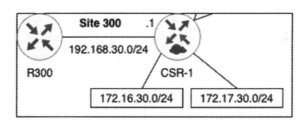

***Figure 10-7.*** *Adding R300*

Set up R300 with the following configuration:

```
R300#sh run
!
hostname R300
!
```

```
enable password Test123
!
username sd-admin password 0 Test123
!
interface GigabitEthernet0/0
 ip address 192.168.30.30 255.255.255.0
 no shut
 ip ospf 1 area 3
!
router ospf 1
!
ip http server
ip http secure-server
!
ip route 0.0.0.0 0.0.0.0 192.168.30.1
!
line vty 0 4
 login local
 transport input telnet ssh
!
end

R300#
```

Next, we need to configure CSR-1, and what we will do here is add another loopback interface and configure GigabitEthernet3.

Firstly, create a new feature template for a VPN interface, called c-Internal-LAN which references the physical interface GigabitEthernet3 and has an IP address of 192.168.30.1/24 (Figure 10-8).

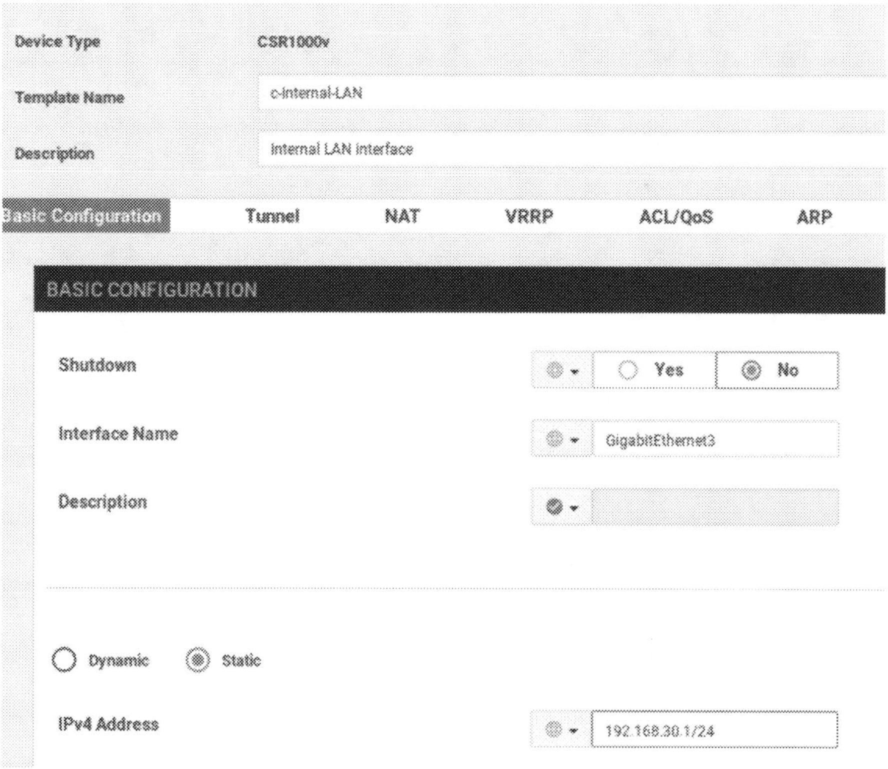

| Device Type | CSR1000v |
|---|---|
| Template Name | c-Internal-LAN |
| Description | Internal LAN interface |

| Basic Configuration | Tunnel | NAT | VRRP | ACL/QoS | ARP |
|---|---|---|---|---|---|

**BASIC CONFIGURATION**

| Shutdown | ⊕ ▾ | ○ Yes | ⊙ No |
|---|---|---|---|

| Interface Name | ⊕ ▾ | GigabitEthernet3 |
|---|---|---|

| Description | ⊘ ▾ | |
|---|---|---|

○ Dynamic  ⊙ Static

| IPv4 Address | ⊕ ▾ | 192.168.30.1/24 |
|---|---|---|

***Figure 10-8.*** *The c-Internal-LAN template*

Create another interface called c-Loopback3, this time referencing (you guessed it) Loopback3, with an IP address of 172.16.31.1/24 (Figure 10-9).

289

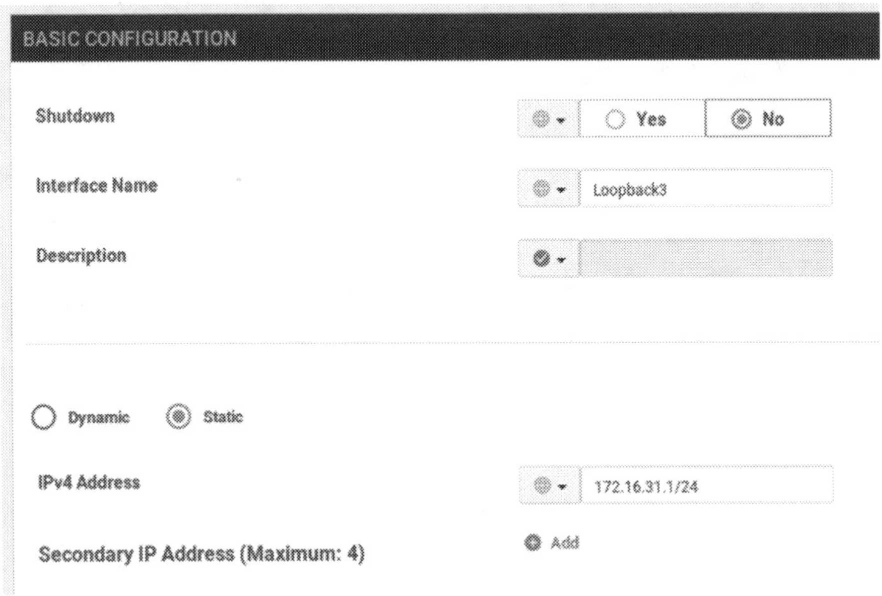

*Figure 10-9.* *The new loopback interface on CSR-1*

Save this, and then edit the c-v-OSPF feature template, adding a new interface under the Area section. Only add the GigabitEthernet3 interface at the moment, not the new loopback (Figure 10-10).

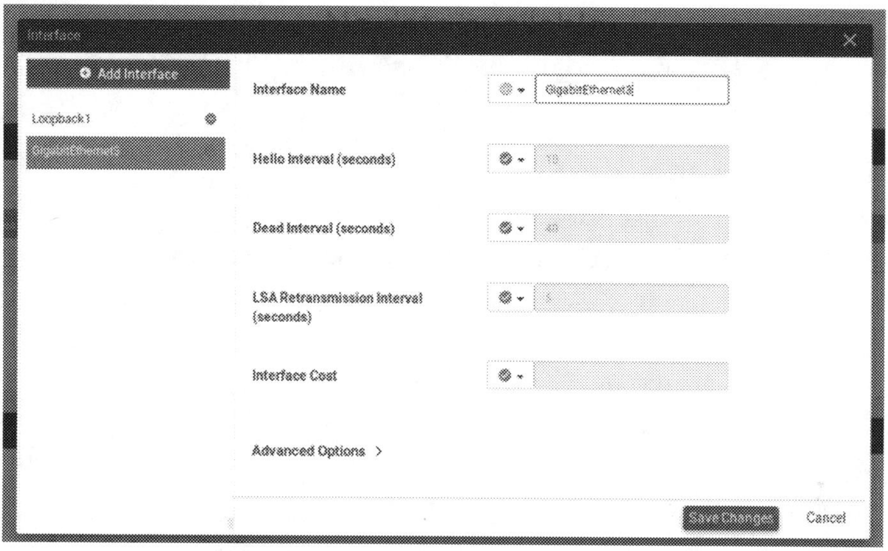

*Figure 10-10.  Editing the OSPF template*

Go back up to Redistribute, and click New Redistribute. Select Connected from the drop-down, and then click Add. Save the template.

Now, edit the CSR device template adding the new templates (Figure 10-11).

*Figure 10-11.  Adding the new interface templates to the CSR template*

291

Save and apply the template. Once the changes have been pushed to the device, we should get a good result when we try pinging CSR-1 from R300:

```
R300#ping 192.168.30.1
Type escape sequence to abort.
Sending 5, 100-byte ICMP Echos to 192.168.30.1, timeout is 2
seconds:
.!!!!
Success rate is 80 percent (4/5), round-trip min/avg/max =
1/6/21 ms
R300#
*May  7 11:01:47.812: %OSPF-5-ADJCHG: Process 1, Nbr 3.3.3.3 on
GigabitEthernet0/0 from LOADING to FULL, Loading Done
GigabitEthernet0/0 is up, line protocol is up
R300#
```

Once OSPF forms an adjacency, we should see CSR-1's new loopback interface in the routing table of R300:

```
R300#sh ip route ospf | b Gateway
Gateway of last resort is not set

      172.16.0.0/16 is variably subnetted, 2 subnets, 2 masks
O        172.16.30.1/32 [110/2] via 192.168.30.1, 01:36:32, Gi0/0
O E2     172.16.31.0/24
            [110/20] via 192.168.30.1, 01:11:07, Gi0/0
R300#
R300#sh ip route 172.16.31.0
Routing entry for 172.16.31.0/24
  Known via "ospf 1", distance 110, metric 20, type extern 2,
  forward metric 1
  Last update from 192.168.30.1 on GigabitEthernet0/0,
  01:11:45 ago
```

```
  Routing Descriptor Blocks:
  * 192.168.30.1, from 3.3.3.3, 01:11:45 ago, via GigabitEthernet0/0
      Route metric is 20, traffic share count is 1
R300#
```

The new 192.168.30.0/24 prefix has also been advertised up to the
other edge routers:

```
vEdge02# show ip routes 192.168.30.0/24 detail
Codes Proto-sub-type:
  IA -> ospf-intra-area, IE -> ospf-inter-area,
  E1 -> ospf-external1, E2 -> ospf-external2,
  N1 -> ospf-nssa-external1, N2 -> ospf-nssa-external2,
  e -> bgp-external, i -> bgp-internal
Codes Status flags:
  F -> fib, S -> selected, I -> inactive,
  B -> blackhole, R -> recursive

---------------------------------------------
VPN 1       PREFIX 192.168.30.0/24
---------------------------------------------

proto           omp
distance        250
metric          0
uptime          0:01:50:32
tloc-ip         70.100.100.1
tloc-color      mpls
tloc-encap      ipsec
nexthop-label   1001
status          F,S
```

```
---------------------------------------------
VPN 1       PREFIX 192.168.30.0/24
---------------------------------------------
proto           omp
distance        250
metric          0
uptime          0:01:50:32
tloc-ip         70.100.100.1
tloc-color      biz-internet
tloc-encap      ipsec
nexthop-label   1001
status          F,S

vEdge02#
```

Now, let's use some policies to tweak this new route. We start by going to *Configuration* ➤ *Policies* and selecting the localized policies option (Figure 10-12).

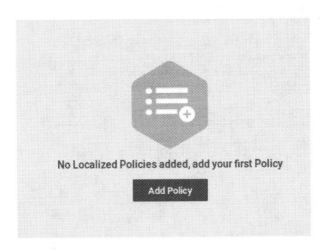

*Figure 10-12.* *Localized policies*

Click Add Policy. With any policy, be it localized or centralized, we need to create our "Groups of Interest." These are the building blocks of any route maps or access lists that we will be creating; these lists allow the solution to scope policies and can be used through the entire network. We can match the following information as shown in Table 10-1.

***Table 10-1.*** *The Groups of Interest*

| List type | Purpose |
|---|---|
| AS Paths | List AS paths |
| Communities | List one or more BGP communities |
| Extended Communities | List one or more BGP extended communities |
| Prefixes | List one or more IP prefixes |

It is important to note that these are not the only Groups of Interest. They are the only ones applicable for *this* task, as you can see in Table 10-4 later on.

Within the "Create Groups of Interest" section, click "Prefix" and select the "New Prefix List" option. Create a prefix list with the name Site300-172-16-31, and then add the prefix 172.16.31.0/24 (Figure 10-13).

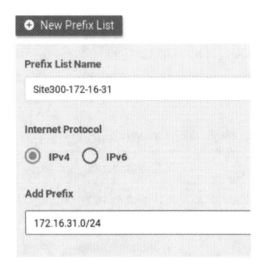

***Figure 10-13.***  *Creating a prefix list*

Click Add so that it is added to the template (Figure 10-14).

| Name | Entries | Internet Protocol |
| --- | --- | --- |
| Site300-172-16-31 | 172.16.31.0/24 | IPv4 |

***Figure 10-14.***  *The prefix listc is added to the template*

Click Next. We are not going to do any QoS mapping or policy rewriting, so click Next past that screen. Likewise, we are not going to configure any access lists, so click Next again.

The type of policy we will be creating is a localized control policy, which affects the BGP or (in our case) OSPF routing in the local site. The other type of local policy is called a localized data policy, which uses access lists applied to an interface (or interfaces) to permit or deny traffic based on a six-tuple match (source and destination IP addresses, source and destination ports, DSCP fields, and the protocol number).

Click *Add Route Policy* ➤ *Create New*, call it route-pol-172-16-31, and give it a description.

Each policy starts with a default deny action, so we need to add sequences that match our traffic and perform actions on them (Figure 10-15).

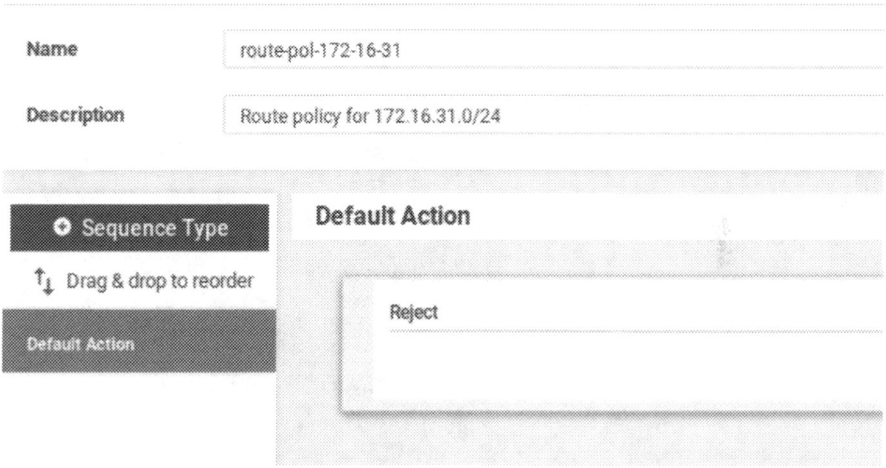

| Name | route-pol-172-16-31 |
| Description | Route policy for 172.16.31.0/24 |

| ⊕ Sequence Type | **Default Action** |
| ↑↓ Drag & drop to reorder | |
| Default Action | Reject |

*Figure 10-15.* *The default policy*

We can match the following (Table 10-2).

*Table 10-2.*  *Our match options*

| Option | Matches |
|--------|---------|
| Address | IP prefix list |
| AS Path List | BGP AS path list |
| Community List | BGP community list |
| Extended Community List | BGP extended community list |
| BGP Local Preference | BGP local preference |
| Metric | Route metric (0 – 4294967295) |
| Next Hop | IP prefix list |
| OMP Tag | OMP tag (0 – 4294967295) |
| Origin | BGP origin code (ebgp, igp, incomplete) |
| OSPF Tag | OSPF tag (0 – 4294967295) |
| Peer | IP address |

Click Sequence Type, select Address as the match option, and select the Site300-172-16-31 prefix list from the list (Figure 10-16).

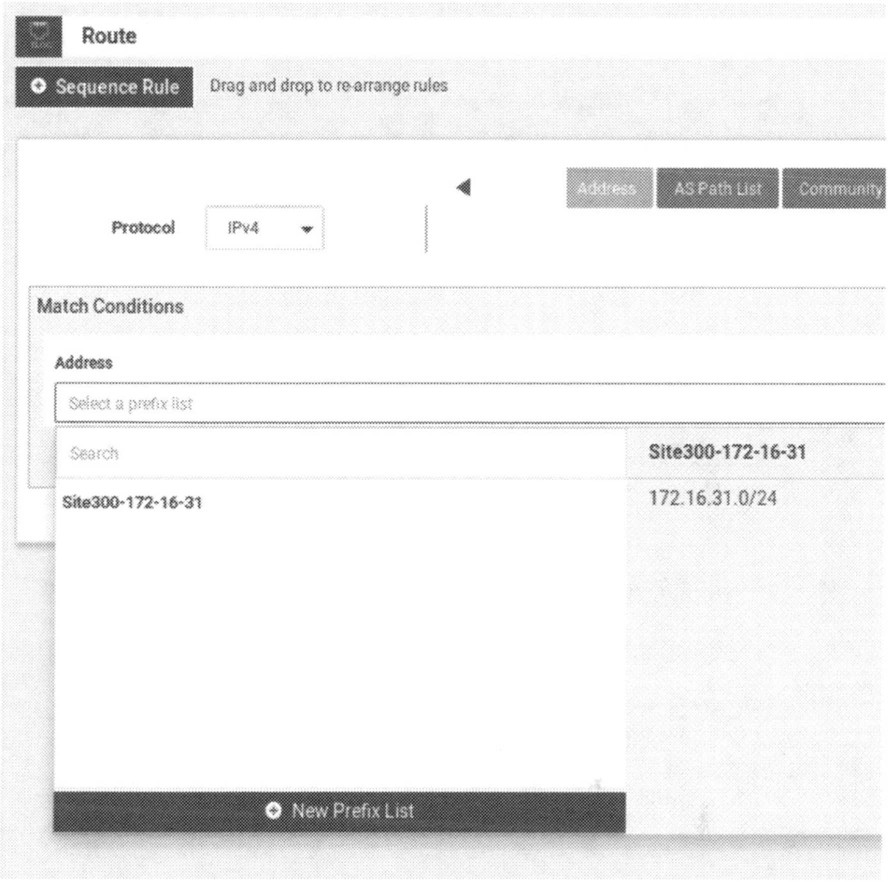

***Figure 10-16.*** *Selecting the prefix list*

Select Actions. By default, all the sequences are set to have an action of Reject. Set the action to Accept (Figure 10-17).

***Figure 10-17.*** *Set the action to Accept*

The actions we can set are shown in Table 10-3.

***Table 10-3.*** *The actions we can set*

| Option | Action |
|---|---|
| Aggregator | Set the AS number and IP address of the BGP route aggregator |
| AS Path | Set an AS number or series of AS numbers to either exclude or prepend to the AS path |
| Atomic Aggregate | Set the BGP atomic aggregate |
| Community | Set the BGP Community |
| Local Preference | Set the BGP local preference |
| Metric | Set the metric value |
| Metric Type | Set the metric type |
| Next Hop | Set the next-hop IP address |
| OMP Tag | Set the OMP tag that OMP will use |
| Origin | Set the BGP origin |
| Originator | Set the IP address from which the route was learned |
| OSPF Tag | Set the OSPF tag |
| Weight | Set the BGP weight |

Select Metric and set it to 25 (Figure 10-18).

*Figure 10-18.* *Setting the Metric*

Click "Save Match and Actions" (Figure 10-19).

*Figure 10-19.* *Saving the match conditions*

Edit the Default Action, and set it to "Accept" (because we want our other traffic to pass) (Figure 10-20).

*Figure 10-20.* *Setting the Default Action*

Click "Save Route Policy," and then click Next. In the final screen, name the policy "Policy-Site-300" (Figure 10-21).

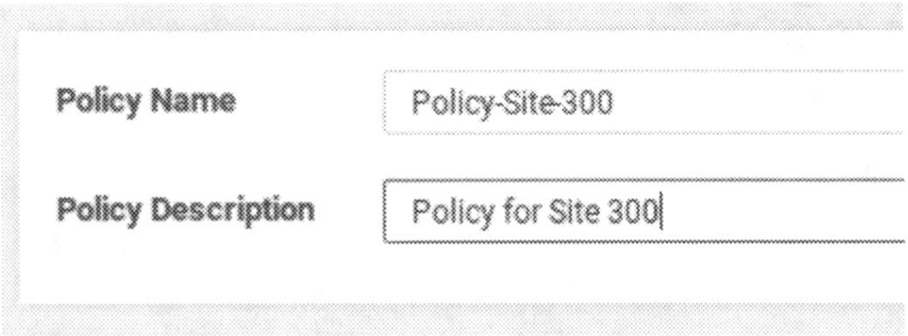

| Policy Name | Policy-Site-300 |
| --- | --- |
| Policy Description | Policy for Site 300 |

***Figure 10-21.*** *Setting the policy name*

Click "Save Policy." We need to now attach this to our templates. Edit the t-CSR1000v device template and scroll to Additional Templates. From the Policy drop-down, select the Policy-Site-300 policy (Figure 10-22).

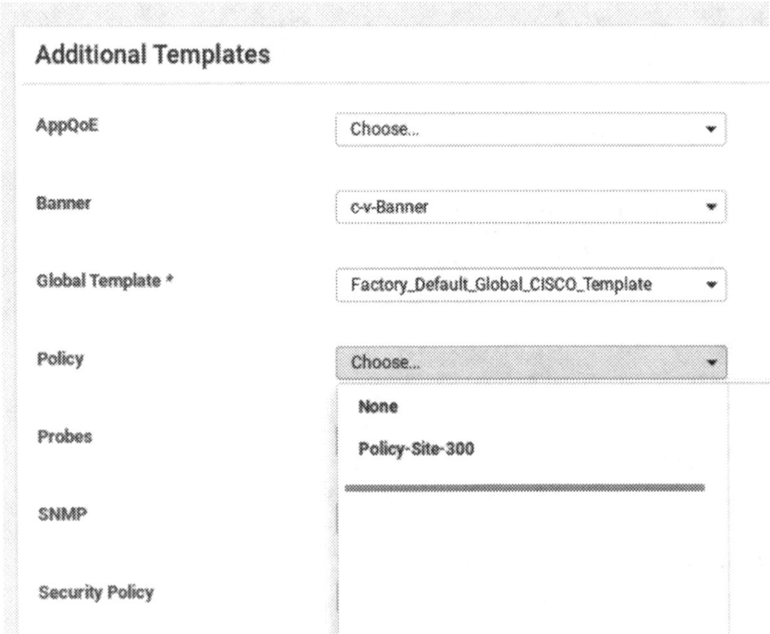

## Additional Templates

| AppQoE | Choose... |
| --- | --- |
| Banner | c-v-Banner |
| Global Template * | Factory_Default_Global_CISCO_Template |
| Policy | Choose... |
| | None |
| Probes | Policy-Site-300 |
| SNMP | |
| Security Policy | |

***Figure 10-22.*** *Adding the policy to the device template*

Update the template and configure the device.

Once this has been completed, go back to the c-v-OSPF template, and edit the redistribute section we created earlier, this time adding a route policy of "route-pol-172.16-31" (Figure 10-23).

**Figure 10-23.** *Setting the route policy*

Click "Save Changes" (Figure 10-24).

**Figure 10-24.** *The redistribute settings*

Update the template and apply it to the devices.

The result is that R300 now has the same route (172.16.31.0/24), but with a metric of 25 (instead of 20 as it was before):

```
R300#sh ip route 172.16.31.0
Routing entry for 172.16.31.0/24
  Known via "ospf 1", distance 110, metric 25, type extern 2,
  forward metric 1
  Last update from 192.168.30.1 on GigabitEthernet0/0,
  00:02:03 ago
```

```
Routing Descriptor Blocks:
* 192.168.30.1, from 3.3.3.3, 00:02:03 ago, via
GigabitEthernet0/0
    Route metric is 25, traffic share count is 1
R300#
```

While this is a very simplistic example, the control we can leverage over our local routing is very complex, such as changing the metric on all routes received for a particular peer, so that our traffic is routed over higher-speed links.

Let's see what we can do with a centralized policy.

# Centralized Policies

Centralized policies affect our routing in the overlay network, these are a compound of data and control policies together. Although they are configured on the vManage NMS (as everything is), they are handled by the vSmart controllers (as the vSmart controller is our "routing brain").

Once we have onboarded the vEdge devices, they begin to advertise their routes to the vSmart controller. The controller builds up the routing table and advertises these back out, a little similar to BGP route reflectors.

We can see the routes received using the command "show omp routes received"; the output is quite lengthy, so I have truncated it just to show the prefixes received:

```
vSmart01# show omp routes received | i vpn
omp route entries for vpn 1 route 172.16.10.0/24
omp route entries for vpn 1 route 172.16.20.0/24
omp route entries for vpn 1 route 172.16.30.0/24
omp route entries for vpn 1 route 172.16.31.0/24
```

```
omp route entries for vpn 1 route 192.168.30.0/24
omp route entries for vpn 2 route 172.17.10.0/24
omp route entries for vpn 2 route 172.17.20.0/24
omp route entries for vpn 2 route 172.17.30.0/24
vSmart01#
```

We can also see the prefixes that the vSmart controller advertises back out:

```
vSmart01# show omp routes advertised | b VPN
VPN     PREFIX
----------------------------
1       172.16.10.0/24
1       172.16.20.0/24
1       172.16.30.0/24
1       172.16.31.0/24
1       192.168.30.0/24
2       172.17.10.0/24
2       172.17.20.0/24
2       172.17.30.0/24

vSmart01#
```

Let's dig in deeper by looking at a Wireshark capture of a ping between vEdge01 and R300 (R300-pre-qos.pcapng) (Figure 10-25).

```
↦    11 24.583390     172.16.10.1                       192.168.30.30

▶ Frame 11: 98 bytes on wire (784 bits), 98 bytes captured (784 bits) on interface 0
▶ Ethernet II, Src: 50:00:00:04:00:02 (50:00:00:04:00:02), Dst: 50:00:00:08:00:00 (50:00:00:08:00:00)
▼ Internet Protocol Version 4, Src: 172.16.10.1 (172.16.10.1), Dst: 192.168.30.30 (192.168.30.30)
    0100 .... = Version: 4
    .... 0101 = Header Length: 20 bytes (5)
  ▼ Differentiated Services Field: 0x00 (DSCP: CS0, ECN: Not-ECT)
      0000 00.. = Differentiated Services Codepoint: Default (0)
      .... ..00 = Explicit Congestion Notification: Not ECN-Capable Transport (0)
    Total Length: 84
    Identification: 0x3289 (12937)
  ▶ Flags: 0x4000, Don't fragment
    ...0 0000 0000 0000 = Fragment offset: 0
    Time to live: 63
    Protocol: ICMP (1)
    Header checksum: 0x7448 [validation disabled]
    [Header checksum status: Unverified]
    Source: 172.16.10.1 (172.16.10.1)
    Destination: 192.168.30.30 (192.168.30.30)
▶ Internet Control Message Protocol
```

***Figure 10-25.*** *Our first PCAP*

As expected, we have no QoS applied. Let's use a centralized policy to implement a little quality of service.

The creation of a centralized profile is very similar to a local one; we head to *Configuration* ➤ *Policies* (Figure 10-26).

No Centralized Policies added, add your first Policy

**Add Policy**

***Figure 10-26.*** *Adding a centralized policy*

Click Add Policy. We need to create our Groups of Interest and these can be as shown in Table 10-4.

***Table 10-4.*** *Groups of Interest*

| List type | Purpose |
|---|---|
| Application | There are inbuilt application lists for Microsoft and Google apps, or you can create your own list from the applications on the system |
| Color | Create a list of VPN colors |
| Data Prefix | IP prefix list used in data policies |
| Policer | Configure burst and exceed traffic rules |
| Prefix | IP prefix list used in control policies |
| Site | A list of sites |
| SLA Class | Used with application-aware routing, defines jitter, latency, and loss |
| TLOC | A list of TLOCs |
| VPN | A list of VPNs |

Click the Site option, and click "New Site List." Call it Site-300 and enter 300 in the box below (Figure 10-27).

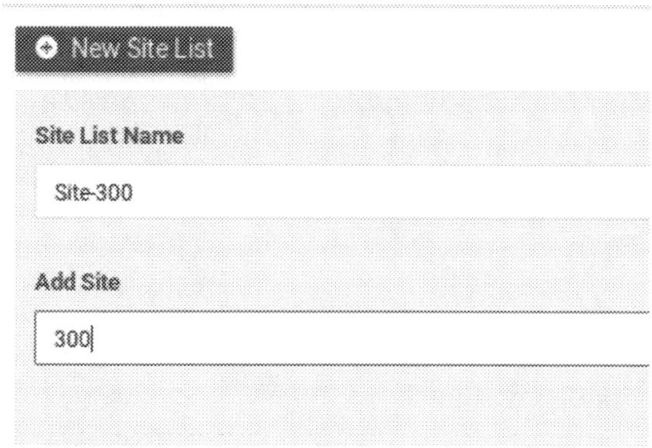

***Figure 10-27.*** *A site list*

Click Add. Repeat this for sites 200 and 100 (Figure 10-28).

| Name | Entries | Reference Count |
|------|---------|-----------------|
| Site-300 | 300 | 0 |
| Site-100 | 100 | 0 |
| Site-200 | 200 | 0 |

***Figure 10-28.*** *Three site lists*

Click VPN and then "New VPN List." Enter 1 in the box below, and click "Add." Create another for VPN-2 (Figure 10-29).

| Name | Entries | Reference Count |
|------|---------|-----------------|
| VPN-1 | 1 | 0 |
| VPN-2 | 2 | 0 |

***Figure 10-29.*** *VPN lists*

Click Next. We then need to configure a topology and VPN membership. Our options for topology are *Hub-and-Spoke, Mesh, Custom Control (Route & TLOC),* or *"Import Existing Topology."* Hub-and-Spoke and Mesh are the typical network designs, and Route and TLOC give us options for matching OMP routes, or TLOCs.

While the options are listed as "and," as in "Topology **and** VPN membership" or "Route **&** TLOC," in reality, they are more of an "and/or." So, for the moment, let's just create a rule based on the VPN membership.

VPN memberships match sites to VPNs; once these are applied, then interfaces can only be in the VPNs listed. For example, if site 100 only has VPNs 1 and 2, and we were to add a loopback interface in VPN 100, then while the edge device may be provisioned with this new loopback interface, it would be isolated from the rest of the overlay. Without a VPN membership policy, routers can have any VPN deployed without any restrictions.

Select VPN Membership, and click "Add VPN Membership Policy." Create a VPN list matching each site to the two VPNs (Figure 10-30).

***Figure 10-30.*** *Creating a VPN membership policy*

Click "Save," and then click "Next." Now, we need to create our traffic rules, which can be based on Application-Aware Routing, Traffic Data, or Cflowd (which is used for monitoring traffic flows). Select Traffic Data, and click Add Policy and then Create New.

Give the new policy a name of Site-300-Central-Pol and a description. Click the button to add a new Sequence Type (Figure 10-31).

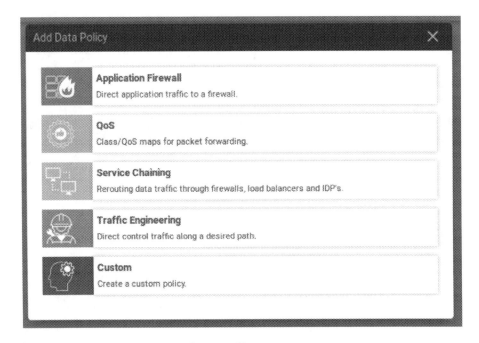

*Figure 10-31.* *Creating a data policy*

We have five options. We can send application traffic to a firewall, implement QoS, or manipulate traffic to send it through a service such as a firewall or a load balancer, or we can send the traffic along the path of our choosing. We can also have a custom policy.

QoS is the easiest for us to test, given our environment. We can use the policies to change the drop probability of our traffic. By default, none of our traffic will have a differentiated services code point (DSCP) value, which is used by DiffServ to mark traffic for classification, or any other marker. These markers are separated into levels of "drop probability," where a lower drop probability is better, whereas a higher drop probability means the traffic is more likely to be dropped. There are different markers, and these originate from different quality of service implementations throughout the years. We have the class selector (CS0, CS1, and so on) which maps to the IP precedence, a field used before DiffServ. We also have AF values, for Assured Forwarding, an IETF standard for the assurance of delivery, as long as the traffic does not exceed a subscribed rate. If it does, then that traffic has a higher probability of being dropped if there is congestion in the network.

The values possible are as follows (along with EF, or expedited forwarding, which is DSCP 46).

| Drop probability | Assured forwarding | DSCP | Binary | Class |
|---|---|---|---|---|
| Low | AF11 | 10 | 001010 | 1 |
| Low | AF21 | 18 | 010010 | 2 |
| Low | AF31 | 26 | 011010 | 3 |
| Low | AF41 | 34 | 100010 | 4 |
| Medium | AF12 | 12 | 001100 | 1 |
| Medium | AF22 | 20 | 010100 | 2 |
| Medium | AF32 | 28 | 011100 | 3 |
| Medium | AF42 | 36 | 100100 | 4 |
| High | AF13 | 14 | 001110 | 1 |
| High | AF23 | 22 | 010110 | 2 |
| High | AF33 | 30 | 011110 | 3 |
| High | AF43 | 38 | 100110 | 4 |

We are going to use these to make the traffic from vEdge01 have the highest importance available. Start by selecting QoS, and click the option to create a new sequence rule. Create a new rule with the following settings:

Match:

- Source Data Prefix: 172.16.10.0/24

- Protocol: 1

- Destination Data Prefix: 192.168.30.0/24

- DSCP: 0

Set:

- DSCP: 10

We are matching any source IP address in the 172.16.10.0/24 network, sending any ICMP traffic (protocol 1) to any IP in the 192.168.30.0/24 network, with a DSCP value of 0. If the traffic matches, then it will have a DSCP value of 10 applied (Figure 10-32).

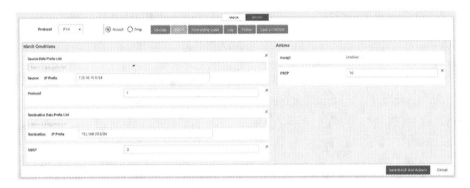

***Figure 10-32.***  *Our QoS rule*

Click "Save Match and Actions," and set the default action to Accept. Click "Save Data Policy" once this has been done. On the last page, name the policy "Site-300-QoS," and give it a description. Next, create a "New Site List and VPN List." Select "From Service" and add all three sites and VPN-1 (Figure 10-33).

Site-300-Central-Pol

**⊕ New Site List and VPN List**

◉ From Service   ○ From Tunnel   ○ All

Select Site List

Site-300 ×   Site-100 ×   Site-200 ×

Select VPN List

VPN-1 ×

***Figure 10-33.*** *The site and VPN list*

Click Add to save the VPN list. Next, click Preview and look through the settings. Then click Save Policy. On the next page, click the three dots and select "Activate."

Run Wireshark on R300's Gi0/0 interface (by right-clicking R300, selecting "Capture," and then selecting the Gi0/0 interface), and ping from vEdge01 (`ping vpn 1 192.168.30.30`) (Figure 10-34). Then do the same from vEdge02 (Figure 10-35). We can see the difference (R300-post-qos. pcapng).

```
     6 10.278266    172.16.10.1                    192.168.30.30

▶ Frame 6: 98 bytes on wire (784 bits), 98 bytes captured (784 bits) on interface 0
▶ Ethernet II, Src: 50:00:00:04:00:02 (50:00:00:04:00:02), Dst: 50:00:00:08:00:00 (50:00:00:08:00:00)
▼ Internet Protocol Version 4, Src: 172.16.10.1 (172.16.10.1), Dst: 192.168.30.30 (192.168.30.30)
    0100 .... = Version: 4
    .... 0101 = Header Length: 20 bytes (5)
  ▼ Differentiated Services Field: 0x28 (DSCP: AF11, ECN: Not-ECT)
      0010 10.. = Differentiated Services Codepoint: Assured Forwarding 11 (10)
      .... ..00 = Explicit Congestion Notification: Not ECN-Capable Transport (0)
    Total Length: 84
    Identification: 0xeade (60126)
  ▶ Flags: 0x4000, Don't fragment
```

***Figure 10-34.*** *Pinging from vEdge01*

```
   55 120.603754    172.16.20.1                     192.168.30.30

▶ Frame 55: 98 bytes on wire (784 bits), 98 bytes captured (784 bits) on interface 0
▶ Ethernet II, Src: 50:00:00:04:00:02 (50:00:00:04:00:02), Dst: 50:00:00:08:00:00 (50:00:00:08:00:00)
▼ Internet Protocol Version 4, Src: 172.16.20.1 (172.16.20.1), Dst: 192.168.30.30 (192.168.30.30)
      0100 .... = Version: 4
      .... 0101 = Header Length: 20 bytes (5)
    ▼ Differentiated Services Field: 0x00 (DSCP: CS0, ECN: Not-ECT)
      0000 00.. = Differentiated Services Codepoint: Default (0)
      .... ..00 = Explicit Congestion Notification: Not ECN-Capable Transport (0)
      Total Length: 84
      Identification: 0x7220 (29216)
    ▶ Flags: 0x4000, Don't fragment
```

***Figure 10-35.*** *Pinging from vEdge02*

We are matching the traffic and assigning a DSCP value of 10 (AF11) to the traffic coming from vEdge01, but leaving the traffic from vEdge02 unchanged. So let's change that.

# Configuring Policies Through the CLI

If you are hankering after some good old-fashioned CLI fun, then fear not, the vManage NMS will let you do this as well.

Let's start by looking at and breaking down our existing policy. You can see the existing policy by clicking the View option when you click the three dots next to the policy.

We start with a policy declaration:

```
policy
```

We then have our VPN membership (which we set up in Figure 10-30):

```
vpn-membership vpnMembership_1206778820
   sequence 10
   match
    vpn-list VPN-1
    !
   action accept
    !
```

```
   !
   sequence 20
    match
     vpn-list VPN-2
    !
    action accept
    !
   !
 default-action reject
!
```

Next, we have our match and set statements, which we created in Figure 10-32:

```
data-policy _VPN-1_Site-300-Central-Pol
 vpn-list VPN-1
   sequence 1
    match
     source-ip 172.16.10.0/24
     protocol 1
     destination-ip 192.168.30.0/24
     dscp 0
    !
    action accept
     set
      dscp 10
     !
    !
   !
 default-action accept
!
```

We then have the lists we created first, for our sites and VPNs (Figures 10-28 and 10-29):

```
lists
 site-list Site-100
  site-id 100
 !
 site-list Site-200
  site-id 200
 !
 site-list Site-300
  site-id 300
 !
 vpn-list VPN-1
  vpn 1
 !
 vpn-list VPN-2
  vpn 2
 !
 !
!
```

The next section is where we apply our policy to the sites:

```
apply-policy
 site-list Site-100
  data-policy _VPN-1_Site-300-Central-Pol from-service
  vpn-membership vpnMembership_1206778820
 !
 site-list Site-200
  data-policy _VPN-1_Site-300-Central-Pol from-service
  vpn-membership vpnMembership_1206778820
 !
```

```
site-list Site-300
 data-policy _VPN-1_Site-300-Central-Pol from-service
 vpn-membership vpnMembership_1206778820
 !
!
```

We list each site and then apply the data policy (_VPN-1_Site-300-Central-Pol) and the VPN membership vpnMembership_1206778820.

Let's use this as a template to add a sequence for vEdge02. Firstly, let's see if we can insert a sequence into our existing data policy.

From the Policies page, click the Custom Options menu on the top right-hand side, and select CLI Policy (Figure 10-36).

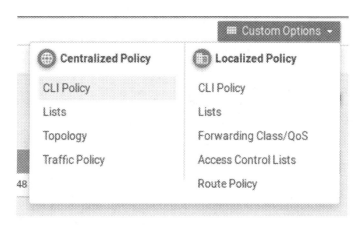

***Figure 10-36.***   *Creating a CLI policy*

Click "Add Policy." Call the policy Site-200-Policy, give it a description, and paste in the following:

```
data-policy _VPN-1_Site-300-Central-Pol
  vpn-list VPN-1
    sequence 2
    match
      source-ip 172.16.20.0/24
```

317

```
    protocol 1
    destination-ip 192.168.30.0/24
    dscp 0
    !
   action accept
    set
     dscp 12
     !
    !
   !
  default-action accept
 !
```

Click "Add."

When you try to activate the policy, it will fail (Figure 10-37).

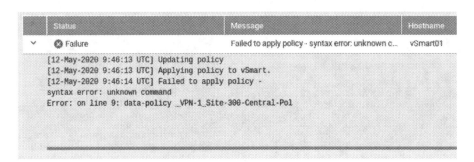

***Figure 10-37.*** *Policy failure*

We have an "unknown command"; let's edit the new policy to use "exit" instead of the exclamation marks:

```
data-policy _VPN-1_Site-300-Central-Pol
  vpn-list VPN-1
    sequence 2
    match
```

```
      source-ip 172.16.20.0/24
      protocol 1
      destination-ip 192.168.30.0/24
      dscp 0
    exit
    action accept
     set
      dscp 12
     exit
    exit
   exit
  default-action accept
 exit
```

Click "Update," and go back into CLI Policy from Custom Options and activate it (as you cannot activate it from the main page).

It still fails. What if we try removing the "exits"?

```
data-policy _VPN-1_Site-300-Central-Pol
  vpn-list VPN-1
    sequence 2
    match
     source-ip 172.16.20.0/24
     protocol 1
     destination-ip 192.168.30.0/24
     dscp 0
    action accept
     set
      dscp 12
  default-action accept
```

It will still fail, again with the same error of "unknown command."

So, what is the answer here? Well, despite the error pointing to an erroneous word, which seems like a simple enough fix, it turns out that we can't use the CLI to insert new rules into existing policies (especially when one is created in the UI). Instead, we need to enter the entire policy (including our additions).

To get the full configuration, click the three dots next to our UI-created policy and choose preview, and then copy them into a notepad document.

Add our new sequence, so that the data-policy section looks like this:

```
data-policy _VPN-1_Site-300-Central-Pol
  vpn-list VPN-1
   sequence 1
    match
     source-ip       172.16.10.0/24
     destination-ip 192.168.30.0/24
     protocol        1
     dscp            0
    !
    action accept
     set
      dscp 10
     !
    !
   !
   sequence 2
    match
     source-ip       172.16.20.0/24
     destination-ip 192.168.30.0/24
```

```
    protocol         1
    dscp             0
    !
   action accept
    set
     dscp 12
     !
    !
   !
  default-action accept
 !
!
```

Then paste the whole thing back into the CLI policy configuration (Figure 10-38).

**CLI Configuration**

```
 1   policy
 2    vpn-membership vpnMembership_1206778820
 3       sequence 10
 4        match
 5         vpn-list VPN-1
 6        !
 7        action accept
 8        !
 9       !
10       sequence 20
11        match
12         vpn-list VPN-2
13        !
14        action accept
15        !
16      !
17     default-action reject
18    !
19    data-policy _VPN-1_Site-300-Central-Pol
20     vpn-list VPN-1
21        sequence 1
22         match
23          source-ip 172.16.10.0/24
24          protocol 1
25          destination-ip 192.168.30.0/24
26          dscp 0
27         !
28         action accept
29          set
30           dscp 10
31          !
32         !
33        !
34        sequence 2
35         match
36          source-ip 172.16.20.0/24
37          protocol 1
38          destination-ip 192.168.30.0/24
39          dscp 0
40         !
41         action accept
42          set
43           dscp 12
44          !
45         !
46        !
47     default-action accept
48    !
```

***Figure 10-38.*** *The completed policy*

Now, activation should be successful (Figure 10-39).

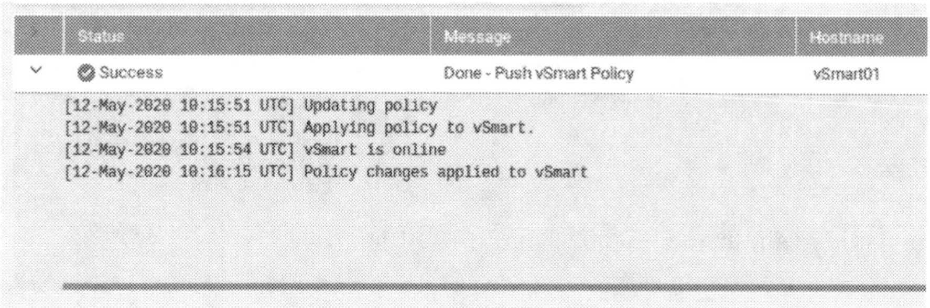

| | Status | Message | Hostname |
|---|---|---|---|
| ∨ | ⊘ Success | Done - Push vSmart Policy | vSmart01 |

```
[12-May-2020 10:15:51 UTC] Updating policy
[12-May-2020 10:15:51 UTC] Applying policy to vSmart.
[12-May-2020 10:15:54 UTC] vSmart is online
[12-May-2020 10:16:15 UTC] Policy changes applied to vSmart
```

***Figure 10-39.*** *A successful policy change*

If we head back to our Policies main page, we will see that our original (UI-created) policy is no longer active, but our new one is (Figure 10-40).

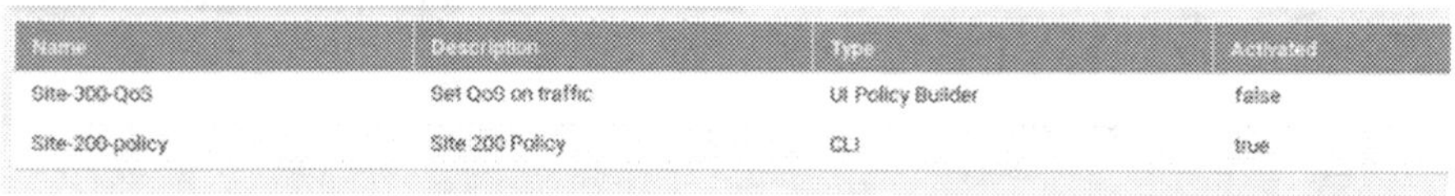

| Name | Description | Type | Activated |
|---|---|---|---|
| Site-300-QoS | Set QoS on traffic | UI Policy Builder | false |
| Site-200-policy | Site 200 Policy | CLI | true |

***Figure 10-40.*** *The policies page*

It is important to plan your policies carefully as adding a new policy can deactivate an existing one. We can, for instance, have only one centralized policy active at any one time.

Now, let's test it. Fire up a Wireshark capture of R300's Gi0/0, and ping it from vEdge01 and vEdge02. We should see two different AF values, AF11 (which is decimal 10) and AF12 (which is decimal 12), as you can see in R300-dual-policy.pcapng.

Firstly, vEdge01 (Figure 10-41).

```
    5  9.684090      172.16.10.1                        192.168.30.30
 ▶ Frame 5: 98 bytes on wire (784 bits), 98 bytes captured (784 bits) on interface 0
 ▶ Ethernet II, Src: 50:00:00:04:00:02 (50:00:00:04:00:02), Dst: 50:00:00:08:00:00 (50:00:00:08:00:00)
 ▼ Internet Protocol Version 4, Src: 172.16.10.1 (172.16.10.1), Dst: 192.168.30.30 (192.168.30.30)
     0100 .... = Version: 4
     .... 0101 = Header Length: 20 bytes (5)
   ▶ Differentiated Services Field: 0x28 (DSCP: AF11, ECN: Not-ECT)
     Total Length: 84
```

*Figure 10-41.* *AF11*

Then again from vEdge02 (Figure 10-42).

```
   15  14.543828     172.16.20.1                        192.168.30.30
 ▶ Frame 15: 98 bytes on wire (784 bits), 98 bytes captured (784 bits) on interface 0
 ▶ Ethernet II, Src: 50:00:00:04:00:02 (50:00:00:04:00:02), Dst: 50:00:00:08:00:00 (50:00:00:08:00:00)
 ▼ Internet Protocol Version 4, Src: 172.16.20.1 (172.16.20.1), Dst: 192.168.30.30 (192.168.30.30)
     0100 .... = Version: 4
     .... 0101 = Header Length: 20 bytes (5)
   ▶ Differentiated Services Field: 0x30 (DSCP: AF12, ECN: Not-ECT)
     Total Length: 84
```

*Figure 10-42.* *AF12*

Our policies are successful!

# Summary

While our topology is a little small to test more policies, hopefully, you
can see, in this chapter, how powerful they can be at controlling the data
moving around the network.

In the next chapter, we will look at upgrades.

# CHAPTER 11

# Upgrades

Before we can set up the security policies in the next chapter, we need to upgrade our environment. The reason for this is that the 19.2 and 19.3 images do not support some of the features we need, but version 20.1 does.

## Managing Software Images

The vManage NMS handles the software distribution and upgrades for all of our SD-WAN devices throughout the network; it is our software repository. In this chapter, we are going to upgrade all of our devices. There are a couple of best practices that we should follow when performing upgrades:

- Use vManage to perform upgrades, rather than the CLI.

- The network overlay must be up and operational if you are upgrading a remote vManage server.

- Upgrades should be performed in the order of

    1: vManage servers.

    2: vBond orchestrators.

    3: Half of the vSmart controllers. Then wait 24 hours to ensure that the network is stable.

    4: The other half of the vSmart controllers.

© Stuart Fordham 2021
S. Fordham, *Learning SD-WAN with Cisco*, https://doi.org/10.1007/978-1-4842-7347-0_11

5: Upgrade 10% of the vEdge routers. Then wait 24 hours.

6: Upgrade the remaining vEdge routers.

Now, while these are best practices, real life is sometimes different, as we will see. But, for the moment, let's do it "the Cisco way."

The steps we need to take are to first add the new software to the repository, upgrade the software image, and then activate the software image.

# Adding Images to the Repository

To add the new software images, navigate to *Maintenance* ➤ *Software Repository* ➤ *Software Images* ➤ *Add New Software*. We can choose from "vManage" (locally stored images), Remote Server (an FTP or HTTP server), or "Remote Server – vManage" where, as the name suggests, images are stored on a remote vManage server.

As we do not have the images locally on our Linux box, we are going to use the Remote Server option. However, we do not have access to a remote server. We have hit a bit of a catch-22 in our learning path. In order to complete the next chapter on security, we need to upgrade our devices, yet, in order to upgrade our devices, we need to do part of the next chapter. Jump ahead and complete the first part, which is the NAT configuration. Once you have done that, come back here.

We add a new repository by setting the controller version, the software version, and the full path to the upgrade file. In this case, I am running a very simple web server on my Mac, which you can do by opening a terminal prompt, cd'ing to the folder containing the upgrade image, and then typing "`python -m SimpleHTTPServer 8000`". Other FTP and HTTP servers are available. You can then add the new software to the repository (Figure 11-1).

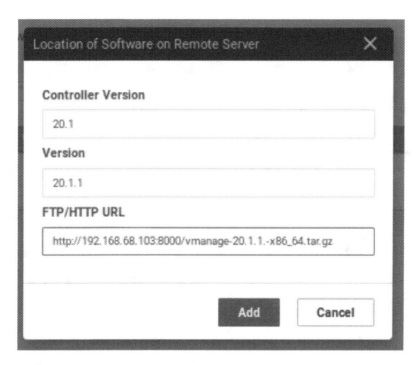

**Figure 11-1.** *Adding software to the repository*

Our images will appear in the list (Figure 11-2).

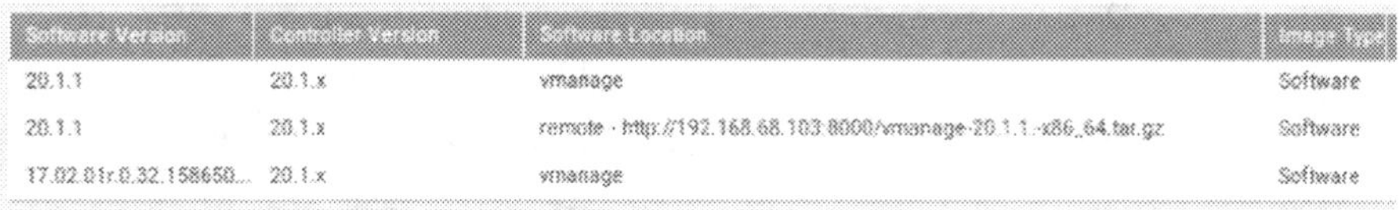

| Software Version | Controller Version | Software Location | Image Type |
|---|---|---|---|
| 20.1.1 | 20.1.x | vmanage | Software |
| 20.1.1 | 20.1.x | remote - http://192.168.68.103:8000/vmanage-20.1.1-x86_64.tar.gz | Software |
| 17.02.01r.0.32.158650... | 20.1.x | vmanage | Software |

**Figure 11-2.** *Our software list*

Once the image repositories have been selected, we can upgrade the image.

# Upgrading Images

Navigate to *Maintenance* ➤ *Software Upgrade*, and select the devices to be upgraded. Then click the "Upgrade" button. Select the version you want to upgrade to from the drop-down menu (Figure 11-3).

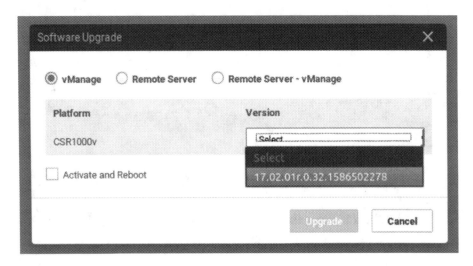

***Figure 11-3.*** *Performing an upgrade*

You can skip to directly activating the new software image and rebooting the device using the "Activate and Reboot" option. If you do not select this option, then you will need to go to the next section. If you select the Remote Server option, then you will need to select the correct VPN to use. The final step is to click "Upgrade."

# Activating Software Images

If you did not select the "Activate and Reboot" option, then navigate to *Maintenance* ➤ *Software Upgrade*, and select the devices that you wish to activate the new software on. Click the Activate button.

---

**Note**   Make sure that your devices are all upgraded to a minimum of 20.1.1 (and 17.02.01r0.32 for the CSR device).

---

Upgrading with vManage sounds simple enough, and yes, when it works, it is simplicity (such as in the official Cisco documentation[1]). However, occasionally, using the CLI is unavoidable.

## Upgrading via the CLI

While best practice says "use the NMS, not the CLI," sometimes the CLI is king, such as when I was writing this book.

Attempting to upgrade the vManage servers via vManage resulted in an error. Every time. While the following output is for a remote server upload, the same occurred when running the upgrade in vManage mode.

Let's step through the process. I have truncated the output as each line starts with the date and "[vManage01]", so this has been removed for readability. I have also used initials to replace some items:

DAM = DeviceActionManager

GTMT = Global Task Monitor Thread

DASDAO = DeviceActionStatusDAO

IAP = InstallActionProcessor

TMSI = Task Monitor Software Install

IIDAO = InstallImageDAO

---

[1] https://sdwan-docs.cisco.com/Product_Documentation/vManage_Help/
Release_18.3/Maintenance/Software_Upgrade

SIAP = SoftwareInstallActionProcessor

DDAP = DefaultDeviceActionProcessor

ADAP = AbstractDeviceActionProcessor

We start with the action of install:

```
[DAM] (software_install Thread) |default| Processing device
action Software Install
[DAM] (software_install Thread) |default|
*#*#*#*#*#*#*#*#*#*#*#**#*# Message received for processing
deviceAction: software_install
```

Then we do some checks and the upgrade task starts:

```
[DAM] (GTMT) |default| Checking any unique device action which
require processing
[DASDAO] (GTMT) |default| Found device action software_install
[DAM] (GTMT) |default| After [1] atttempt to fetch In progress
tasks from DB. Got 1 device actions in 'in_progress' state
[DASDAO] (GTMT) |default| Found device action software_install
[DAM] (GTMT) |default| After [2] atttempt to fetch In progress
tasks from DB. Got 1 device actions in 'in_progress' state
[DASDAO] (GTMT) |default| Found device action software_install
[DAM] (GTMT) |default| After [3] atttempt to fetch In progress
tasks from DB. Got 1 device actions in 'in_progress' state
[DefaultDeviceActionProcessor] (GTMT) |default| Starting Task
Monitor - Software Install
```

Once this starts, we get our image list and location and our targets (which are our vManage servers):

```
[IAP] (TMSI) |default| Software upgrade vmanage thread pool
size  20 Server CPU core 4 VDaemon count 4
[IIDAO] (TMSI) |default| Getting uploaded image info
for {versionType=remote, versionTypeName=software,
networkFunctionType=ROUTER, versionName=20.1.1}
[IIDAO] (TMSI) |default| Found uploaded image info
list: [InstallImageInfo [nfType=ROUTER, vType=remote,
versionTypeName=software, version=20.1.1, softwareUrl=ht
tp://192.168.68.103:8000/vmanage-20.1.1-x86_64.tar.gz]]
[SIAP] (TMSI) |default| Validating input for installImageInfo
InstallImageInfo [nfType=ROUTER, vType=remote,
versionTypeName=software, version=20.1.1, softwareUrl=ht
tp://192.168.68.103:8000/vmanage-20.1.1-x86_64.tar.gz]
[IIDAO] (TMSI) |default| Getting uploaded image info
for {versionType=remote, versionTypeName=software,
networkFunctionType=ROUTER, versionName=20.1.1}
[IIDAO] (TMSI) |default| Found uploaded image info
list: [InstallImageInfo [nfType=ROUTER, vType=remote,
versionTypeName=software, version=20.1.1, softwareUrl=ht
tp://192.168.68.103:8000/vmanage-20.1.1-x86_64.tar.gz]]
[SIAP] (TMSI) |default| Validating input for installImageInfo
InstallImageInfo [nfType=ROUTER, vType=remote,
versionTypeName=software, version=20.1.1, softwareUrl=ht
tp://192.168.68.103:8000/vmanage-20.1.1-x86_64.tar.gz]
[DDAP] (TMSI) |default| Performing Device Action- Software
Install for devices- Vbonds: [],Vsmarts: [],vManages:
[100.100.1.2, 100.100.1.22],vEdges: [],
[ADAP] (TMSI) |default| Processing vmanage list
```

```
[ADAP] (TMSI) |default| Start process device action for device list
[ADAP] (TMSI) |default| Adding device 100.100.1.22 for device
action processing
```

We then try to connect to the second vManage device:

```
[IAP] (TMSI) |default| Software upgrade timeout - 60
[DDAP] (TMSI) |default| Software activate timeout - 30
[IAP] (TMSI) |default| Software upgrade vmanage thread pool
size  20 Server CPU core 4 VDaemon count 4
[NetConfClient] (device-action-software_install-0) |default|
Failed to connect to device : 100.100.1.22 Port: 830 user :
vmanage-admin error : Authentication failed
[SoftwareInstallActionProcessor] (device-action-software_
install-0) |default| Failed to process install action: com.
viptela.vmanage.server.device.common.NetConfClientException:
org.apache.sshd.common.RuntimeSshException: Failed to get the
session.
```

This fails. But why? Well, there were no issues with the cluster. Everything was green. Both vManage servers could SSH to each other using the admin account, with the same password, so connectivity and credentials were fine. Yet we still have an "Authentication failed" error.

Truth be told, I never found the solution. Googling the last line of the earlier output results in a whopping eight results. I tried, but in the end, resorted to a more manual method for the vManages (and the vBond and vSmart).

If we have the software in our repository, then we can pull them from there. We just need to find them. To do this, we can turn to the REST API (Representational State Transfer Application Programming Interface) and call *https://<vmanageIP>/dataservice/device/action/software* and get a list of the software in the repository (Figure 11-4).

**Figure 11-4.** *Using the API to list the software images*

So, we can access the images using the URL *http://10.1.1.2:8080/software/packages/viptela-20.1.1-x86_64.tar.gz* and then use the command "request software install" along with the path to perform the upgrade:

```
vManage02# request software install http://10.1.1.2:8080/
software/package/vmanage-20.1.1-x86_64.tar.gz
--2020-06-08 14:42:12--  http://10.1.1.2:8080/software/package/
vmanage-20.1.1-x86_64.tar.gz
Connecting to 10.1.1.2:8080... connected.
HTTP request sent, awaiting response... 206 Partial Content
Length: 1120120144 (1.0G) [application/octet-stream]
Saving to: 'vmanage-20.1.1-x86_64.tar.gz'
```

```
vmanage-20.1.1-x86_ 100%[====================>]    1.04G
214KB/s    in 93m 46s
```

```
2020-06-08 16:15:57 (194 KB/s) - 'vmanage-20.1.1-x86_64.tar.gz'
saved [1120120144/1120120144]
```

```
Signature verification Succeeded.
Successfully installed version: 20.1.1
```

```
vManage02#
```

OK, so EVE-NG might not be the fastest for file transfers, but it works. The next step is to set the new version as the default:

```
vManage02# request software set-default 20.1.1
This will change the default software version.
Are you sure you want to proceed? [yes,NO] yes
vManage02#
```

Finally, we activate the software:

```
vManage02# request software activate 20.1.1
This will reboot the node with the activated version.
Are you sure you want to proceed? [yes,NO] yes
```

The software will install, and the device will reboot into the new version.

Another option is to use SCP. I started by copying the files to the same Linux server used for the certificates, and for this, you can use the CD-ROM method we used to get the serial file into our network; just make sure you use the "-joliet" option so that the file names are not truncated.

Once you have the files on the Linux server, you can use SCP or FTP to copy them to the vManage01 device (Figure 11-5).

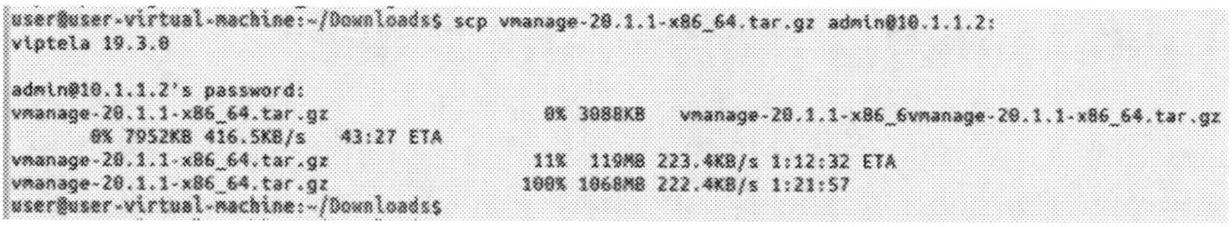

```
user@user-virtual-machine:~/Downloads$ scp vmanage-20.1.1-x86_64.tar.gz admin@10.1.1.2:
viptela 19.3.0

admin@10.1.1.2's password:
vmanage-20.1.1-x86_64.tar.gz                        0% 3088KB    vmanage-20.1.1-x86_6vmanage-20.1.1-x86_64.tar.gz
        0% 7952KB 416.5KB/s   43:27 ETA
vmanage-20.1.1-x86_64.tar.gz                       11%  119MB 223.4KB/s 1:12:32 ETA
vmanage-20.1.1-x86_64.tar.gz                      100% 1068MB 222.4KB/s 1:21:57
user@user-virtual-machine:~/Downloads$
```

***Figure 11-5.*** *Using SCP to copy images to vManage01*

We then run through the same set of steps, just replacing the location:

Request software install /home/admin/vmanage-20.1.1_x86-64.tar.gz

Request software set-default 20.1.1

Request software active 20.1.1

After vManage02 rebooted, the application service would not start. On a hunch, I upgraded vManage01, and once they were both at the same software version, the cluster started up.

Next, I used the SCP method to upgrade vBond01 and then vSmart01.

Once the "backbone" of the SD-WAN was all on 20.1.1, I was able to use the vManage NMS to upgrade the edge devices, which went nice and smoothly (Figure 11-6).

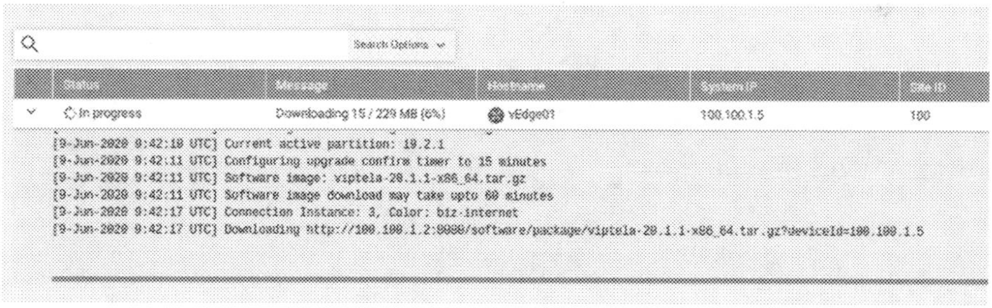

***Figure 11-6.*** *Upgrading the edge devices using vManage*

# Troubleshooting Image Upgrades

We all know that upgrades can be tricky from time to time, especially when performed remotely, which, as I am sure, can be a bit nerve-wracking while devices reboot, and we have no eyes on what's happening. Because of this, we do have a fixed time window for upgrades to complete, as upgrades that take longer than 60 minutes to complete will time out. We cannot extend this value, but we can shorten it if we so desire, such as setting it to 45 minutes:

```
vManage01# config
Entering configuration mode terminal
vManage01(config)# system upgrade-confirm ?
Description: Configure software upgrade confirmation timeout
Possible completions:
  <5..60> minutes
vManage01(config)# system upgrade-confirm 45
vManage01(config-system)# commit
Commit complete.
vManage01(config-system)# end
vManage01#
```

If the control connection to the vManage server takes longer than 15 minutes to come back up, then vManage will automatically revert to the previous (working) image.

# Summary

We have seen how to add new images to the repository and also how to use HTTP and SCP to load images onto devices and use both vManage and the CLI to perform upgrades.

Now that we have our upgrades all done, we can implement some security rules.

# CHAPTER 12

# Security

Now that we are a little more up to date after our upgrades, we can have some fun with security. I know that sounds like an oxymoron (like "only choice"), but Security can be fun. I promise.

In this chapter, we are going to implement security rules to permit and deny traffic. Mainly deny because, well, it is easier to test.

To get the real benefit in this chapter (and so that we can do the upgrades in the previous chapter), we need to extend the network again, by adding real Internet access and another Linux node.

## Setting Up Internet Access

Start by shutting down the ISP-R router. Connect a new network object by right-clicking the EVE-NG canvas and selecting "Network" in the "Add a new object" options. Make the network a Management(Cloud0) one, and call it "Internet." Connect this new object to ISP-R's Gi0/2 interface by dragging the orange network icon. Start the router up.

Enter the following settings:

```
ISP-R#conf t
ISP-R(config)#int gi 0/2
ISP-R(config-if)#ip address dhcp
ISP-R(config-if)#ip nat outside
ISP-R(config-if)#no shut
ISP-R(config-if)#int gi 0/0
```

© Stuart Fordham 2021
S. Fordham, *Learning SD-WAN with Cisco*, https://doi.org/10.1007/978-1-4842-7347-0_12

```
ISP-R(config-if)#ip nat inside
ISP-R(config-if)#int gi 0/1
ISP-R(config-if)#ip nat inside
ISP-R(config-if)#int gi 0/3
ISP-R(config-if)#ip nat inside
ISP-R(config-if)#exit
ISP-R(config)#access-list 1 permit 50.11.11.0 0.0.0.255
ISP-R(config)#access-list 1 permit 50.10.10.0 0.0.0.255
ISP-R(config)#access-list 1 permit 50.12.12.0 0.0.0.255
ISP-R(config)#access-list 1 permit 10.1.1.0 0.0.0.255
ISP-R(config)#access-list 1 permit 10.2.1.0 0.0.0.255
ISP-R(config)#
ISP-R(config)#ip nat inside source list 1 interface gi0/2
overload
ISP-R(config)#
```

The preceding configuration sets the Gi0/2 interface for DHCP. It then sets the same address as the outbound interface for NAT (the interface we'll be translating to). The gi0/0, gi0/1, and 0/3 interfaces are set up as the NAT source interfaces. Then we have an access list to match the traffic we are going to perform NAT for and, lastly, a NAT command to NAT the source addresses from the access list to the GI0/2 interface.

The Internet connection should join ISP-R onto your local network through EVE-NG. The Gi0/2 interface will get an IP address on your local network (assuming you have DHCP running), and we will also get a default route.

```
ISP-R#sh ip int bri | i 0/2
GigabitEthernet0/2    192.168.68.121  YES DHCP    up      up
ISP-R#
ISP-R#sh ip route | i 0.0.0.0/0
S*    0.0.0.0/0 [254/0] via 192.168.68.1
ISP-R#
```

The details you will have will differ from the preceding ones, but hopefully, you get the gist of what we are trying to achieve. We can test our connectivity:

```
ISP-R#sh ip cef 8.8.8.8
0.0.0.0/0
  nexthop 192.168.68.1 GigabitEthernet0/2
ISP-R#
ISP-R#ping 8.8.8.8
Type escape sequence to abort.
Sending 5, 100-byte ICMP Echos to 8.8.8.8, timeout is 2
seconds:
!!!!!
Success rate is 100 percent (5/5), round-trip min/avg/max =
44/111/266 ms
ISP-R#
```

The next step is to give ourselves a machine to play with. To do that, we can add a machine onto CSR-1.

# Linux VM

Adding a new connection to an edge device in vManage should be very familiar to you now, so without the aid of screenshots, shut down CSR-1 and connect its Gi4 interface to a new Linux node. In vManage, create a new interface template, giving it an IP address of 192.168.33.1/24. Add the template onto the main device template, and push it to the router.

The Linux node should have an IP of 192.168.33.33/24, and its default gateway should be the IP address assigned to CSR-1's Gi4 interface (192.168.33.1). We should have connectivity between the Linux node and CSR-1.

The next step is to get CSR-1 to do some network address translation (NAT) for us, as ISP-R will not NAT for the 192.168.33.0/24 subnet.

# CSR-1 NAT

Edit the t-CSR1000v interface template (the one that controls the Gi1 interface), and select the NAT tab and enable the option. Set the refresh mode to bidirectional, and enable Respond To Ping (Figure 12-1).

*Figure 12-1.* *Enabling NAT*

Then edit the service template for VPN1 (c-v-VPN1) and add a default route, pointing to the VPN (Figure 12-2).

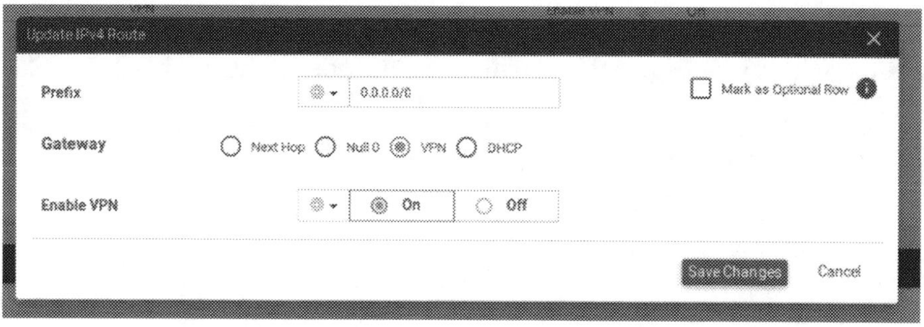

*Figure 12-2.* *Adding a default route for VPN1*

Once the template is applied, we should get this result in the configuration on CSR-1:

```
interface GigabitEthernet1
 ip address 50.10.10.1 255.255.255.0
 no ip redirects
 ip nat outside
 negotiation auto
 arp timeout 1200
 no mop enabled
 no mop sysid
!
ip nat settings central-policy
ip nat route vrf 65528 0.0.0.0 0.0.0.0 global
ip nat route vrf 1 0.0.0.0 0.0.0.0 global
ip nat translation tcp-timeout 3600
ip nat translation udp-timeout 60
!
ip nat inside source list nat-dia-vpn-hop-access-list int
GigEth1 overload
```

I shortened the last line of output for the sake of formatting. If you are familiar with VRF route leaking, which is common in the world of MPLS, then this is what is happening here.

If we generate some traffic from the new Linux node, we should start to see some NAT translations:

```
CSR-1#sh ip nat trans
Pro  Inside global    Inside local         Outside local
Outside global
tcp  50.10.10.1:5120 192.168.33.33:57242 62.252.60.2:443
62.252.60.2:443
udp  50.10.10.1:5090 192.168.33.33:57764
8.8.8.8:53        8.8.8.8:53
icmp 50.10.10.1:6049 192.168.33.33:6049   14.31.75.1:6049
14.31.75.1:6049
udp  50.10.10.1:5088 192.168.33.33:57682
8.8.8.8:53        8.8.8.8:53
udp  50.10.10.1:5089 192.168.33.33:40085
8.8.8.8:53        8.8.8.8:53
Total number of translations: 5

CSR-1#
```

Now, to get the best out of this chapter, we need to migrate our CSR template, but only if you started with version 19.2 and have upgraded to 20.1 as we did in the previous chapter. If you started with version 20.1, then you are good already.

The reason we need to migrate our template is that we need to use the CLI feature, which is unavailable on the older template. You may have already seen this due to the banner displayed in vManage (Figure 12-3).

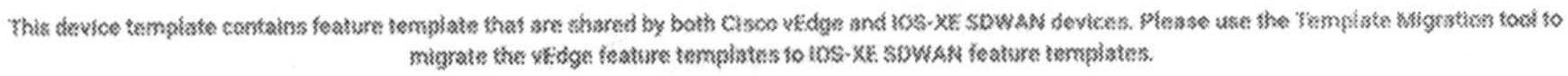

This device template contains feature template that are shared by both Cisco vEdge and IOS-XE SDWAN devices. Please use the Template Migration tool to migrate the vEdge feature templates to IOS-XE SDWAN feature templates.

*Figure 12-3. The migration banner*

Click the Template Migration link (Figure 12-4).

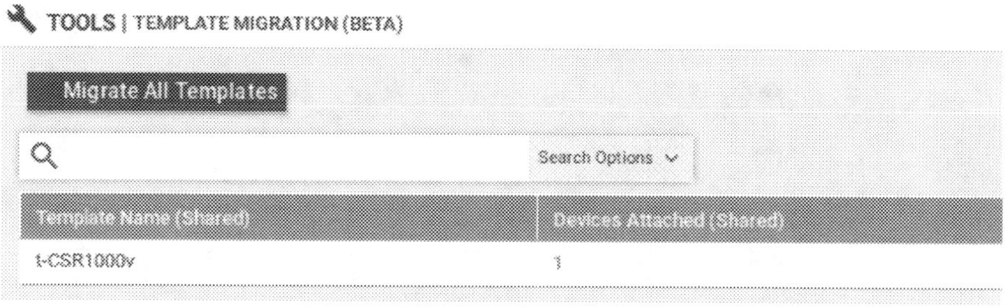

**TOOLS | TEMPLATE MIGRATION (BETA)**

| Migrate All Templates | |
| --- | --- |
| Q | Search Options ∨ |
| Template Name (Shared) | Devices Attached (Shared) |
| t-CSR1000v | 1 |

***Figure 12-4.*** *Migrating the t_CSR100v template*

Click "Migrate All Templates." In the next window, tick the bottom option, and then click "Migrate" (Figure 12-5).

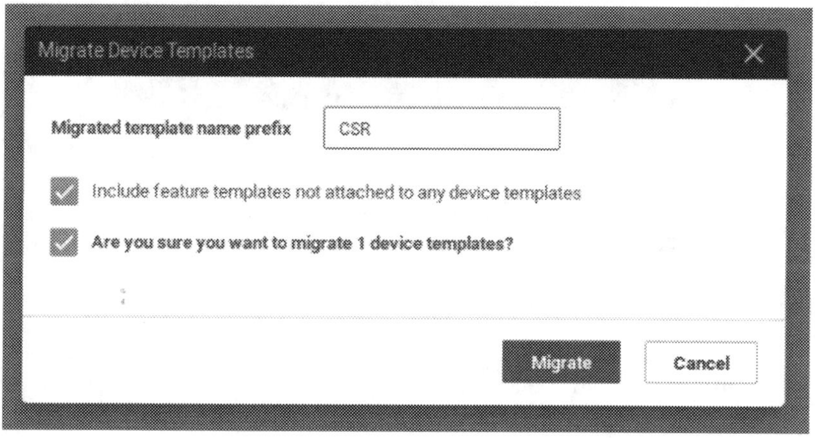

Migrate Device Templates                                                    ✕

Migrated template name prefix          CSR

☑ Include feature templates not attached to any device templates

☑ Are you sure you want to migrate 1 device templates?

                                                    Migrate        Cancel

***Figure 12-5.*** *Click to migrate*

The migrated template name prefix can be anything we like, and during migration, vManage will take our existing template (t-CSR1000v in this case) and create a new one with the prefix (CSR_t-CSR1000v); all of its feature templates will also be migrated.

We can now add a CLI add-on feature template. Create one called CSR-DNS, and add in "ip dns server" and "ip domain-lookup" (Figure 12-6).

***Figure 12-6.*** *The CLI Add-On Template*

Now, our CSR should act as a DNS server. Save this and add it to the new CSR_t-CSR1000v template in the Additional Templates section (Figure 12-7).

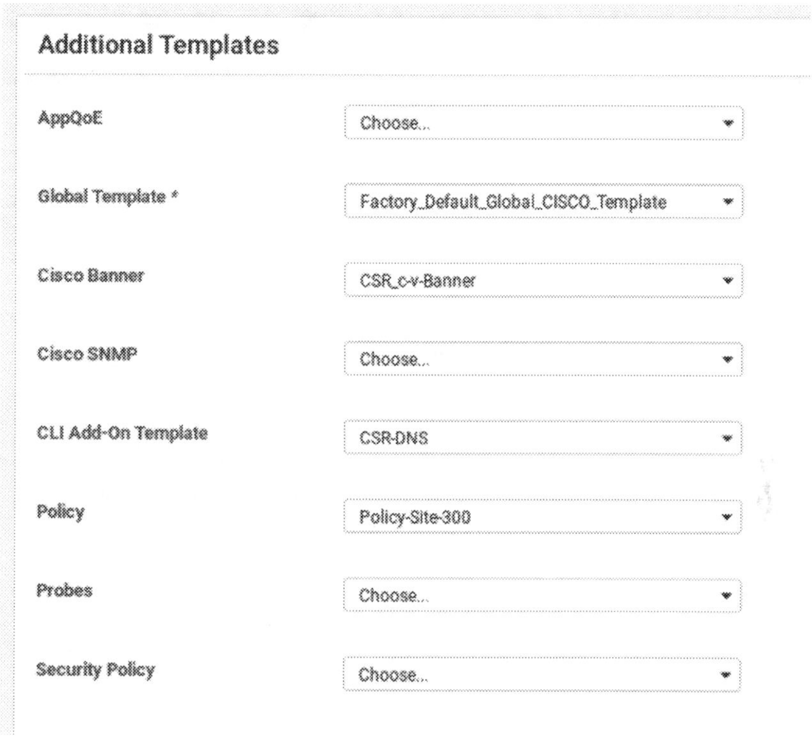

**Additional Templates**

| | |
|---|---|
| AppQoE | Choose... ▼ |
| Global Template * | Factory_Default_Global_CISCO_Template ▼ |
| Cisco Banner | CSR_c-v-Banner ▼ |
| Cisco SNMP | Choose... ▼ |
| CLI Add-On Template | CSR-DNS ▼ |
| Policy | Policy-Site-300 ▼ |
| Probes | Choose... ▼ |
| Security Policy | Choose... ▼ |

***Figure 12-7.*** *Adding the CLI Add-On Template*

We now need to switch our CSR device to use this new template. We do this as we have done before, by clicking the three dots next to the template name and selecting Attach Devices. We then select the device to attach and click through the dialog boxes (Figure 12-8).

**Figure 12-8.** *Attaching CSR-1 to the new template*

Pay close attention to the config diff here, as if we carry on now, we will lose our NAT configuration (Figure 12-9).

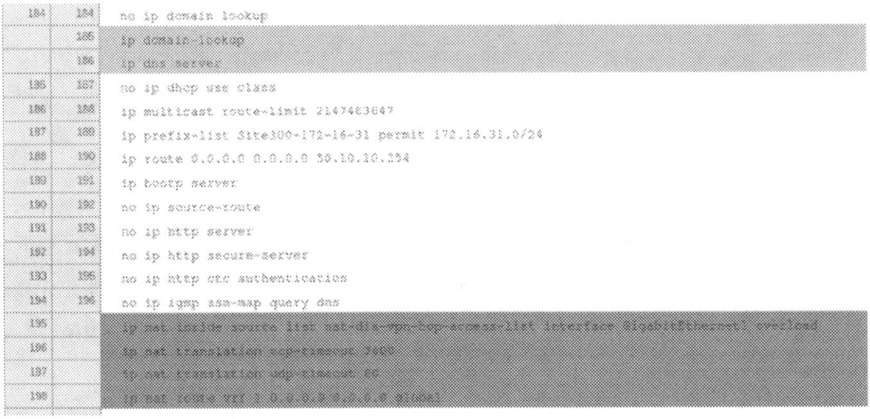

**Figure 12-9.** *We will lose the NAT configuration*

The interesting thing is that the templates were (after migration) still set to perform NAT. Going through the new template, clicking Update (without making any changes), and attaching the CSR-1 device again seemed to do the trick, and the second time I tried to apply the template to the device, the NAT statements were not due to be removed (Figure 12-10).

```
        185   ip domain-lookup
        186   ip dns server
185     187   no ip dhcp use class
186     188   ip multicast route-limit 2147483647
187     189   ip prefix-list Site300-172-16-31 permit 172.16.31.0/24
188     190   ip route 0.0.0.0 0.0.0.0 90.10.10.254
189     191   ip bootp server
190     192   no ip source-route
191     193   no ip http server
192     194   no ip http secure-server
193     195   no ip http ctc authentication
194     196   no ip igmp ssm-map query dns
195     197   ip nat inside source list nat-dia-vpn-hop-access-list interface GigabitEthernet1 overload
196     198   ip nat translation tcp-timeout 3600
197     199   ip nat translation udp-timeout 60
198     200   ip nat route vrf 1 0.0.0.0 0.0.0.0 global
199     201   interface GigabitEthernet1
200     202    no shutdown
201     203    arp timeout 1200
202     204    ip address 90.10.10.1 255.255.255.0
203     205    no ip redirects
204     206    ip mtu   1500
205     207    ip nat outside
206     208    mtu 1500
207     209    negotiation auto
208     210   exit
```

**Figure 12-10.** *We still have NAT*

Your mileage on this might vary, but you may also see that pushing the template fails, with an application error. If you remove the CLI Add-On Template, then pushing the device template works, so clearly, something is wrong with the CLI Add-On Template. The reason for this is that not all CLI commands can be pushed into the device this way, as they are not supported. "`ip domain-lookup`" is one of these unsupported commands. So if you hit this issue, then remove the command from the Add-On Template, and push it to the device again. It is worth keeping an eye on the Cisco website for the template as the number of supported commands gets updated with each IOS-XE version. The really long link to follow is *www. cisco.com/c/en/us/td/docs/routers/sdwan/configuration/system-interface/ios-xe-17/systems-interfaces-book-xe-sdwan/m-cli-add-on-feat.html*. By the time you read this, the command may be supported on newer versions.

We should, now, have our CSR router acting as a DNS server:

```
CSR-1# sh run | i dns
no ip igmp ssm-map query dns
no ip nat service dns tcp
no ip nat service dns udp
no ip nat service dns-reset-ttl
ip dns server
CSR-1#
```

The last step of our basic configuration is to set our external DNS servers. Edit the CSR_c-VPN0 template, and add the DNS servers 208.67.222.222 and 208.67.220.220 (which are the Cisco Umbrella DNS servers) (Figure 12-11).

*Figure 12-11.* *Using the Umbrella servers*

Repeat the process for CSR_c-v-VPN1, and then apply the template. Those template changes get us the following:

```
CSR-1#sh run | i name-server
ip name-server 208.67.220.220 208.67.222.222
ip name-server vrf 1 208.67.220.220 208.67.222.222
ip name-server vrf 65528 208.67.220.220 208.67.222.222
CSR-1#
```

And, more importantly, the Linux node inside site 300 can access the Internet (Figure 12-12).

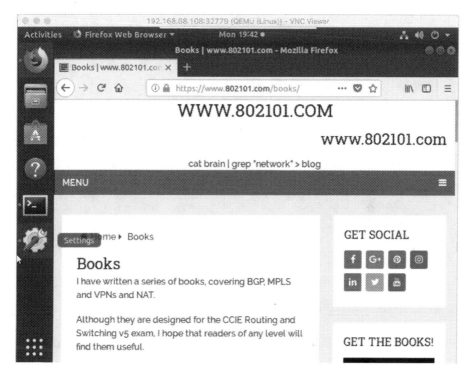

***Figure 12-12.***  *We have Internet access!*

Now that we have the basics in place, we can configure some security rules.

# Applying Security Rules

Let's start with something simple. As you know, SSH is good and Telnet is bad. So, in our first example, we are going to block Telnet access from the Linux node to R300. Currently, this access is permitted (Figure 12-13).

```
user@user-virtual-machine:~$
user@user-virtual-machine:~$ telnet 192.168.30.30
Trying 192.168.30.30...
Connected to 192.168.30.30.
Escape character is '^]'.

*****************************************************************************
* IOSv is strictly limited to use for evaluation, demonstration and IOS  *
* education. IOSv is provided as-is and is not supported by Cisco's       *
* Technical Advisory Center. Any use or disclosure, in whole or in part,  *
* of the IOSv Software or Documentation to any third party for any        *
* purposes is expressly prohibited except as otherwise authorized by      *
* Cisco in writing.                                                       *
*****************************************************************************

User Access Verification

Username: sd-admin
Password:
*****************************************************************************
* IOSv is strictly limited to use for evaluation, demonstration and IOS  *
* education. IOSv is provided as-is and is not supported by Cisco's       *
* Technical Advisory Center. Any use or disclosure, in whole or in part,  *
* of the IOSv Software or Documentation to any third party for any        *
* purposes is expressly prohibited except as otherwise authorized by      *
* Cisco in writing.                                                       *
*****************************************************************************
R300>
```

***Figure 12-13.*** *Telnet is permitted*

Let's deny it instead. Start by heading to *Configuration* ➤ *Security,* and click "Add Security Policy" (Figure 12-14).

No policies added, add your first security policy

Add Security Policy

***Figure 12-14.*** *Adding a security policy*

We are going to use Direct Internet Access (DIA), as this gives us all
the cool features, such as application firewall, intrusion prevention, URL
filtering, malware protection, DNS security, and TLS/SSL decryption
(Figure 12-15).

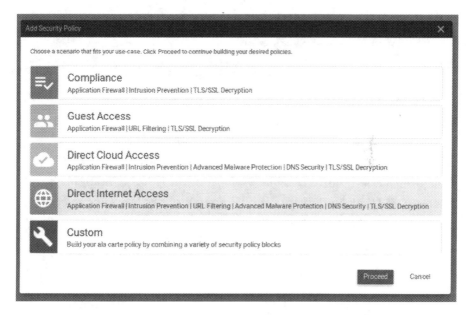

***Figure 12-15.***  *Select Direct Internet Access*

We need to create our VPN zones, the 5-tuple that will do our traffic
matching, and any application behaviors. Click "Add Firewall Policy"
(Figure 12-16).

*Figure 12-16.* We need to define some targets

The first step is to define our zone pairs, which are our source and destination VPNs (Figure 12-17). As all our traffic (for the moment) is within VPN 1 (R300 and the new Linux machine), we are going to create a zone for this. Click "Apply Zone-Pairs."

*Figure 12-17.* We need to set our zone pairs

Click in the Source Zone box, and select "New Zone List" from the drop-down (Figure 12-18).

**Figure 12-18.**   *Creating the source zone*

Create a new zone, called "Zone-list," specifying VPN 1, and click Save (Figure 12-19).

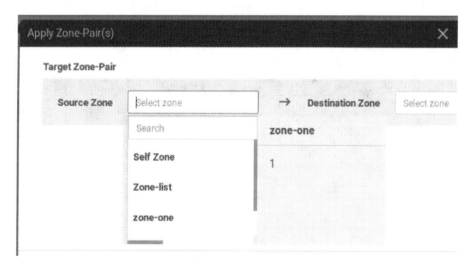

**Figure 12-19.**   *Setting the source zone*

We can define multiple VPNs within these zones, such as "1,2,3,10-20", if we need to. Set both the source and destination zones to the newly created zone list (Figure 12-20).

***Figure 12-20.*** *Our zones are set*

Click Save. We now have our zone pair set (Figure 12-21).

***Figure 12-21.*** *The zone pairs are set*

Name the firewall policy in the next box, calling it "Site-300-FW-Pol." The next step is to start adding some rules. Give the rule a name, such as "Deny-Telnet," and set the action to "Deny" (Figure 12-22).

***Figure 12-22.*** *The Deny-Telnet rule*

Now we need to define our 5-tuple. Click the plus sign next to Source Data Prefix, and add a new prefix of 192.168.33.0/24 (Figure 12-23).

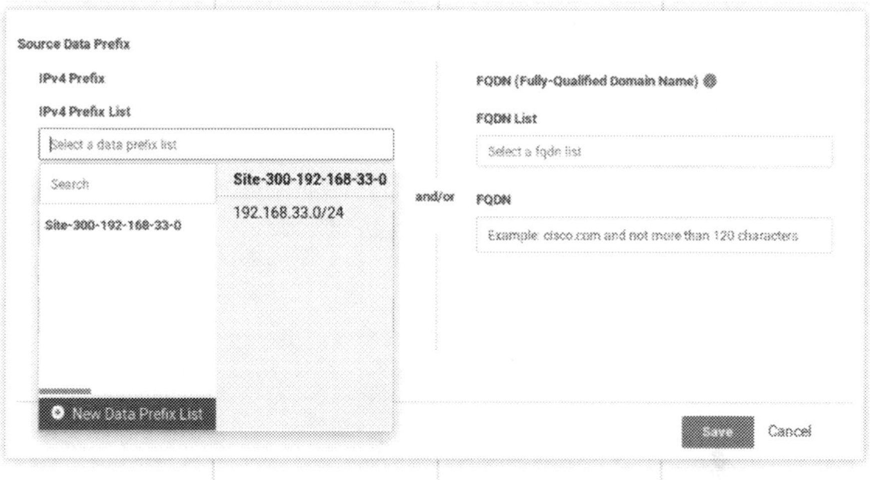

***Figure 12-23.*** *The source prefix*

Select it and click Save (Figure 12-24).

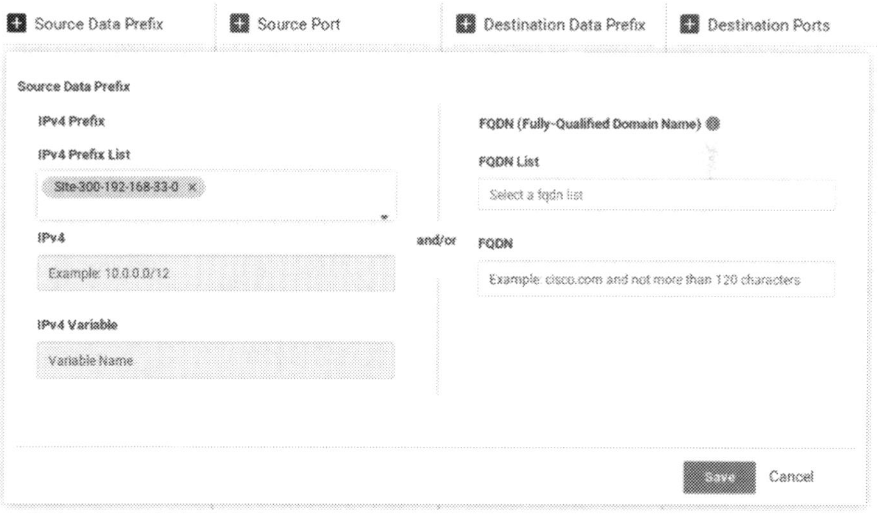

***Figure 12-24.*** *The source prefix is set*

We are going to leave the source port as Any. For the Destination Data Prefix, click the plus sign and enter the subnet 192.168.30.0/24 in the IPv4 field (Figure 12-25). We don't have to create an object every time; it depends on how often you are going to reference the same prefixes.

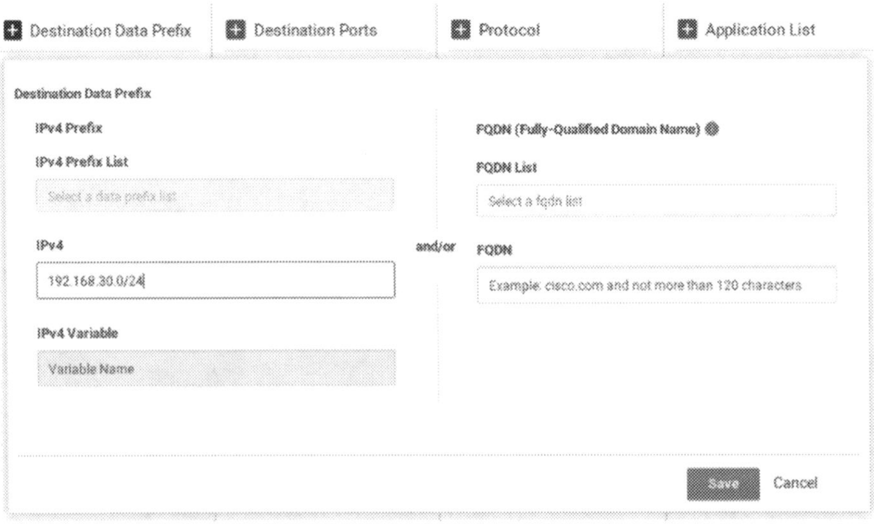

***Figure 12-25.*** *The destination prefix*

Click Save. Now, for the rest of the details, we could use the destination port (23), the protocol (6), or we can define an application list. We are going to use the destination port (Figure 12-26).

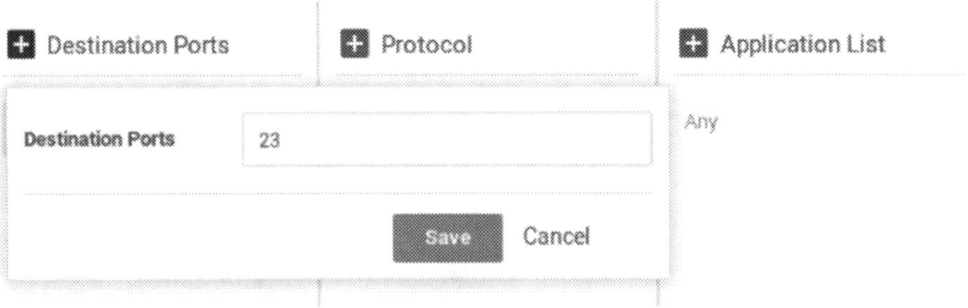

***Figure 12-26.*** *Setting the destination port*

We should end up with the same details as Figure 12-27.

***Figure 12-27.***  *The completed 5-tuple*

Click Save. Now we need to create an allow rule for all the other traffic; otherwise, everything will be denied. Click Add Rule and fill in the details, setting all the fields to "Any" (Figure 12-28).

***Figure 12-28.***  *Our Allow rule*

Save it and we have two rules (Figure 12-29).

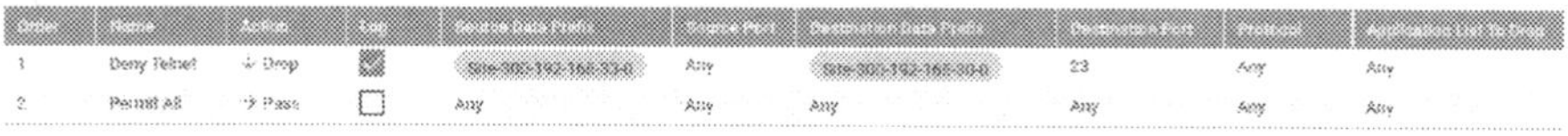

| Order | Name | Action | Log | Source Data Prefix | Source Port | Destination Data Prefix | Destination Port | Protocol | Application List To Drop |
|---|---|---|---|---|---|---|---|---|---|
| 1 | Deny Telnet | ↓ Drop | ✓ | Site-300-192-168-33-0 | Any | Site-300-192-168-30-0 | 23 | Any | Any |
| 2 | Permit All | → Pass | ☐ | Any | Any | Any | Any | Any | Any |

***Figure 12-29.***  *Our completed rules*

Click Save Firewall Policy, and then click Next. We are not going to add any intrusion prevention policies, so click Next. We are going to implement URL filtering, though.

# URL Filtering

Click "Add URL Filtering Policy" (Figure 12-30).

***Figure 12-30.*** *Adding a URL policy*

Click "Add New." The default policy is to block sites with a risk rating of moderate and to redirect those sites to a block page (Figure 12-31).

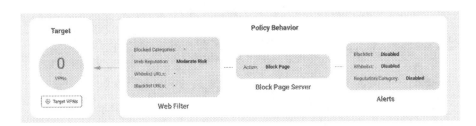

***Figure 12-31.*** *The default URL filtering policy behavior*

Click Target VPNs and add VPNs 0 and 1 (Figure 12-32).

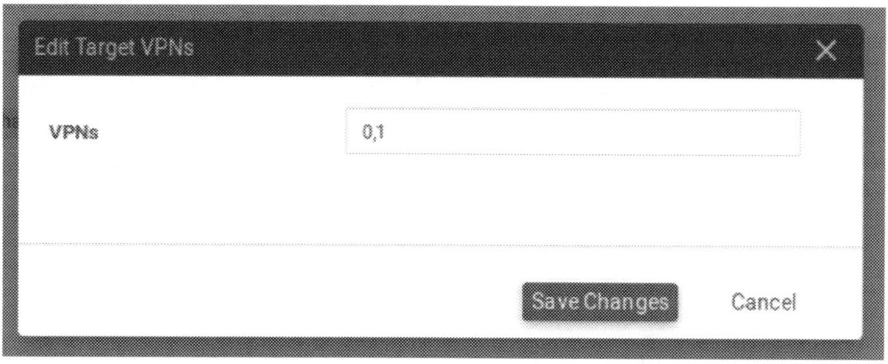

Edit Target VPNs ✕

VPNs            0,1

Save Changes    Cancel

***Figure 12-32.*** *Adding target VPNs*

Give the policy a name, and set the following web categories:

- adult-and-pornography

- hate-and-racism

- illegal

Leave the block page as it is, and tick Blacklist and Reputation/ Category. We should see this at the top of the page (Figure 12-33).

***Figure 12-33.*** *Our URL filtering policy*

Click Save and then Next. Click Next past the advanced Malware Protection screen and again past the DNS security and the TLS/SSL decryption screens. Finally, give the policy a name of "Sec-pol" and a description (Figure 12-34).

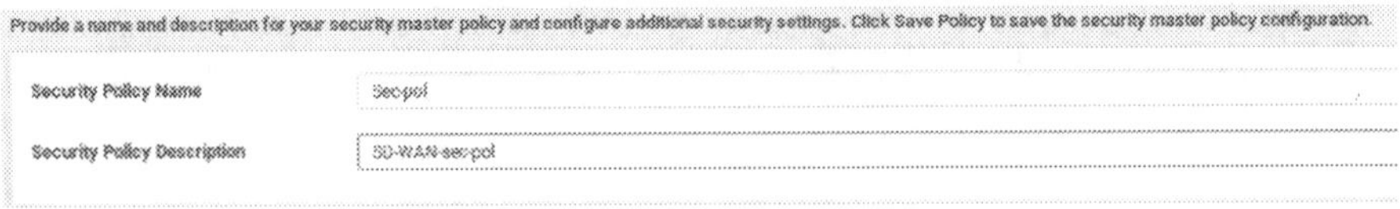

**Figure 12-34.** *Naming our security policy*

There are a number of options on this page, such as logging. We can leave these at their defaults (for the moment). If we preview the policy, it looks like this:

```
policy
 url-filtering URL-filtering-policy
  web-category-action block
  web-categories adult-and-pornography hate-and-racism illegal
  block-threshold moderate-risk
  block text Access to the requested page has been denied.
Please contact your Network Administrator
  alert categories-reputation blacklist
  target-vpns 0 1
 !
 zone-based-policy Site-300-FW-Pol
   sequence 1
    match
     source-data-prefix-list Site-300-192-168-33-0
     destination-data-prefix-list Site-300-192-168-33-0
     destination-port 23
    !
    action drop
     log
    !
   !
   sequence 11
    action pass
```

```
    !
     !
  default-action drop
 !
  zone Zone-list
   vpn 1
   !
  zone-pair ZP_zone-one_zone-one_-1002302744
   source-zone zone-one
   destination-zone zone-one
   zone-policy Site-300-FW-Pol
   !
 lists
  data-prefix-list Site-300-192-168-30-0
   ip-prefix 192.168.30.0/24
   !
  data-prefix-list Site-300-192-168-33-0
   ip-prefix 192.168.33.0/24
   !
  !
 zone-to-nozone-internet deny
 failure-mode open
 !
```

Save the policy. As per the warning on the URL filtering screen, we need to upload a file to the router. The file we need is sec-app-ucmk9.16.12.02r.1.0.10_SV2.9.13.0_XE16.12.x86_764.tar, and you can get this from the Cisco.com website and then copy it to the Linux server.

Follow the same steps to create a CD ROM as we have done in previous chapters, copying the file to a folder called /tmp/sd-avc on the EVE-NG server and creating an ISO image (using the -J flag to specify Joliet, so we get the long file name support):

```
root@eve-ng:~# ls /tmp/sd-avc/
secapp-ucmk9.16.12.02r.1.0.10_SV2.9.13.0_XE16.12.x86_64.tar
root@eve-ng:~#
root@eve-ng:~# mkisofs -J -l -R -o cdrom.iso /tmp/sd-avc/
 18.73% done, estimate finish Wed May 13 14:58:03 2020
 37.47% done, estimate finish Wed May 13 14:58:03 2020
 56.14% done, estimate finish Wed May 13 14:58:03 2020
 74.88% done, estimate finish Wed May 13 14:58:03 2020
 93.55% done, estimate finish Wed May 13 14:58:03 2020
Total translation table size: 0
Total rockridge attributes bytes: 300
Total directory bytes: 434
Path table size(bytes): 10
Max brk space used 0
26731 extents written (52 MB)
root@eve-ng:~# ls
cdrom.iso
root@eve-ng:~# mv cdrom.iso /opt/unetlab/addons/qemu/linux-
ubuntu-desktop-17.10.1/
root@eve-ng:~#
```

Stop and start the Linux server so that it picks up the CD-ROM. Back in vManage, go to *Maintenance ➤ Software Repository ➤ Virtual Images*, click Upload Virtual Image, and select the vManage option. Upload the secapp file (Figure 12-35).

| Software Version | Available Files | Software Location | Network Function Type |
|---|---|---|---|
| 1.0.10_SV2.9.13.0_XE16.12 | app-hosting_UTD-Snort-Feature-x86_64_1.0.10_... | vmanage | App-Hosting |

***Figure 12-35.*** *Uploading the sec-app file*

Now we can add the security policy to our device template. Go to the template CSR_t-CSR1000v, and select Additional Templates. Under Security Policy, select "Sec-pol," and select "UTD-CSR1000v" within the Container Profile drop-down (Figure 12-36).

| Security Policy | Sec-pol ▼ |
| Container Profile * | UTD-CSR1000v ▼ ⬤ |

*Figure 12-36.  Adding the container profile*

Push this configuration to CSR-1. You may get the following error when it tries to install the new container:

```
UTC ERROR [vManage01] [LxcInstallActionProcessor] (device-
action-lxc_install-0) |default| On device CSR-0502AB1A-7DED-
13AE-3AB1-776B741BB137-70.100.100.1, Failed to install 1/1
lxc container (app-hosting-UTD-Snort-Feature-x86_64-1.0.10_
SV2.9.13.0_XE16.12).
```

```
Pre config validation failed. Device is not configured to
accept new configuration. Available memory insufficient,
required CPU:7 percent, reserved CPU:0 percent, available
CPU:7 percent, required memory:2097152 KB, reserved memory:0
KB, available memory:1048576 KB, required capacity:861 MB,
reserved capacity:0 MB, available harddisk:0 MB, available
bootflash:4867 MB, available logical volume:0 MB
```

By default, the CSR devices are set to have 4GB of memory, which is less than we need to run the UTD application:

```
CSR-1#sh ver | beg memory
cisco CSR1000V (VXE) processor (revision VXE) with
2080408K/3075K bytes of memory.
Processor board ID 9NVWF6PVA8D
4 Gigabit Ethernet interfaces
32768K bytes of non-volatile configuration memory.
3978448K bytes of physical memory.
6188032K bytes of virtual hard disk at bootflash:.
OK bytes of WebUI ODM Files at webui:.
```

So shut down CSR-1 and add more memory (8GB is a good number), by right-clicking the device in the EVE-NG GUI and selecting the properties. Increase the memory and start it up again.

```
CSR-1#sh ver | beg memory
cisco CSR1000V (VXE) processor (revision VXE) with
2296472K/3075K bytes of memory.
Processor board ID 9NVWF6PVA8D
4 Gigabit Ethernet interfaces
32768K bytes of non-volatile configuration memory.
8107212K bytes of physical memory.
6188032K bytes of virtual hard disk at bootflash:.
OK bytes of WebUI ODM Files at webui:
```

Now we can apply the configuration again, click the three dots, and select "Change Device Values." Don't change anything, just next through it, and vManage will update the CSR router as well as push the UTD file. We are going to walk through the process, starting with the initial download request.

```
%IOSXE-5-PLATFORM: RO/0: VCONFD_NOTIFIER: Install status:
d5ba3356-b49d-4ff3-834a-15f4b2b4cae2 download-start.
Message Downloading http://100.100.1.2:8080/software/package/
lxc/app-hosting_UTD-Snort-Feature-x86_64_1.0.10_SV2.9.13.0_
XE16.12_secapp-ucmk9.16.12.02r.1.0.10_SV2.9.13.0_XE16.12.
x86_64.tar?deviceId=70.100.100.1

%Cisco-SDWAN-CSR-1-action_notifier-6-INFO-1400002: RO/0:
VCONFD_NOTIFIER: Notification: 5/13/2020 15:8:3 system-
software-install-status severity-level:minor host-name:CSR-1
system-ip:70.100.100.1 status:download-start install-
id:d5ba3356-b49d-4ff3-834a-15f4b2b4cae2 message:Downloading
http://100.100.1.2:8080/software/package/lxc/app-hosting_
UTD-Snort-Feature-x86_64_1.0.10_SV2.9.13.0_XE16.12_
secapp-ucmk9.16.12.02r.1.0.10_SV2.9.13.0_XE16.12.x86_64.
tar?deviceId=70.100.100.1
CSR-1#
```

After a while, you should see a long list of messages on the CSR's console, starting with vManage logging in:

```
%DMI-5-AUTH_PASSED: RO/0: dmiauthd: User 'vmanage-admin'
authenticated successfully from 100.100.1.2:59787 and was
authorized for netconf over ssh. External groups:
```

The NETCONF messages passed from vManage to CSR-1 have instructed our router to download the app:

```
%IOSXE-5-PLATFORM: RO/0: VCONFD_NOTIFIER: Install status:
d5ba3356-b49d-4ff3-834a-15f4b2b4cae2 download-complete. Message
Downloaded app image to /bootflash/.UTD_IMAGES/app-hosting_
UTD-Snort-Feature-x86_64_1.0.10_SV2.9.13.0_XE16.12_secapp-
ucmk9.16.12.02r.1.0.10_SV2.9.13.0_XE16.12.x86_64.tar
```

The download finishes and we install the app:

```
%Cisco-SDWAN-CSR-1-action_notifier-6-INFO-1400002: R0/0:
VCONFD_NOTIFIER: Notification: 5/13/2020 15:13:16 system-
software-install-status severity-level:minor host-name:CSR-1
system-ip:70.100.100.1 status:download-complete install-
id:d5ba3356-b49d-4ff3-834a-15f4b2b4cae2 message:Downloaded
app image to /bootflash/.UTD_IMAGES/app-hosting_UTD-
Snort-Feature-x86_64_1.0.10_SV2.9.13.0_XE16.12_secapp-
ucmk9.16.12.02r.1.0.10_SV2.9.13.0_XE16.12.x86_64.tar
%IOSXE-5-PLATFORM: R0/0: VCONFD_NOTIFIER: Install status:
d5ba3356-b49d-4ff3-834a-15f4b2b4cae2 verification-complete.
Message NOOP
```

The installation finishes:

```
%Cisco-SDWAN-CSR-1-action_notifier-6-INFO-1400002: R0/0:
VCONFD_NOTIFIER: Notification: 5/13/2020 15:13:18 system-
software-install-status severity-level:minor host-name:CSR-1
system-ip:70.100.100.1 status:verification-complete install-
id:d5ba3356-b49d-4ff3-834a-15f4b2b4cae2 message:NOOP
%VMAN-5-PACKAGE_SIGNING_LEVEL_ON_INSTALL: R0/0: vman: Package
'iox-utd_1.0.10_SV2.9.13.0_XE16.12.tar' for service container
'utd' is 'Cisco signed', signing level cached on original
install is 'Cisco signed'
%VMAN-2-MEMORY_LIMIT_WARN: R0/0: vman: Virtual service (utd)
profile (urlf-medium) defines 4096 MB of Memory exceeding the
maximum 3072 MB.
%VIRT_SERVICE-5-INSTALL_STATE: Successfully installed virtual
service utd
%IOSXE-5-PLATFORM: R0/0: VCONFD_NOTIFIER: Install status:
d5ba3356-b49d-4ff3-834a-15f4b2b4cae2 install-start. Message
Success, App state: DEPLOYED
```

```
%Cisco-SDWAN-CSR-1-action_notifier-6-INFO-1400002: R0/0:
VCONFD_NOTIFIER: Notification: 5/13/2020 15:14:6 system-
software-install-status severity-level:minor host-name:CSR-1
system-ip:70.100.100.1 status:install-start install-
id:d5ba3356-b49d-4ff3-834a-15f4b2b4cae2 message:Success, App
state: DEPLOYED
%IM-6-INSTALL_MSG: R0/0: ioxman: app-hosting: Install
succeeded: utd installed successfully Current state is deployed
```

vManage logs in again, pushing through the new configuration:

```
%DMI-5-AUTH_PASSED: R0/0: dmiauthd: User 'vmanage-admin'
authenticated successfully from 100.100.1.2:59849 and was
authorized for netconf over ssh. External groups:
%SYS-5-CONFIG_P: Configured programmatically by process iosp_
vty_100001_dmi_nesd from console as NETCONF on vty32131
%DMI-5-CONFIG_I: R0/0: nesd: Configured from NETCONF/RESTCONF
by vmanage-admin, transaction-id 321
```

Now we start to see some virtual port groups coming up:

```
%LINEPROTO-5-UPDOWN: Line protocol on Interface
VirtualPortGroup0, changed state to up
%LINEPROTO-5-UPDOWN: Line protocol on Interface
VirtualPortGroup1, changed state to up
```

We have another login from vManage and we see some Snort action. Snort is where we will get the application detection abilities:

```
%DMI-5-AUTH_PASSED: R0/0: dmiauthd: User 'vmanage-admin'
authenticated successfully from 100.100.1.2:59873 and was
authorized for netconf over ssh. External groups:
%ONEP_BASE-6-SS_ENABLED: ONEP: Service set Vty was enabled by
Platform
```

```
%ONEP_BASE-6-CONNECT: [Element]: ONEP session Application:utd_
snort Host:CSR-1 ID:3818 User: has connected.
%ONEP_BASE-6-DISCONNECT: [Element]: ONEP session
Application:utd_snort Host:CSR-1 ID:3818 User: has disconnected.
%ONEP_BASE-6-CONNECT: [Element]: ONEP session Application:utd_
snort Host:CSR-1 ID:8443 User: has connected.
%ONEP_BASE-6-DISCONNECT: [Element]: ONEP session
Application:utd_snort Host:CSR-1 ID:8443 User: has disconnected.
%ONEP_BASE-6-CONNECT: [Element]: ONEP session Application:utd_
snort Host:CSR-1 ID:7470 User: has connected.
%ONEP_BASE-6-DISCONNECT: [Element]: ONEP session
Application:utd_snort Host:CSR-1 ID:7470 User: has disconnected.
```

UTD is now installed and activated:

```
%VIRT_SERVICE-5-ACTIVATION_STATE: Successfully activated
virtual service utd
%IM-6-START_MSG: R0/0: ioxman: app-hosting: Start succeeded:
utd started successfully Current state is running
```

We get a little Snort update:

```
%ONEP_BASE-6-CONNECT: [Element]: ONEP session Application:utd_
snort Host:CSR-1 ID:4577 User: has connected.
%IOSXE_UTD-4-MT_CONFIG_DOWNLOAD: UTD MT configuration download
has started% UTD: Received appnav notification from LXC
for    (src 192.0.2.1, dst 192.0.2.2)
% UTD successfully registered with Appnav (src 192.0.2.1, dst
192.0.2.2)
% UTD redirect interface set to VirtualPortGroup1 internally
%IOSXE_UTD-4-MT_CONFIG_DOWNLOAD: UTD MT configuration download
has completed
```

A quick bounce of the service and everything is green again:

```
%IOSXE-1-PLATFORM: R0/0: cpp_cp: QFP:0.0 Thread:000
TS:00000000865384064983 %UTD-1-UTD_HEALTH_CHANGE: Service node
changed state Down => Green (3)
%LINEPROTO-5-UPDOWN: Line protocol on Interface Tunnel6000001,
changed state to up
%IOSXE-1-PLATFORM: R0/0: cpp_cp: QFP:0.0 Thread:000
TS:00000000866135564670 %UTD-1-UTD_HEALTH_CHANGE: Service node
changed state Green => Down (0)
%IOSXE-1-PLATFORM: R0/0: cpp_cp: QFP:0.0 Thread:000
TS:00000000876327852984 %UTD-1-UTD_HEALTH_CHANGE: Service node
changed state Down => Green (3)
```

Now, if we test our Telnet again, we can see that our security policies
are in place and working (Figure 12-37).

```
user@user-virtual-machine:~$ telnet 192.168.30.30
Trying 192.168.30.30...
telnet: Unable to connect to remote host: Connection timed out
user@user-virtual-machine:~$ ▮
```

***Figure 12-37.*** *Telnet is denied*

If we look at the console output on the CSR router, we can see that the
Telnet traffic is being dropped and that this is due to the Site-300-FW-Pol:

```
%IOSXE-6-PLATFORM: R0/0: cpp_cp: QFP:0.0 Thread:000
TS:00000141275333373800 %FW-6-LOG_SUMMARY: 7 tcp packets
were dropped from GigabitEthernet4 192.168.33.33:34490 =>
192.168.30.30:23 (target:class)-(ZP_zone-one_zone-one_-
1002302744:Site-300-FW-Pol-seq-1-cm_)  (srcvrf:dstvrf)-(1:1)
```

However, other traffic is also being dropped:

```
%IOSXE-6-PLATFORM: RO/O: cpp_cp: QFP:0.0 Thread:000
TS:00000141335337138264 %FW-6-LOG_SUMMARY: 5 tcp packets
were dropped from GigabitEthernet4 192.168.33.33:41877 =>
35.232.111.17:80 (target:class)-(none:none)  (srcvrf:dstvrf)-
(1:global)
```

The reason for this is because we have no rule to permit traffic from VPN 1 to the global VRF. Before we go and fix that, let's have a little look at some verification commands we can use to confirm what the firewall on CSR-1 is doing. To get an idea of all the drops, we can use the following command:

```
CSR-1#show platform hardware qfp active feature firewall drop
-------------------------------------------------------------
Drop Reason                             Packets
-------------------------------------------------------------
Zone-pair without policy                12066
Policy drop:classify result               7
Firewall invalid zone                   4749
CSR-1#
```

To see the amount of traffic dropped due to policy, we can use this command:

```
CSR-1#show sdwan zbfw drop-statistics policy-action-drop
zbfw drop-statistics policy-action-drop 7

CSR-1#
```

And to get a long list of all the statistics, we can use "show sdwan zbfw zonepair-statistics". I have removed the connection statistics to make it easier to read (and also as they were all zero):

```
CSR-1#show sdwan zbfw zonepair-statistics
zbfw zonepair-statistics ZP_zone-one_zone-one_-1002302744
 src-zone-name zone-one
 dst-zone-name zone-one
 policy-name   Site-300-FW-Pol
 fw-traffic-class-entry Site-300-FW-Pol-seq-1-cm_
  zonepair-name              ZP_zone-one_zone-one_-1002302744
  class-action               "Inspect Drop"
  pkts-counter               7
  bytes-counter              518
    fw-tc-match-entry Site-300-FW-Pol-seq-1-acl_ 3
   match-type "access-group name"
  l7-policy-name             NONE
 fw-traffic-class-entry Site-300-FW-Pol-seq-11-cm_
  zonepair-name              ZP_zone-one_zone-one_-1002302744
  class-action               "Inspect Pass"
  pkts-counter               95
  bytes-counter              8551
    fw-tc-match-entry Site-300-FW-Pol-seq-11-acl_ 3
   match-type "access-group name"
  l7-policy-name             NONE
 fw-traffic-class-entry class-default
  zonepair-name              ZP_zone-one_zone-one_-1002302744
  class-action               "Inspect Pass"
  pkts-counter               403
  bytes-counter              42977
  l7-policy-name             NONE

CSR-1#
```

Let's just check that other traffic within VPN still passes, therefore showing that the zone one to zone one allow rule is working (Figure 12-38).

```
user@user-virtual-machine:~$ ssh sd-admin@192.168.30.30
*********************************************************************
* IOSv is strictly limited to use for evaluation, demonstration and IOS  *
* education. IOSv is provided as-is and is not supported by Cisco's       *
* Technical Advisory Center. Any use or disclosure, in whole or in part,  *
* of the IOSv Software or Documentation to any third party for any        *
* purposes is expressly prohibited except as otherwise authorized by      *
* Cisco in writing.                                                        *
*********************************************************************Passw
ord:

*********************************************************************
* IOSv is strictly limited to use for evaluation, demonstration and IOS  *
* education. IOSv is provided as-is and is not supported by Cisco's       *
* Technical Advisory Center. Any use or disclosure, in whole or in part,  *
* of the IOSv Software or Documentation to any third party for any        *
* purposes is expressly prohibited except as otherwise authorized by      *
* Cisco in writing.                                                        *
*********************************************************************
R300>
```

***Figure 12-38.*** *SSH is permitted*

Good. So, how do we fix the outbound traffic? Thankfully, it is a super simple fix. Head back to Security, and edit the Sec-pol policy. Under the Policy Summary is a little tick box for *"Bypass firewall policy and allow all Internet traffic to/from VPN 0"* (Figure 12-39). Tick it and then click "Save Policy Changes."

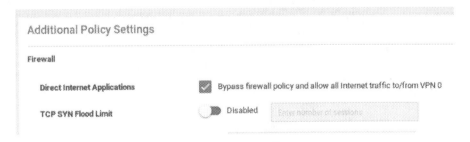

***Figure 12-39.*** *Bypass the firewall for VPN 0*

Once this is pushed out again, we have Internet access (Figure 12-40).

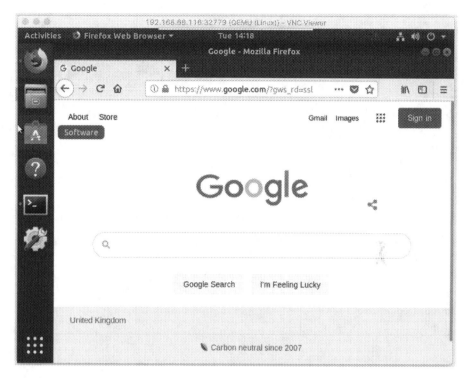

*Figure 12-40.*  *Internet is still working*

More importantly, our URL filtering is also working. We can check this by trying to get to 4Chan as this appears on several of our blocked categories (adult themes, nudity, pornography, and tasteless) (Figure 12-41).

---

**Caution**    Only try this website if it is safe to do so. It is probably best not to try if it's going to get you flagged by your employer's DNS history. I don't want to get you in trouble.

---

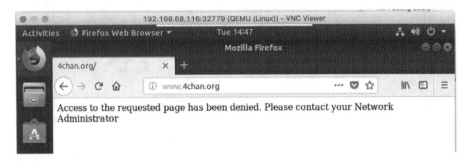

**Figure 12-41.** *4Chan is blocked*

From a monitoring perspective, we can see the amount of traffic being prevented by our filters from the Monitoring page. Go to *Monitoring* ➤ *Network,* and select the CSR-1 device (Figure 12-42).

**Figure 12-42.** *The network monitoring page*

Clicking URL filtering shows us the number of sessions that have been blocked (Figure 12-43).

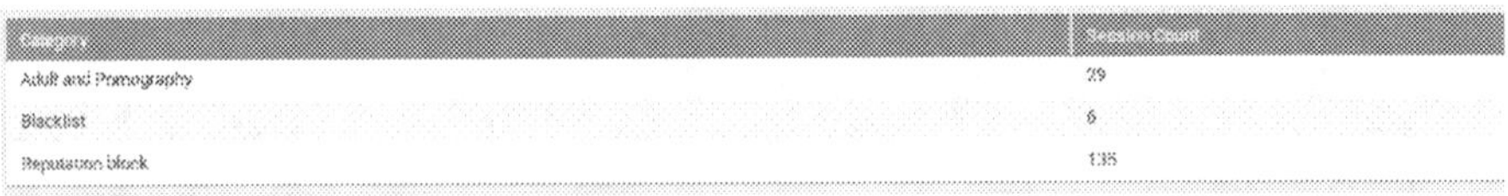

| Category | Session Count |
|---|---|
| Adult and Pornography | 29 |
| Blacklist | 6 |
| Reputation block | 138 |

**Figure 12-43.** *Blocked session information*

While we cannot, from this page, drill down into the data to see what sites have been blocked, or for whom they have been blocked, it does give us a little insight into what is happening within our network.

# Summary

In this chapter, we implemented some simple firewall rules to block traffic and used the application plugin to block a website based on what categories it is in.

In our next chapter, we will be looking at management and operations of the SD-WAN.

# CHAPTER 13

# Management and Operations

In our penultimate chapter, we are going to look at monitoring through the use of email alerts, logging, SNMP, and setting up maintenance windows, and we will finish by exploring the REST API. We will start with the basic requirements of any good network: alerting and logging.

## Email Alerts

To set up email alerts, navigate to *Administration* ➤ *Settings*. Scroll down to Email Notifications, and click Edit on the right-hand side.

Set email notifications to be enabled, and enter the details of the SMTP server (either the name or IP address and the port) and the from and reply-to email addresses. Remember to set any authentication if it is required (Figure 13-1).

© Stuart Fordham 2021
S. Fordham, *Learning SD-WAN with Cisco*, https://doi.org/10.1007/978-1-4842-7347-0_13

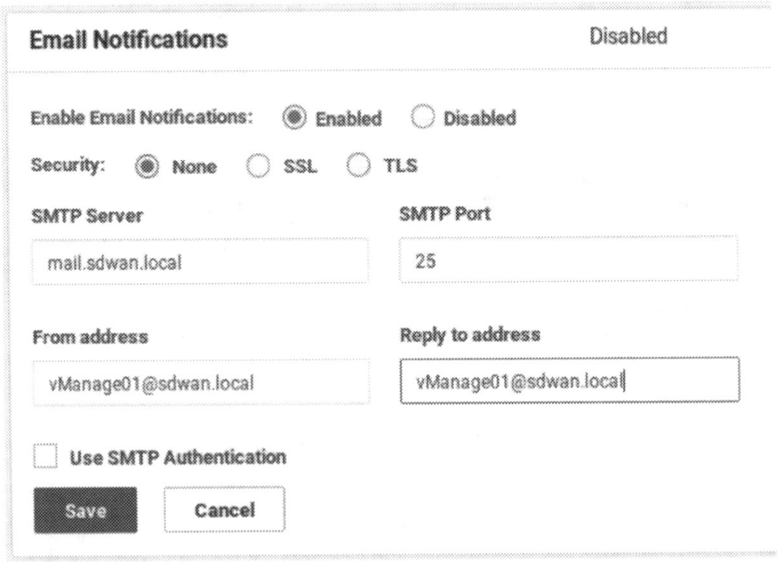

**Email Notifications**                                          Disabled

Enable Email Notifications:    ⦿ Enabled    ◯ Disabled

Security:    ⦿ None    ◯ SSL    ◯ TLS

SMTP Server                                 SMTP Port

mail.sdwan.local                            25

From address                                Reply to address

vManage01@sdwan.local                       vManage01@sdwan.local

☐ Use SMTP Authentication

[ Save ]    [ Cancel ]

*Figure 13-1.  Setting up email notifications*

Save the settings. Next, we have to set what we would like to receive emails about. Go to *Monitor ➤ Alarms*, and click Email Notifications on the top right-hand corner. Click "Add Email Notification." Enter a name for the notification, and select the severity levels to alert on as well as the alarms we want to alert on (Figure 13-2).

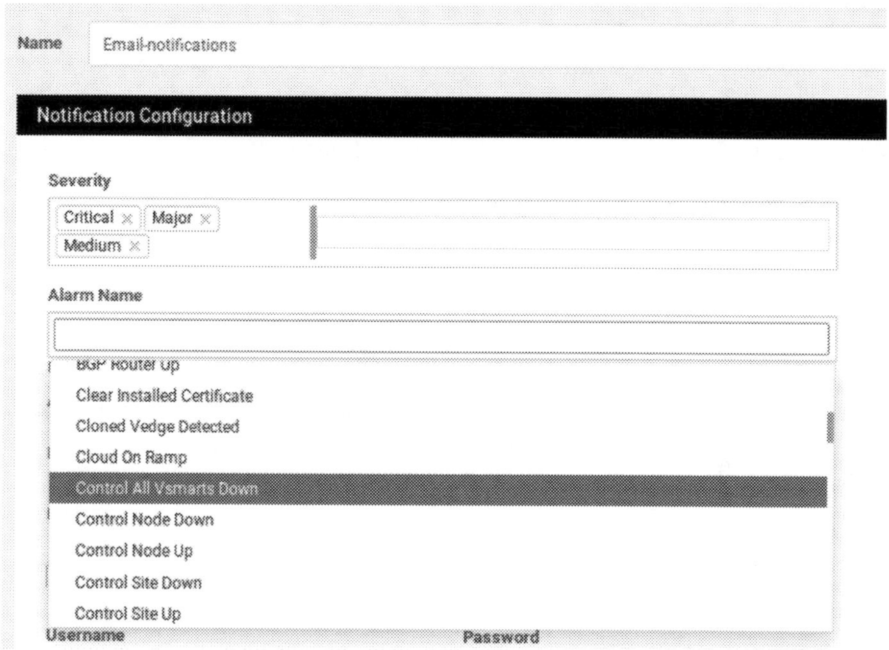

**Figure 13-2.**  *Selecting severity and alarms*

Add in the email addresses to send to (Figure 13-3).

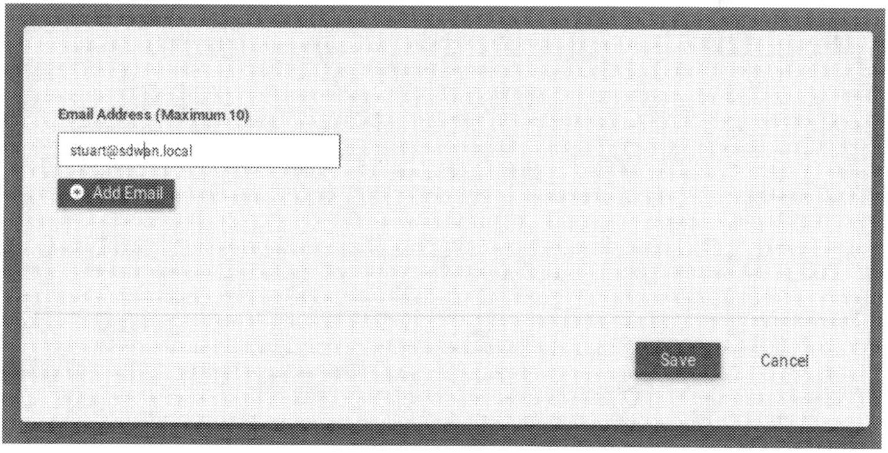

**Figure 13-3.**  *Setting the recipient email address*

This can also invoke a webhook (such as posting to a custom Microsoft Teams channel), or be tailored to only include certain devices, so you could, for example, set up a particular alert for just the edge devices (Figure 13-4). This would be useful if you had particular people looking after the edge routers and another set of people looking after the control plane (vManage, vSmart, and vBond), for instance.

*Figure 13-4.*  *Device selection*

Click Save once completed.

# Audit Logs

If you head over to the Monitor section and select "Audit Log," you will see a list of all of the configurations that have occurred over the selected time period, by all users (Figure 13-5).

| Timestamp | User | User IP | Message | Module | Feature | Device |
|---|---|---|---|---|---|---|
| 19 Jul 2021 5:35:32 PM CEST | admin | 10.1.1.100 | Email Notification Email-notifications added and email ... | Email | Email | -- |
| 19 Jul 2021 5:33:08 PM CEST | admin | 10.1.1.100 | Created emailNotificationSettings setting successfully | settings | settings | 100.100.1.2 |
| 19 Jul 2021 5:32:08 PM CEST | admin | 10.1.1.100 | Authentication succeeded for admin,source IP:10.1.1.1... | user | user | 100.100.1.2 |
| 19 Jul 2021 5:18:13 PM CEST | admin | 10.1.1.100 | Template t-CSR1000v successfully attached to device ... | template | template-device-... | 70.100.100.1 |
| 19 Jul 2021 5:17:10 PM CEST | admin | 10.1.1.100 | Device Validation Template device config - Validation s... | template | template-device-... | Validation |
| 19 Jul 2021 5:14:34 PM CEST | admin | 10.1.1.100 | Template t-CSR1000v edited | template | device | -- |
| 19 Jul 2021 5:13:43 PM CEST | admin | 10.1.1.100 | Template cEdge-VPN2 edited | template | general | -- |
| 19 Jul 2021 5:13:28 PM CEST | admin | 10.1.1.100 | Template cEdge-VPN2 created | template | general | -- |

*Figure 13-5.*  *The audit log*

You can click the green arrow above the entries to download the events in a CSV format.

# Syslog

Another essential aspect of proper network caretaking is to have centralized logging. To do this, we return to our templates. Add a new Logging feature template called "CSR-logging" (Figure 13-6).

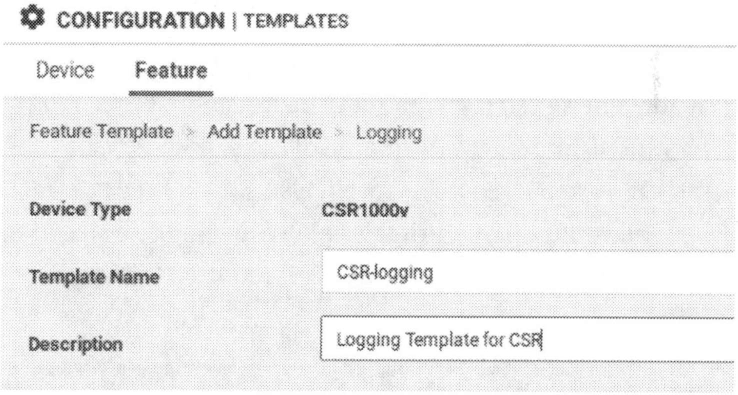

⚙ CONFIGURATION | TEMPLATES

Device    **Feature**

Feature Template  >  Add Template  >  Logging

| | |
|---|---|
| **Device Type** | **CSR1000v** |
| **Template Name** | CSR-logging |
| **Description** | Logging Template for CSR |

*Figure 13-6.*  *A logging template*

By default, logging to disk is enabled, we can log a maximum of 10MB to each log file, and we can have ten log files. These will be rotated, and the oldest will be deleted once a new one is created (Figure 13-7).

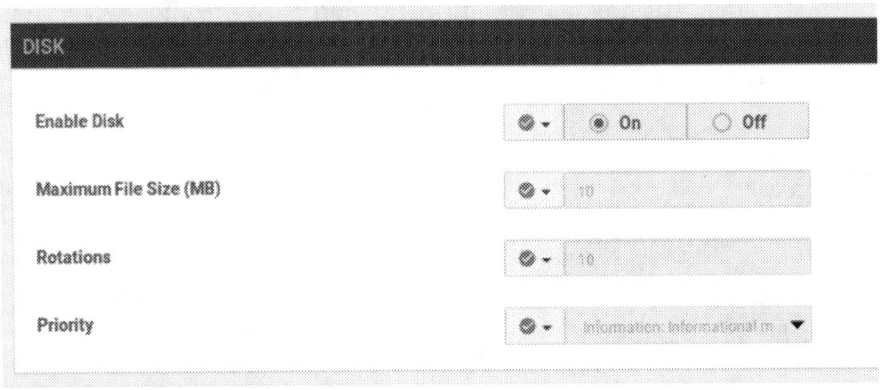

**Figure 13-7.** *Logging to disk*

We can add a new syslog server in the next section, by clicking "New Server." Enter the IP address or hostname of the syslog server, along with the ID of the VPN used to reach it. We can also set a source interface (which if you follow the CIS security templates, having a source interface for logging is recommended) and a priority if required (Figure 13-8).

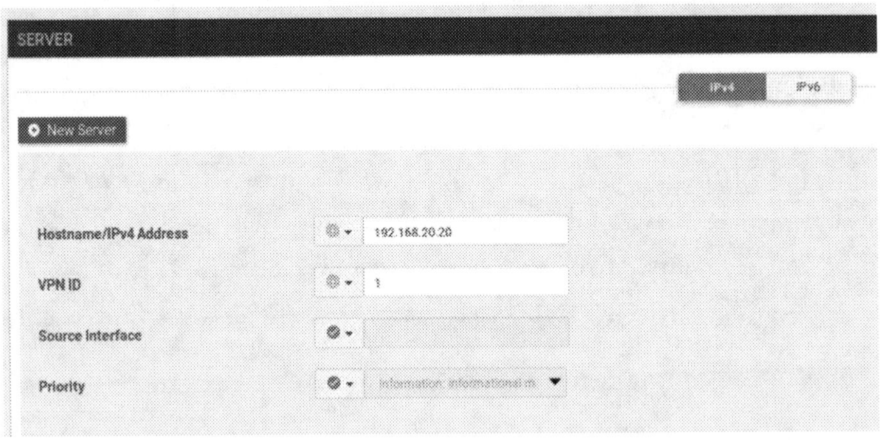

**Figure 13-8.** *Setting a Syslog server*

Once you have saved the template, edit the device template and set it to use the new logging template (Figure 13-9).

**Basic Information**

| System * | c-v-System ▾ |
| Logging* | Factory_Default_Logging_Template ▾ |
| | **CSR-logging** |
| | Factory_Default_Logging_Template |

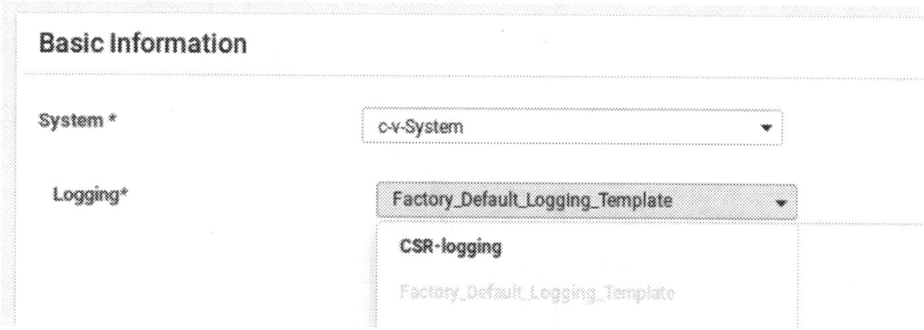

*Figure 13-9.* *Adding the logging template*

Save and apply the template to your devices.

# SNMP

SNMP (Simple Network Management Protocol) allows us to query the devices for certain metrics, or for the devices to send data, such as event notifications, which are known as traps.

Create a new SNMP feature template for CSR1000v routers, name it "CSR_CSR-SNMP", and set a description (I am using this name as originally I called it CSR-SNMP, and that template was migrated as we saw in the previous chapter, but I wanted the screenshot to match). Set the SNMP feature to not be shutdown. We can use a mixture of device-specific values (device name and location) and global variables (contact person) (Figure 13-10).

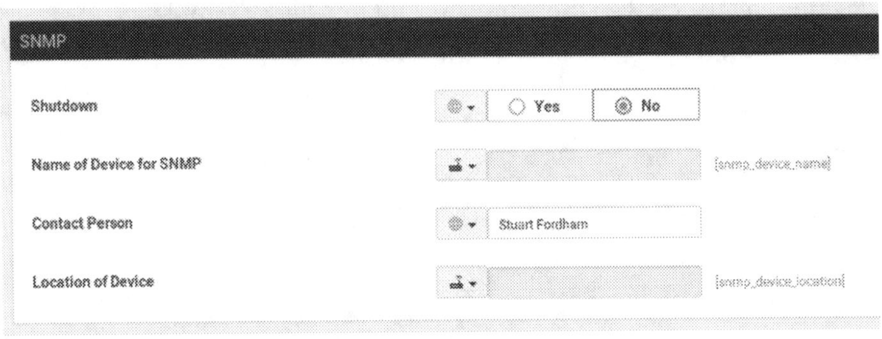

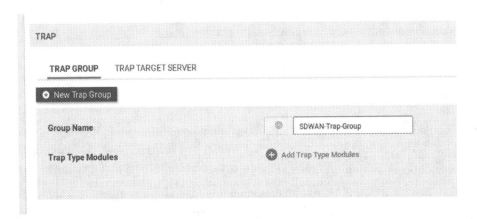

**Figure 13-10.** *An SNMP template*

Create a new trap group, called SDWAN-Trap-Group (Figure 13-11).

**Figure 13-11.** *Creating a trap group*

Add a new trap module (Figure 13-12).

***Figure 13-12.*** *Adding a trap module*

Set the module name and security level you need (Figure 13-13).

***Figure 13-13.*** *Setting the module security level*

Save the changes and click "Add" (Figure 13-14).

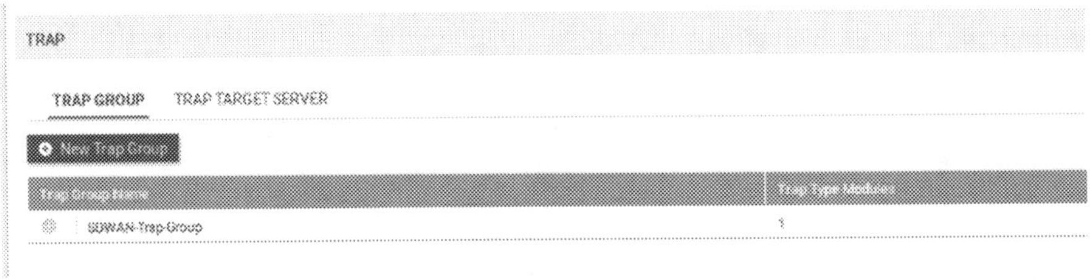

*Figure 13-14.* *The finished trap group*

We can have different SNMP rights, and these can query different aspects of the environment, based on the object identifier (OID), which is a dotted numerical reference to the MIB (Management Information Base), or "tree" of SNMP data. Create a new view, called "Read-Only," and click "Add Object Identifiers" (Figure 13-15).

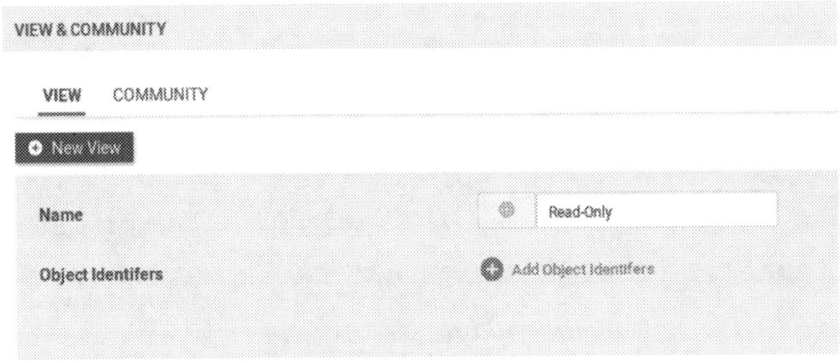

*Figure 13-15.* *Creating a read-only view*

Click "Add Object Identifier" (Figure 13-16).

***Figure 13-16.*** *Adding an OID*

Enter the Object Identifier (OID). Here, we are using 1.3.6.1, which is the Internet portion of the SNMP MIB (Figure 13-17).

***Figure 13-17.*** *The Internet OID*

Click "Add" (Figure 13-18).

VIEW & COMMUNITY

VIEW    COMMUNITY

**New View**

| Name | List of OIDs |
| --- | --- |
| Read-Only | 1 |

*Figure 13-18.* *The read-only view*

SNMP (version 1 and 2) queries reference a "Community," which is the credentials shared between the device and the management station doing the querying. SMNPv3 uses users instead of communities. Click the Community tab, and then click "Add Community." Give the community a name, and select the authorization level, and then select the view to use (Figure 13-19).

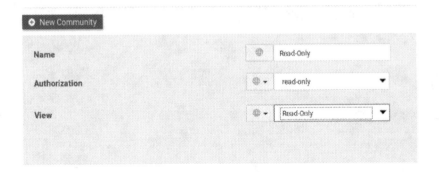

| New Community | |
| --- | --- |
| Name | Read-Only |
| Authorization | read-only |
| View | Read-Only |

*Figure 13-19.* *Setting up the Community*

Click "Add" (Figure 13-20).

**New Community**

| Community | Authorization | View |
| --- | --- | --- |
| Read-Only | read-only | Read-Only |

*Figure 13-20.* *The completed Community*

Now that we have everything else set up, we can create a trap target server. Click the tab and create a new trap target, entering the VPN ID, IP address, port, trap group name, and community name. Enter a source interface if required (Figure 13-21).

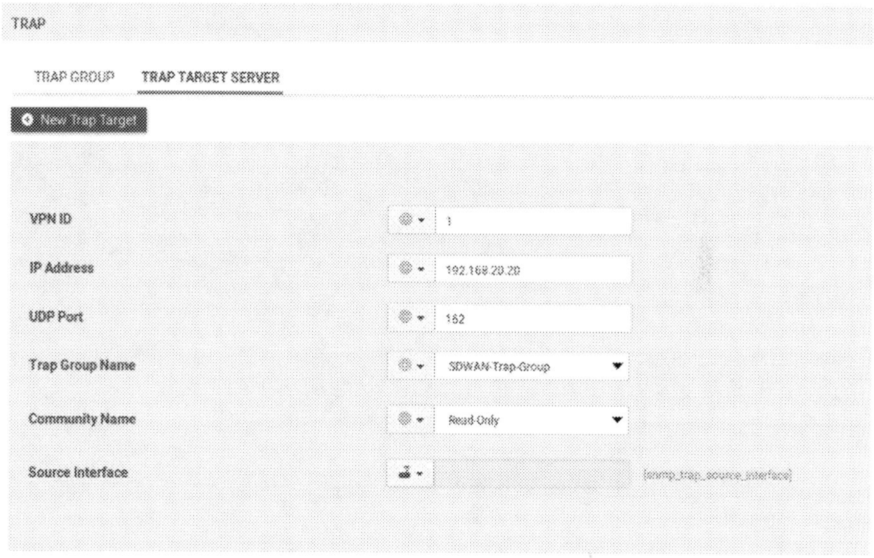

*Figure 13-21.*  *The Trap target settings*

Click "Add" (Figure 13-22).

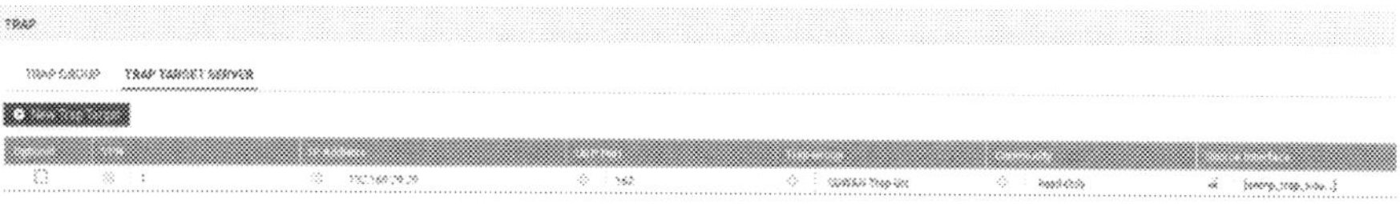

*Figure 13-22.*  *The completed Trap target*

Lastly, go into the CSR1000v device template, and set the SNMP template (under "Additional Templates") to use the new CSR_CSR-SNMP template (Figure 13-23).

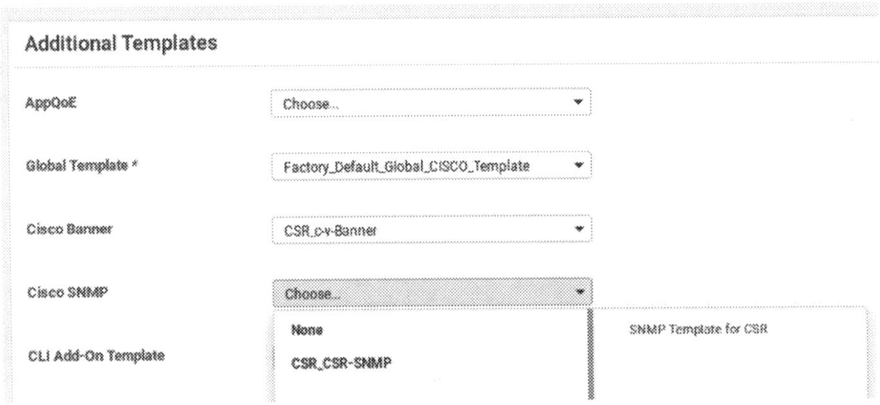

*Figure 13-23.*  *Adding the SNMP feature template*

Now your SNMP monitoring software should start to receive SNMP traps.

# Maintenance Windows

Now that we have set up alerting and logging, we need to look at how to suppress these alerts during a maintenance window.

Navigate to *Administration* ➤ *Settings*, and then scroll down to Maintenance Window, and click the edit button. Select the start date and time (Figure 13-24).

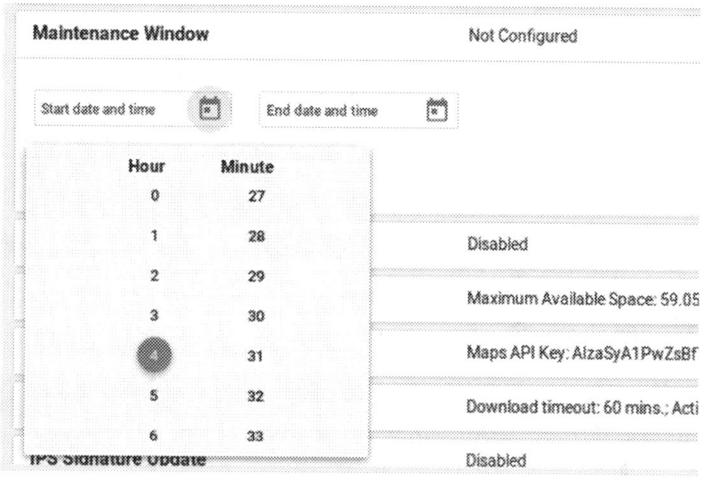

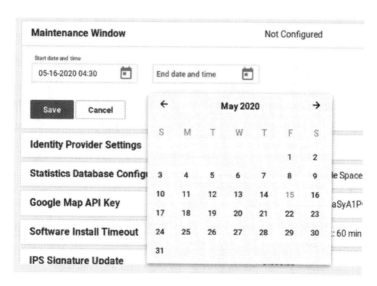

**Figure 13-24.**  *The maintenance window start time*

Set the end date and time (Figure 13-25).

**Figure 13-25.**  *The maintenance window end time*

Click Save (Figure 13-26).

**Figure 13-26.** *The maintenance window*

Maintenance windows are displayed on the vManage NMS dashboard starting two days before the maintenance window.

# REST API

The vManage server provides an extensive REST API (Representational State Transfer Application Programming Interface). Through this API, we can control, configure, and monitor the entire network programmatically, kind of like a software-defined-software-defined WAN. Using REST, we can make the following type of calls:

| Call | Action |
| --- | --- |
| GET | Retrieve or read information |
| PUT | Update an object |
| POST | Create an object |
| DELETE | Remove and object |

We can also use the REST API to perform bulk actions to retrieve state and statistical information, and this uses RESTful bulk API calls.

The easiest way to get started with the REST API is to visit `https://vmanage-ip-address:port/apidocs` (Figure 13-27).

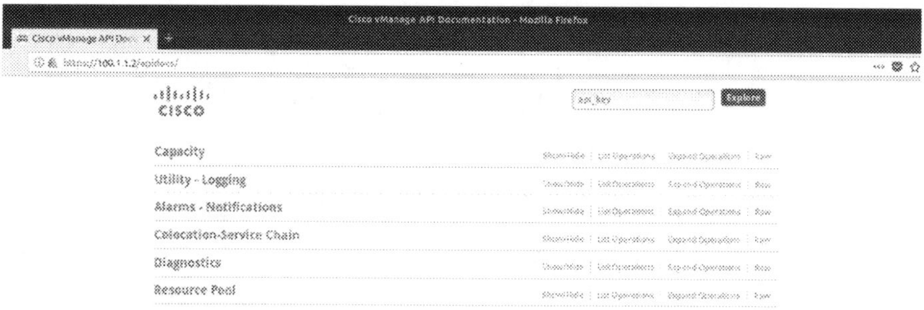

***Figure 13-27.*** *The API docs*

Clicking one of the options drops down a smaller box that will show you the model schema and response codes (Figure 13-28) and will allow you to test it out in your environment.

***Figure 13-28.*** *An example of the REST API*

Create a new user by going to *Administration* ➤ *Manage Users* and call it "api," and set a password of Test123. Make it a member of the operators group.

Start a terminal prompt on one of the Linux boxes. We need to start by authenticating to vManage by specifying the username and password; these need to match the fields on the login page.

```
curl -k -d "j_username=api&j_password=Test123 -X POST
https://10.1.1.2:8443/j_security_check --cookie-jar api-cookie.txt
```

The -k option allows us to make insecure curl commands (we bypass certificate checking, which is useful as we do not have a "proper" CA-signed certificate). The -d flag is the data we are sending. We specify that we are posting this data (the -X flag). We should now have a cookie stored in a text file as we are using the --cookie-jar option to save the result in a file called cookie.txt. We can see this in Figure 13-29.

```
user@user-virtual-machine:~$ curl -k -d "j_username=api&j_password=Test123" -X
POST https://10.1.1.2:8443/j_security_check --cookie-jar api-cookie.txt
user@user-virtual-machine:~$ cat api-cookie.txt
# Netscape HTTP Cookie File
# https://curl.haxx.se/docs/http-cookies.html
# This file was generated by libcurl! Edit at your own risk.

#HttpOnly_10.1.1.2     FALSE   /       TRUE    0       JSESSIONID      Jl71Dix
TBlFKFQJfP6NsGa0r0HyZ1WDmlgEENpWw.a9e8cabb-8259-478a-bcbe-1644753a8f3e
user@user-virtual-machine:~$ █
```

***Figure 13-29.*** *Authenticating to the API*

We have a session life span of 24 hours, but the API session will time out after 30 minutes of inactivity.

From here, we can make a simple GET request, such as to see the banner configured (Figure 13-30).

```
user@user-virtual-machine:~$ curl -k --location --request GET "https://10.1.1.2
:8443/dataservice/settings/banner" --cookie api-cookie.txt
{"data":[{"mode":"on","bannerDetail":"This is a banner"}]}user@user-virtual-mac
hine:~$ 
```

**_Figure 13-30._**  _Retrieving the banner through the API_

So far so good. Let's use the API to create a new user. As the commands get a little long, we can use some tricks to make life easier, such as using files to hold the data we want to use in the command.

Create a file called tester.json, and enter the details as shown in the following:

```
{
  "group": [
  "operator"
  ],
  "description": "An API test user",
  "userName": "tester",
  "password": "Test123"
}
```

Now let's try using this in a command to create a new user. Enter the following:

```
curl -k -H "Content-Type: application/json" -X POST --data
@tester.json --cookie api-cookie.txt https://10.1.1.2:443/
dataservice/admin/user
```

The command will fail with the following error: "SessionTokenFilter: Token provided via HTTP Header does not match the token generated by the server" (Figure 13-31).

```
user@user-virtual-machine:~$ curl -k -H "Content-Type: application/json" -X POS
T --data @tester.json --cookie api-cookie2.txt https://10.1.1.2:443/dataservice
/admin/user
<html><head><title>Error</title></head><body>SessionTokenFilter: Token provided
via HTTP Header does not match the token generated by the server.</body></html
>user@user-virtual-machine:~$
```

***Figure 13-31.*** *Session error*

The reason for this error is that since version 19.2, the API requires
a token in any POST, PUT, or DELETE commands. So, how do we get
this token? We just need to make a GET command (curl -k -X GET
https://10.1.1.2:443/dataservice/client/token --cookie api-
cookie.txt). The result is a long alphanumeric string (Figure 13-32).

```
user@user-virtual-machine:~$ curl -k -X  GET https://10.1.1.2:443/dataservice/c
lient/token --cookie api-cookie2.txt
0497CD2B3D2D7C8B47DB45006E98A1B216B2474D683EC9BCCBF5B28242E78DB918EE8CCD0C168FD
0396720FF576F69BBEF46user@user-virtual-machine:~$
```

***Figure 13-32.*** *The session token*

From now on (at least for anything more exciting than a GET request),
we need to specify this session token. This does make the command rather
long though, so I have truncated it in the following, but check Figure 13-33
for the full command. Now our command to create the user becomes

curl -k -H "Content-Type: application/json" -X POST --data
@tester.json --cookie api-cookie.txt https://10.1.1.2:443/
dataservice/admin/user -H "X-XSRF-TOKEN:0497CD"

```
user@user-virtual-machine:~$ curl -k -H "Content-Type: application/json" -X POS
T --data @tester.json --cookie api-cookie2.txt https://10.1.1.2:443/dataservice
/admin/user -H "X-XSRF-TOKEN:0497CD2B3D2D7C8B47DB45006E98A1B216B2474D683EC9BCCB
F5B28242E78DB918EE8CCD0C168FD0396720FF576F69BBEF46"
Access forbidden: role not allowed{"error":{"message":"Forbidden","details":"Us
er does not have permission to access this resource","code":"DS0001"}}user@user
-virtual-machine:~$
```

***Figure 13-33.*** *Using the session token*

Our command works, but we are denied. Our API user does not have the correct permissions to perform creations, updates, or deletions in vManage as the operator group that it belongs to only has read permissions.

Head back to the GUI, and go into User Groups (you should already be there, but if you have navigated away, it's under *Administration* ➤ *Manage Users*). Create a new group called "api-user-admin" with write permissions on the Manage Users feature (Figure 13-34).

*Figure 13-34.* *The api-user-admin group*

Create a new user, called "api2," with a password of Test123, and make them a member of this new group (Figure 13-35).

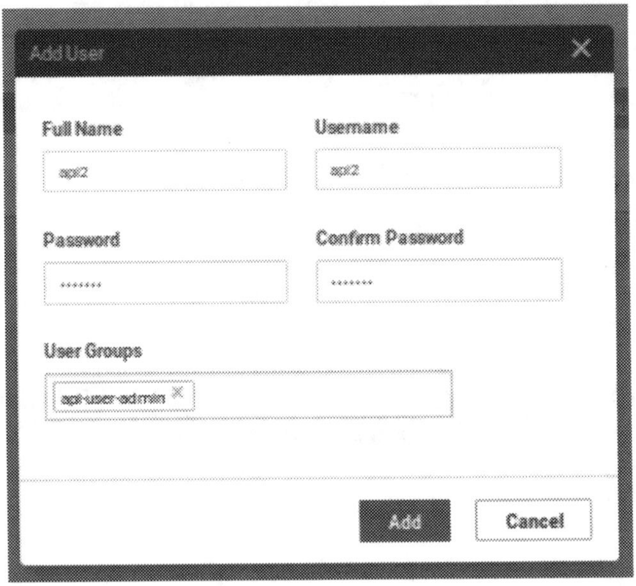

*Figure 13-35.* *The new api2 user*

We need to run through the authentication again with this new user and create the session cookie (Figure 13-36).

```
user@user-virtual-machine:~$ curl -k -d "j_username=api2&j_password=Test123" -X
 POST https://10.1.1.2:8443/j_security_check --cookie-jar api-cookie.txt
user@user-virtual-machine:~$
user@user-virtual-machine:~$ curl -k -X  GET https://10.1.1.2:443/dataservice/c
lient/token --cookie api-cookie.txt
B1A5C4B12E23765203DFAC98DB2738EDE8BCE478E2574797BFDA4E9300A78CA57011B2BA43D666D
E3338B3EC0A6F6B736FADuser@user-virtual-machine:~$
user@user-virtual-machine:~$
```

*Figure 13-36.* *Authenticating with the api2 user*

Now, we can create our user (Figure 13-37).

```
user@user-virtual-machine:~$ curl -k -H "Content-Type: application/json" -X POS
T --data @tester.json --cookie api-cookie.txt https://10.1.1.2:443/dataservice/
admin/user -H "X-XSRF-TOKEN:B1A5C4B12E23765203DFAC98DB2738EDE8BCE478E2574797BFD
A4E9300A78CA57011B2BA43D666DE3338B3EC0A6F6B736FAD"
{}user@user-virtual-machine:~$ ▮
```

***Figure 13-37.***  *Creating a user via the API*

Nothing is returned, so we could either use the API to list all the users or return to the GUI (Figure 13-38).

| Name | Username | User Groups |
|---|---|---|
| -- | admin | |
| api | api | operator |
| api2 | api2 | api-user-admin |
| Monitoring | monitoring | basic |
| An API test user | tester | operator |

***Figure 13-38.***  *The new user*

# Summary

In this chapter, we set up email alerts, looked at audit logs, and configured SYSLOG, SNMP, and maintenance windows, before we finished with how we can use the REST API to retrieve data and perform creative tasks, such as managing users.

In the final chapter, we will look at troubleshooting.

# CHAPTER 14

# Troubleshooting

This chapter is a collection of basic troubleshooting steps, as well as looking at some of the issues I came across while writing this book.

## Basic Troubleshooting Techniques

### Pinging

Ping is a great way to confirm basic connectivity. The gotcha is that when pinging, we must specify the VPN to use:

```
vManage01# ping 100.1.1.3 ?
Possible completions:
  count      Number of ping packets
  fragment   do(prohibit fragmentation, even local
one),        dont(do not set DF flag)
  rapid      Rapid ping
  size       Size of packets, in bytes
  source     Source interface or IP address
  vpn        VPN ID
  wait       Time to wait for a response, in seconds
  |          Output modifiers
  <cr>
vManage01# ping 100.1.1.3 vpn 512
Ping in VPN 512
PING 100.1.1.3 (100.1.1.3) 56(84) bytes of data.
```

© Stuart Fordham 2021
S. Fordham, *Learning SD-WAN with Cisco*, https://doi.org/10.1007/978-1-4842-7347-0_14

```
64 bytes from 100.1.1.3: icmp_seq=1 ttl=64 time=0.872 ms
64 bytes from 100.1.1.3: icmp_seq=2 ttl=64 time=0.366 ms
^C
--- 100.1.1.3 ping statistics ---
2 packets transmitted, 2 received, 0% packet loss, time 1000ms
rtt min/avg/max/mdev = 0.366/0.619/0.872/0.253 ms
vManage01#
```

# Traceroute

Similar to ping, we need to specify which VPN to use when performing traceroutes:

```
Edge01# traceroute vpn 1 172.16.20.1
Traceroute   172.16.20.1 in VPN 1
traceroute to 172.16.20.1 (172.16.20.1), 30 hops max, 60 byte
packets
 1   172.16.20.1 (172.16.20.1)   2.615 ms   3.195 ms   3.252 ms
vEdge01#
```

# Troubleshooting vManage

vManage is fairly easy to set up; however, it is easy to run into issues when setting up clustering.

One such issue is where the second vManage server's application server stays in a waiting state. We can check the status of all of our running processes using the command "request nms all status".

```
vManage02# request nms all status
NMS application server
        Enabled: true
        Status:  waiting
```

```
NMS configuration database
        Enabled: true
        Status:  running PID:5617 for 55s
NMS coordination server
        Enabled: true
        Status:  running PID:5629 for 55s
NMS messaging server
        Enabled: true
        Status:  running PID:7558 for 39s
NMS statistics database
        Enabled: true
        Status:  running PID:3090 for 68s
NMS data collection agent
        Enabled: true
        Status:  not running
NMS cloud agent
        Enabled: true
        Status:  running PID:474 for 84s
NMS container manager
        Enabled: false
        Status:  not running
NMS SDAVC proxy
        Enabled: true
        Status:  running PID:556 for 84s
vManage02#
```

Or we can check the status of an individual service:

```
vManage02# request nms application-server status
NMS application server
        Enabled: true
        Status:  waiting
vManage02#
```

To resolve this issue, make sure you allow the Netconf under VPN 0:

```
vManage02# config
Entering configuration mode terminal
vManage02(config)# vpn 0
vManage02(config-vpn-0)# interface eth1
vManage02(config-interface-eth1)# tunnel-interface
vManage02(config-tunnel-interface)# allow-service netconf
vManage02(config-tunnel-interface)#
```

Also check, if you are running in a cluster environment, that both devices can reach each other. While this may seem obvious, assumption is, as they say, the mother of all mistakes. I ran into this when the switch in VPN 0 was turned off and neither cluster member could fully start.

To aid us in our troubleshooting, vManage provides many logs in /var/log/nms, which we can access by dropping into the vshell and reading the logs as we would on any normal Linux machine:

```
vManage01# vshell
vManage01:~$ cd /var/log/nms
vManage01:/var/log/nms$ tail vmanage-elastic-cluster.log
  [2020-05-11T11:43:26,463][WARN ][o.e.d.z.ZenDiscovery    ]
[vManageNode0] not enough master nodes discovered
during pinging (found [[Candidate{node={vManageNode0}
{oOB6ogMoStawKKPsV28zcg}{GiFx8gIBRxC9ryTVCpacFg}{10.1.1.2}
{10.1.1.2:9300}, clusterStateVersion=-1}]], but needed [2]),
pinging again
[2020-05-11T11:43:31,046][INFO ][o.e.c.s.ClusterService  ]
[vManageNode0] detected_master {vManageNode1}
{NHvIaYDGSOK4AmGyVjHgeQ}{LVpacoUwTFmioNM8R6oq9Q}{10.1.1.22}
{10.1.1.22:9300}, added
vManage01:/var/log/nms$
```

We need both members of the cluster to be up and running when the vManage servers are started together.

Once the two vManage servers could talk to each other, the application server started:

```
vManage01# request nms application-server status
NMS application server
        Enabled: true
        Status:  running PID:32725 for 137s
vManage01#
```

# Troubleshooting vBond

As I stated, way back in Chapter 5, if you have the tunnel interface running on the VPN 0 interface, you will get an error when adding vBond to vManage (Figure 14-1).

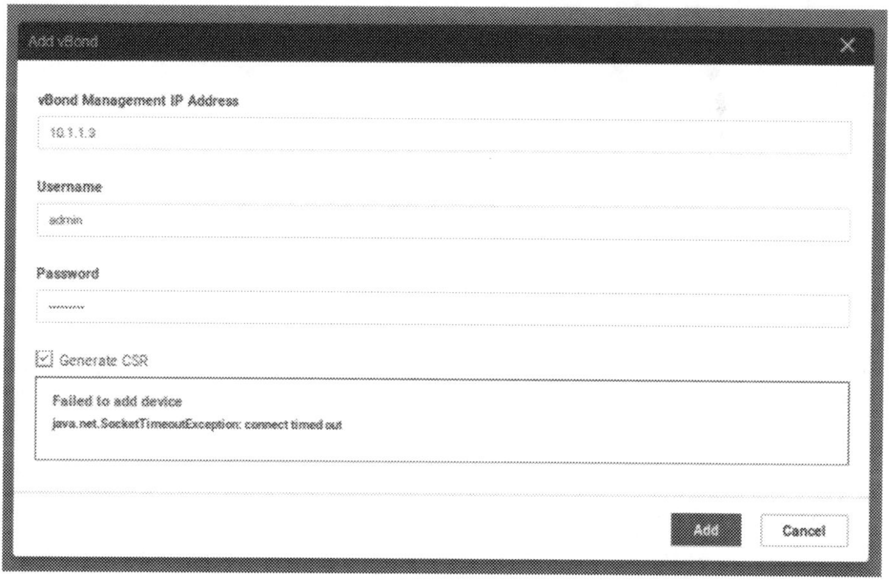

*Figure 14-1.* vBond Java error

In the original configuration, the tunnel interface was declared:

```
vBond01# sh run vpn 0
vpn 0
 interface ge0/0
  ip address 10.1.1.3/24
  ipv6 dhcp-client
  tunnel-interface
   encapsulation ipsec
   no allow-service bgp
   allow-service dhcp
   allow-service dns
   allow-service icmp
   allow-service sshd
   no allow-service netconf
   no allow-service ntp
   no allow-service ospf
   no allow-service stun
   allow-service https
  !
  no shutdown
 !
!
vBond01#
```

We need to remove it:

```
vBond01# config
Entering configuration mode terminal
vBond01(config)# vpn 0
vBond01(config-vpn-0)# interface ge0/0
vBond01(config-interface-ge0/0)# no tunnel-interface
vBond01(config-interface-ge0/0)# end
```

```
Uncommitted changes found, commit them? [yes/no/CANCEL] yes
Commit complete.
vBond01#
```

Another error I faced was that when adding vBond (to vManage), I was informed that we "*Cannot add vEdge as controller*" (Figure 14-2).

***Figure 14-2.***  *Cannot add vEdge as a controller*

The reason for this is that we have missed out the vBond command, so it is defaulting to ZTP mode:

```
vBond01# sh run
system
 host-name             vBond01
 system-ip             100.1.1.3
 site-id               100
 admin-tech-on-failure
```

```
no route-consistency-check
organization-name        Learning_SD-WAN
vbond ztp.viptela.com
```

To fix this, we just need to add the "vBond x.x.x.x local" command (the "vbond-only" is optional):

```
vBond01(config)# system
vBond01(config-system)# vbond 10.1.1.3 local vbond-only
vBond01(config-system)# end
Uncommitted changes found, commit them? [yes/no/CANCEL] yes
Commit complete.
vBond01# sh run system
system
 host-name               vBond01
 system-ip               100.1.1.3
 site-id                 100
 admin-tech-on-failure
 no route-consistency-check
 organization-name       Learning_SD-WAN
 vbond 10.1.1.3 local vbond-only
 aaa
  auth-order local radius tacacs
  usergroup basic
   task system read write
   task interface read write
  !
  usergroup netadmin
  !
  usergroup operator
   task system read
   task interface read
```

```
    task policy read
    task routing read
    task security read
    !
Aborted: by user
vBond01#
```

During the writing of this book, I spent two or three days going over the same issue. I had added the vBond controller, completed the certificate enrolment and assignment. Still, the vBond was not showing the hostname nor the system IP in vManage. I repeated the process, several times, with the same result (Figure 14-3).

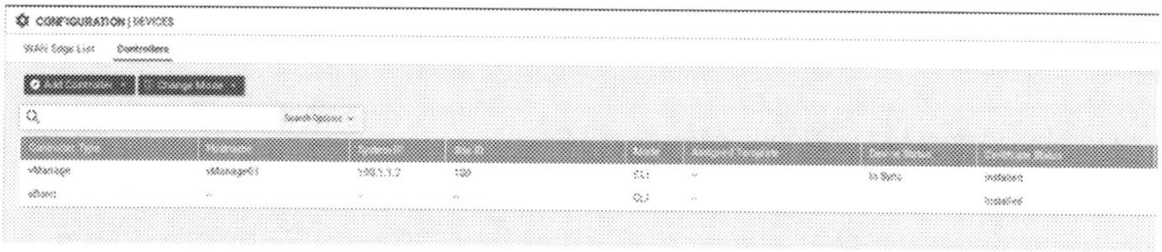

*Figure 14-3.* *No vBond. I expect you to populate*

I had full connectivity (as shown by a ping) and even ran Wireshark, where I could see the SSH traffic when removing and adding the vBond controller. All looked fine.

Eventually, I went onto the CLI and added the vBond IP onto the vManage server:

```
vManage01(config)# system vbond ?
Description: IP address/DNS name
Possible completions:
  <DNS name>
  <IP address>
  port    vBond server port
vManage01(config)# system vbond 10.1.1.3 ?
```

```
Possible completions:
  port    vBond server port
  <cr>
vManage01(config)# system vbond 10.1.1.3
vManage01(config-system)# commit
Commit complete.
vManage01(config-system)#
```

It is important to note that this had already been performed in Chapter 5 and even showed in the CLI configuration on vManage01; hence, it was not the first thing I tried.

So, it just goes to show that although it is shown in the GUI and CLI, it's worth adding it again, just to make sure!

# Troubleshooting vSmart

Similar to the previous vBond issue, you may find that vSmart is not updating with its details in vManage (Figure 14-4).

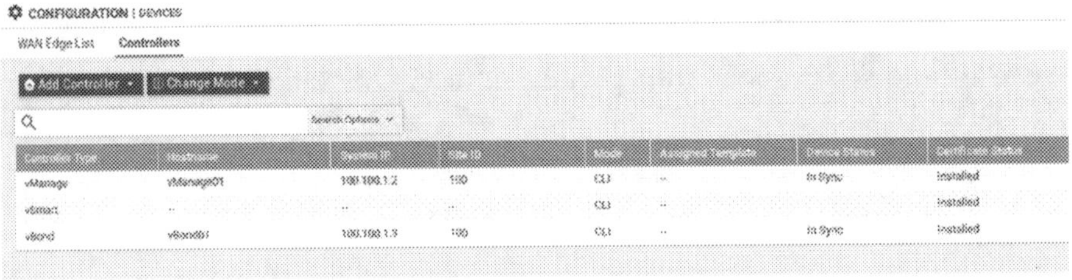

*Figure 14-4.* *vSmart details missing in vManage*

This was due to the system IP missing not being entered:

```
vSmart01(config-system)# system-ip 100.100.1.4
```

# Troubleshooting Edge Devices

If the vEdge device does not have the same root CA certificate as the one used by vBond, then it will not be able to authenticate. We can see this traffic in Wireshark (Figure 14-5).

*Figure 14-5.  Certificate issues*

If we do not have Wireshark handy to help us diagnose such issues, then we have to remember the steps taken in authentication and check that we have the same certificate (I have truncated the output for formatting):

```
CSR-1#show sdwan certificate root-ca-cert | i Issuer
        Issuer: C=US, O=VeriSign, Inc.
        Issuer: OU=Arcturus, O=Cisco
        Issuer: OU=Arcturus, O=Cisco
        Issuer: C=US, O=Symantec Corporation
        Issuer: C=US, O=Symantec Corporation
        Issuer: C=US, O=VeriSign, Inc.
        Issuer: C=US, O=VeriSign, Inc.
        Issuer: C=US, O=VeriSign, Inc.
        Issuer: C=US, O=DigiCert Inc
        Issuer: C=US, O=VeriSign, Inc.
        Issuer: C=US, O=DigiCert Inc
        Issuer: C=US, O=DigiCert Inc
        Issuer: C=US, O=DigiCert Inc
CSR-1#
```

As we can see, we do not have the proper root CA. Once we have copied that over, check that it is there:

```
CSR-1#show sdwan certificate root-ca-cert | i Issuer
        Issuer: C=UK, ST=London, L=London, O=Learning_SD-WAN,
OU=Learning_SD-WAN, CN=vManage01
        Issuer: C=US, O=DigiCert Inc
        Issuer: OU=Arcturus, O=Cisco
        Issuer: OU=Arcturus, O=Cisco
        Issuer: C=US, O=Symantec Corporation
        Issuer: C=US, O=Symantec Corporation
        Issuer: C=US, O=VeriSign, Inc.
        Issuer: C=US, O=VeriSign, Inc.
        Issuer: C=US, O=VeriSign, Inc.
        Issuer: C=US, O=DigiCert Inc
        Issuer: C=US, O=VeriSign, Inc.
        Issuer: C=US, O=DigiCert Inc
        Issuer: C=US, O=DigiCert Inc
        Issuer: C=US, O=DigiCert Inc
CSR-1#
```

This troubleshooting step was brought to you as I missed the "Failed" message when SCP'ing the CA.crt across to the CSR1000v using the same syntax as the vEdge routers. Always check the output!

Another issue I faced was that I lost communications with the vEdge devices, as all the interfaces lost their static IP addresses:

```
interface GigabitEthernet1
 no shutdown
 arp timeout 1200
 ip address dhcp client-id GigabitEthernet1
 ip redirects
 ip dhcp client default-router distance 1
```

```
ip mtu     1500
mtu 1500
negotiation auto
exit
```

This was due to a badly configured template, which reverted all the interfaces to use DHCP. Trying to troubleshoot this, I could see that the vEdges had lost their connection to the vSmart controller, which we can see from the CSR router:

```
CSR-1#show sdwan omp summary
oper-state              UP
admin-state             UP
personality             vedge
omp-uptime              0:00:28:47
routes-received         0
routes-installed        0
routes-sent             0
tlocs-received          2
tlocs-installed         2
tlocs-sent              0
services-received       0
services-installed      0
services-sent           0
mcast-routes-received   0
mcast-routes-installed  0
mcast-routes-sent       0
hello-sent              4
hello-received          1
handshake-sent          1
handshake-received      1
alert-sent              1
```

```
alert-received          0
inform-sent             3
inform-received         3
update-sent             0
update-received         2
policy-sent             0
policy-received         0
total-packets-sent      9
total-packets-received 7
vsmart-peers            0

CSR-1#
CSR-1#show sdwan omp peers
R -> routes received
I -> routes installed
S -> routes sent

                    DOMAIN OVERLAY SITE
PEER          TYPE  ID      ID     ID    STATE      UPTIME R/I/S
----------------------------------------------------------------
100.100.1.4   vsmart 1      1      100   init-in-gr        0/0/0

CSR-1#
```

We can also see this reflected in the dashboard (Figure 14-6).

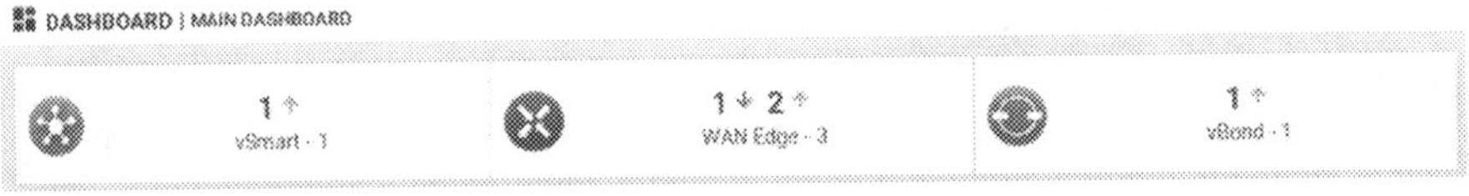

*Figure 14-6.* *No vSmarts*

Clearly, we cannot apply a new template, as we have no control plane connectivity to the vEdges with which to push a new template. We could manually input the IP address again, but this may cause vManage to push the same badly configured template to the devices. Changing the template before setting the IP address has issues, as making template changes tends to not work if vManage cannot complete the process and push the changes to the attached devices. The answer, in this case, was to delete the edge devices from the devices list; this will detach it from any templates allowing you to make the manual changes and then add it back in again. You can also detach them from the device template to achieve the same goal.

# Troubleshooting Certificate Issues

Issues with certificates can be your worst enemy. Guard your certificates carefully, love them, nurture them, and make sure that if they are due to expire, you give yourself plenty of time to replace them!

The CA certificate expired during the writing of this book, so I had to go through the process of updating the CA on the vManage server, then invalidate the vBond and vSmart, and re-add them.

Thankfully, updating the edge devices is not hard; once you update the CA certificates on the edge devices, they will sync up to the rest of the network.

However, once you then send the device list to vBond (which was done for us automatically in Chapter 5 when we added the vBond device), you will need to remove and re-add the edge devices.

Properly managed though, renewing certificates should only result in a short blip in communications while the new certificate takes over from the old certificate. You just need to regenerate the CSRs, sign them, and upload the new certificate **before** the old one expires!

To put it bluntly, certificate expiration can bring down the entire network. It's scary but true.

# vManage Troubleshooting Tools

vManage comes with some inbuilt tools to make our life a little easier.
To access them, head to *Monitor ➤ Network* and select a device, and
then scroll down to Troubleshooting, where you will see options for
troubleshooting Connectivity or Traffic (Figure 14-7).

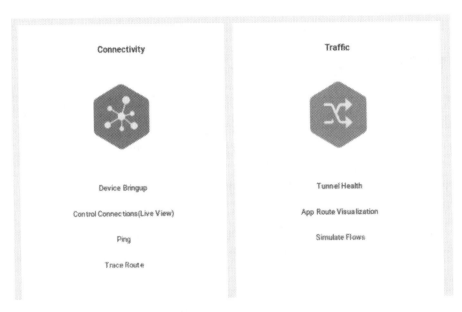

*Figure 14-7.*  *Troubleshooting options*

If we select the Ping option, we can specify the destination IP, the VPN
to use, and the source interface (Figure 14-8).

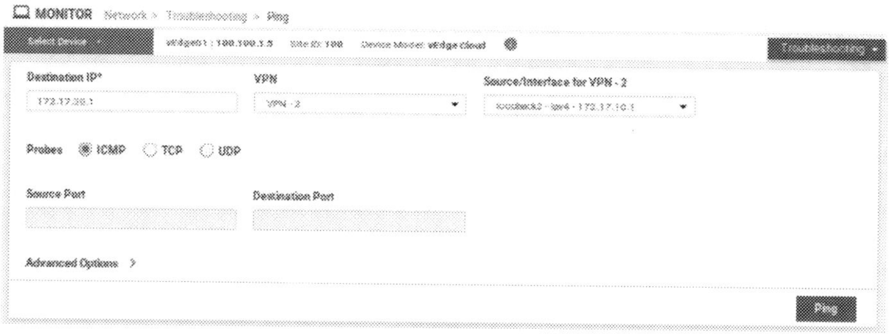

**Figure 14-8.** *Ping!*

Once we press "Ping," the results are shown in the lower half of the page (Figure 14-9).

**Figure 14-9.** *Pong!*

On the traffic side of the page, we can look at our tunnel health, which shows us (by default) the traffic loss between the selected router and another router (Figure 14-10). Clicking the Chart Options link allows us to select Latency/Jitter or the Octets (the amount of traffic sent).

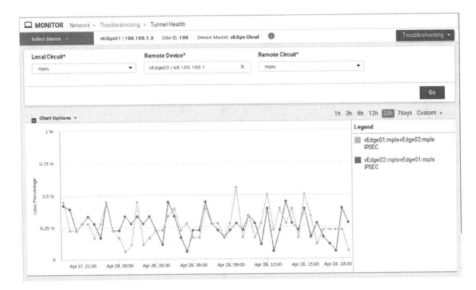

**Figure 14-10.** *The traffic loss*

We can also simulate traffic flows within our network by setting the 5-tuple details (source IP address, destination IP address, source port, destination port, and protocol), along with the application and DSCP value, and clicking "Simulate" (Figure 14-11).

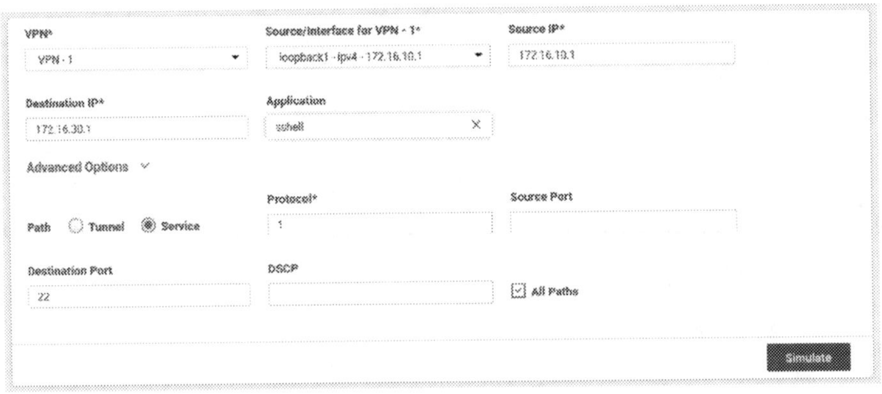

**Figure 14-11.** *The 5-tuple combination needed for simulating traffic*

In the following box will be the results, showing which VPN will be used, the remote system that it will end up on, and the encapsulation (Figure 14-12).

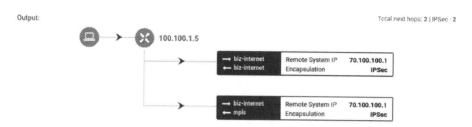

**Figure 14-12.**  *Simulation complete*

There are some hidden troubleshooting options though, which can be revealed if we go to *Administration* ➤ *Settings* and then scroll down to "Data Stream." Set the option to be enabled, and then enter the VPN and IP address of the vManage server that the data stream will be sent to (Figure 14-13). Click Save. This allows extra features, such as packet capture, speed tests, and debug logs.

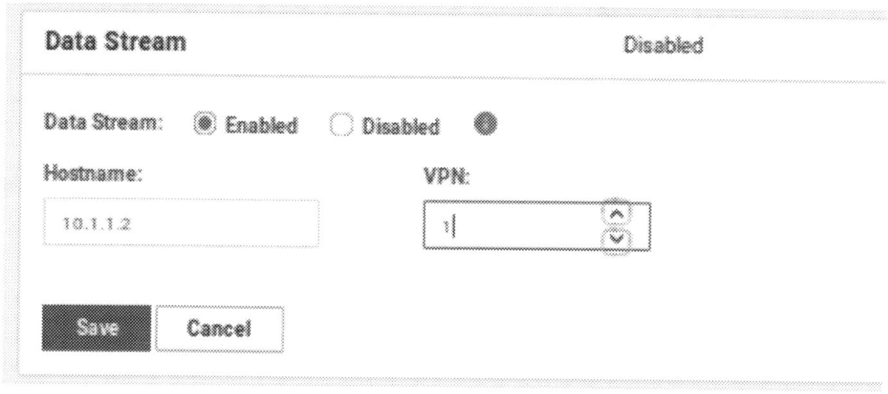

**Figure 14-13.**  *The data stream options*

We now have more troubleshooting options, such as packet capture (Figure 14-14).

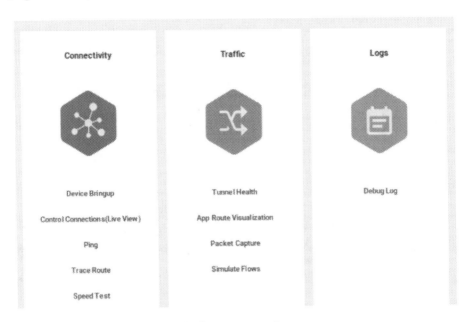

***Figure 14-14.*** *More troubleshooting options*

We will finish the chapter by performing a packet capture, because as the saying goes "PCAP, or it never happened." Click Packet Capture, and then select the VPN and interface (Figure 14-15). We can use additional traffic filters to set a 5-tuple if we want to be very specific about the traffic we are capturing.

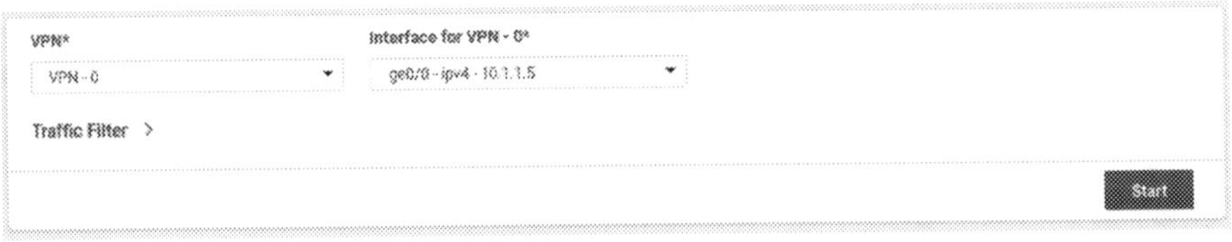

***Figure 14-15.*** *The packet capture settings*

Once the capture starts, it will run for either five minutes, or once the capture file reaches a size of 5MB. You can also stop it manually (Figure 14-16).

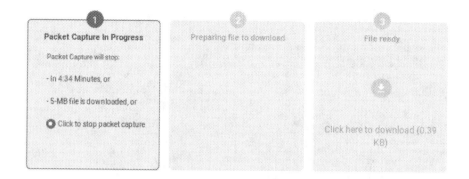

*Figure 14-16.* *The capture in progress*

Once the capture stops, vManage will prepare the file for downloading, and then you can download it. The filenames are very long, so you may want to rename them. The capture is saved as a PCAP file, so will be readable in Wireshark, or TCPDump. Using the latter, we can read the file using the command "sudo tcpdump -ttttnnr <filename>" (Figure 14-17).

```
user@user-virtual-machine:~/Downloads$ mv 932a9a56-e29d-40fd-a428-0f87f07582fe_ge0_0_0.pcap capture3.p
cap
user@user-virtual-machine:~/Downloads$ sudo tcpdump -ttttnnr capture3.pcap
reading from file capture3.pcap, link-type EN10MB (Ethernet)
2021-05-01 18:28:12.571837 IP 10.1.1.2.12646 > 10.1.1.5.60252: UDP, length 261
2021-05-01 18:28:12.572707 IP 10.1.1.2.12646 > 10.1.1.5.60252: UDP, length 181
2021-05-01 18:28:12.574922 IP 10.1.1.5.60252 > 10.1.1.2.12646: UDP, length 101
2021-05-01 18:28:12.574964 IP 10.1.1.5.60252 > 10.1.1.2.12646: UDP, length 341
2021-05-01 18:28:12.577447 IP 10.1.1.2.12646 > 10.1.1.5.60252: UDP, length 101
2021-05-01 18:28:12.578667 IP 10.1.1.5.60252 > 10.1.1.2.12646: UDP, length 101
2021-05-01 18:28:12.579727 IP 10.1.1.2.12646 > 10.1.1.5.60252: UDP, length 101
2021-05-01 18:28:12.635098 IP 10.1.1.5.60252 > 50.10.10.1.12346: UDP, length 129
2021-05-01 18:28:12.637388 IP 50.10.10.1.12346 > 10.1.1.5.60252: UDP, length 122
2021-05-01 18:28:12.746111 IP 10.1.1.5.60252 > 10.1.1.2.12646: UDP, length 140
2021-05-01 18:28:12.746157 IP 10.1.1.5.60252 > 10.1.1.3.12346: UDP, length 140
2021-05-01 18:28:12.746222 IP 10.1.1.5.60252 > 10.1.1.4.12446: UDP, length 140
2021-05-01 18:28:12.747186 IP 10.1.1.4.12446 > 10.1.1.5.60252: UDP, length 154
2021-05-01 18:28:12.747393 IP 10.1.1.2.12646 > 10.1.1.5.60252: UDP, length 182
2021-05-01 18:28:12.768212 IP 10.1.1.3.12346 > 10.1.1.5.60252: UDP, length 111
2021-05-01 18:28:12.945636 IP 10.1.1.5.60252 > 10.1.1.3.12346: UDP, length 16
2021-05-01 18:28:13.086433 IP 50.11.11.1.37246 > 10.1.1.5.60252: UDP, length 129
2021-05-01 18:28:13.086501 IP 10.1.1.5.60252 > 50.11.11.1.37246: UDP, length 122
2021-05-01 18:28:13.137600 IP 10.1.1.5.60252 > 50.11.11.1.37246: UDP, length 129
2021-05-01 18:28:13.139408 IP 50.11.11.1.37246 > 10.1.1.5.60252: UDP, length 122
2021-05-01 18:28:13.258224 IP 50.10.10.1.12346 > 10.1.1.5.60252: UDP, length 129
2021-05-01 18:28:13.258317 IP 10.1.1.5.60252 > 50.10.10.1.12346: UDP, length 122
2021-05-01 18:28:13.411258 IP 10.1.1.5 > 10.1.1.1: ICMP echo request, id 21215, seq 10, length 64
2021-05-01 18:28:13.412898 IP 10.1.1.1 > 10.1.1.5: ICMP echo reply, id 21215, seq 10, length 64
```

**Figure 14-17.**  *The nicely readable PCAP*

As you can see from Figure 14-17, the majority of our traffic is the SD-WAN background traffic, with a ping at the bottom, so unless you want to wade through this "noise" during your troubleshooting, then using the traffic filters is strongly recommended!

# Summary

In this final chapter, we looked at troubleshooting options, starting with the basic tools of ping and traceroute. We then moved on to common issues with vManage, vBond, and vSmart, before moving on to troubleshooting edge devices. We looked at certificate issues and then finished by playing with the troubleshooting tools that vManage gives us.

I hope you have enjoyed the book.

—Stuart

# Index

© Stuart Fordham 2021
S. Fordham, *Learning SD-WAN with Cisco*, https://doi.org/10.1007/978-1-4842-7347-0

Printed in the United States
by Baker & Taylor Publisher Services